Studies in Legal History

Published in association with the
American Society for Legal History

Frederic William Maitland

A Life

C. H. S. Fifoot

Harvard University Press, Cambridge, Massachusetts, 1971

Library of Congress Catalog Card Number 73-145892
SBN 674-31825-0
Printed in the United States of America

Preface

Professor Stanley Katz has suggested that I should offer a short note of books and papers previously published which bear upon Maitland's life, work, or influence. Of this happy thought I now take advantage, adding only a warning that the list does not pretend to be exhaustive.

1908. A. L. Smith, *Frederic William Maitland: Two Lectures and a Bibliography* (Oxford, Clarendon Press).

1910. H. A. L. Fisher, *Frederick* [*sic*] *William Maitland* (Cambridge University Press).

1916. Charles H. Haskins, "Frederic William Maitland" (Proceedings of the American Academy of Arts and Sciences, vol. 51, no. 14).

1923. W. W. Buckland, "F. W. Maitland" (*Cambridge Law Journal,* 1: 279).

1937. G. M. Young, "Maitland," in *Daylight and Champaign* (London, Rupert Hart-Davis).

1951. T. F. T. Plucknett, "Maitland's View of Law and History" (*Law Quarterly Review,* April 1951, pp. 179–194);

reprinted in *Early English Legal Literature* (Cambridge University Press).

1952. R. L. Schuyler, "The Historical Spirit Incarnate: Frederic William Maitland" (*American Historical Review,* 57: 303–322).

1953. H. A. Hollond, *Frederic William Maitland, 1850–1906* (Selden Society Lecture).

1957. Helen M. Cam, *Selected Historical Essays of F. W. Maitland,* Introduction (Cambridge University Press).

1957. E. Maitland, *F. W. Maitland: A Child's-Eye View* (Selden Society).

1961. Sir Cecil Carr, *The Mission of the Selden Society* (Selden Society Lecture).

1962. Frederick Bernays Wiener, *Uses and Abuses of Legal History* (Selden Society Lecture).

1965. H. E. Bell, *Maitland: A Critical Examination and Assessment* (London, Adam and Charles Black).

1965. *The Letters of Frederic William Maitland* (Selden Society; Harvard University Press; Cambridge University Press).

I would like also to call attention to Volume 26 of the Stair Society, now in course of preparation. This is to contain a brief life of George Neilson by Professor E. L. G. Stones, introducing Neilson's treatise on the Laws of the March, edited by Dr. T. I. Rae. It was Maitland who encouraged Neilson's first venture in legal history, *Trial by Combat.*

Most of the books and papers which have already appeared contain some appraisal of Maitland as a man as well as of his work, and no one has approached him with more insight than Helen Cam. But, apart from his daughter's memoir, only three of them are essentially biographical. Buckland drew vignettes of Maitland as he knew him in Cambridge and in the Canaries, at once vivid and charming. Professor Hollond has written a balanced and sympathetic appreciation of the man who won his lasting allegiance when he heard him lecture in 1905. Fisher alone set himself, as in duty bound, to write Maitland's life. He wisely relied, so far as then seemed discreet, upon the letters as the framework of his book, and it would be ungracious not to recognize its value. But it was, as Fisher himself called it, a "biographical sketch"; and, published in 1910, it was written too soon after Maitland's death by one who had stood too close to him.

I had long thought that the time was ripe for a fuller life of Maitland, and I wondered if I dared to attempt it. In 1958 I was asked by the Selden Society to edit his letters, and I thus met his elder daughter, Ermengard. In this task we were in close and frequent touch, and she suggested that I should write her father's life. She put at my disposal family diaries, notebooks, letters, and other papers. Talking and writing to me, she recalled the years in Cambridge, in Gloucestershire, in Madeira, and in the Canaries. She spoke of the winter's tales told by her mother and lent me the parodies of Ibsen contrived and acted as family diversions. She was not a scholar. But she developed her own style in the memoir *A Child's-Eye View,* in the introduction to her sister's little book *Fredegond and Gerald Shove,* which she printed privately in 1952, and in a number of manuscript essays by which she sought to detain the impressions of a day or to catch the flight of imagination. As the reader of my book will see, I have drawn fully upon all that she showed and told me; and without her aid the life of Maitland could not have been written. She inherited much from her father and her mother: a love of music; an eye for eccentricity; a scorn of pretension; warm family affection; shrewd practical judgment; courage in thought, word, and deed. She died in 1968. I have been fortunate to have shared her memories before it was too late and to have known her for her own sake.

Maitland displayed his powers with astonishing richness in books and articles, in lectures and letters. While I have inevitably written of his work—its evolution, its development, and its subsequent fortunes—I have not explored it in depth. For such a task I am not fit. The omission is the less serious in that H. E. Bell was spared, before his early death, to complete a study of Maitland as a historian; and to his book, only too short, we who are left are deeply indebted. My own aim has been to evoke Maitland himself, his qualities of mind and spirit as these are revealed in his writings, among his friends—themselves eminent—and in the midst of his family. I should like also to think that I have offered a sketch, however slight, of Victorian England, with its wealth of intellectual interests and achievements which form an indispensable background to appreciation of the man and of his work. If to these ends I may seem to have accumulated too much detail, I do not feel it necessary to apologize. It was Maitland who insisted that only thus may the life of an idea, a society, or a person be traced and portrayed. Boswell once told Johnson of his fear that he had put into his journals too many little incidents. Dr. Johnson reassured him. "Sir, there is nothing too little for so little a creature as man."

I am warmly sensible of the honor accorded to me in the choice of my book to introduce the series of Studies in Legal History, sponsored jointly by the Harvard University Press and by the American Society for Legal History. I cannot but think how happy Maitland would have been had he foreseen this collaboration. He had himself called in the New World of scholarship to redress the balance of the Old; and, with the passage of years, he felt ever more surely that the future of Anglo-American legal history lay with the United States. When, through illness, he had to decline an invitation to Harvard, he told Charles Gross that he felt as if he "lived in the twelfth century and was rejecting a call to Bologna." Of a worthy edition of the Year Books his hope lay in a company of scholars "trained, if need be, at Paris under masters of the old French language; trained, if need be, at Harvard under masters of the old English law." In the last words of his Rede Lecture he urged the Inns of Court to fulfill their responsibilities as inheritors of the past and as guardians for the future. If they were faithful to their trust, "the glory of Bourges, the glory of Bologna, the glory of Harvard may yet be theirs."

I must pay my debt of gratitude to those who have found for me unpublished material or have allowed me to use it: to two Literary Directors of the Selden Society, the late Professor T. F. T. Plucknett and Professor S. F. C. Milsom, who cordially made me free to examine and to quote the correspondence and other papers of the Society; to Mr. A. E. B. Owen of the Cambridge University Library, who drew my attention to letters of Maitland which I had missed, and to the University Librarian for permission to quote from them; to Professor E. L. G. Stones of the University of Glasgow, who led me to six letters written by Maitland (four of them to George Neilson and two to Albert Venn Dicey), and to Mr. R. O. MacKenna, the University Librarian, who generously sent me copies of the letters and allowed me to use them.

So many have helped me by their knowledge or by their encouragement that it seems invidious to mention individuals. But I cannot deny myself the pleasure of naming, "without prejudice," a few of the many: Mr. Alan S. Bell, Mr. Eric Ronald Guest, Mr. T. Harvatt, Professor H. A. Hollond, Dr. Gareth H. Jones, Professor F. H. Lawson, Professor F. H. Newark, Professor Clive Parry, Professor Dr. Hans Peter, and Professor Samuel E. Thorne.

Finally, I wish to thank my wife. She has read every word of this book (as of all others that I have written) at each of its stages, from tentative approach to final publication; and at times of doubt, difficulty, or despondency she has supported me with warm interest and cool judgment. But for Ermengard Maitland I could not have begun to write the book, and but for my wife I should not have completed it.

C. H. S. Fifoot

Note on the Frontispiece

There is no good portrait of Maitland. His daughter said that faced with a camera he became rigid. The least unsatisfactory photograph is that which Professor Hollond used for his memoir and which he was kind enough to urge should be used again for this book. In the foreword to his memoir he explained that Ermengard Maitland had lent him a copy of this photograph, and continued: "I reproduce it with her permission, because it faintly suggests the magic of Maitland's eyes, and because it was the photograph of him which Mrs. Maitland liked best and always kept by her. Its date cannot be ascertained; but Miss Maitland remembers the dog as a friend of her childhood in the nineties."

C.H.S.F.

Contents

Frederic William Maitland

Chapter I

Parentage

The Parish Register of Tongland, Kircudbrightshire, records the baptism on February 2, 1710, of Robert Maitland. He was the first son and the fourth child of John Maitland, Laird of Barcaple, by his wife Margaret Gordon. Because of John's "profligate character"[1] Robert is said to have been brought up by his maternal grandfather. An adventurous spirit at least was inherited by John's children. A younger son, William, went into the British Army but, "being displeased," sold his commission, entered the Russian service, won the goodwill of the Empress Elizabeth, and was killed in action at some date between 1760 and 1768. Robert, when he was seventeen years old, sailed to America as supercargo of a Glasgow vessel. His voyage proved lucrative. After an interval in the counting house of a Glasgow merchant, he sailed again to America. On the way home the ship was stranded and, though all on board were saved, he reached Glasgow only "after suffering much from want of provisions." While still young he determined, like many of his compatriots, to seek his fortune in London. There, in the vague but impressive words of his grandson, he "established a mercantile house"; and in 1740 at St. Giles without Cripplegate he married Ursula Gorham, whose family speculated in house and land development and through whom London property came to the Maitlands and remained with them for more than a hundred years.

On Robert's death in 1791 his youngest son Alexander succeeded to the control of the business. Six years earlier Alexander had married Caroline Busby,[2] through whom he became lord of the manor of Brookthorpe and Harescombe in Gloucestershire. But he made his home in Peckham, which like Camberwell was, late in the eighteenth and early in the nineteenth century, a congenial place of residence for city merchants who were no longer disposed to live over their counting houses. It was the walled garden of his father's house in Camberwell, with the fields beyond, that Robert Browning borrowed for the setting of *Paracelsus*;[3] and it was in Peckham that Benjamin Jowett, a furrier, made his home in 1814 and where the future Master of Balliol was born in 1817.[4] Alexander Maitland's house was long remembered by family friends for the beauty of its garden,[5] and there in 1792 was born his son Samuel Roffey Maitland.

Alexander, as befitted his ancestry, was a dissenter, and as a dissenter Samuel Roffey was brought up. Until he was fifteen he went to a variety of private schools whose common factor was their inadequacy. "When I left school," he wrote,[6] "I had read very little and had no decent knowledge of any kind of history whatever." In 1807 he became by good fortune the private pupil of Launcelot Sharpe, one of the masters of the Merchant Taylors' School. Sharpe was both an able tutor and—not invariably a concomitant—a man of wide culture. He set his pupil on the path of scholarship and infected him with his own historical and antiquarian enthusiasm. In October 1809 Samuel Roffey went up to St. John's College, Cambridge. His first term he wasted. "Having made up my mind to remove to Trinity, I did not take pains for my December examination and was suspended." In the Lent Term of 1810, in the easy manner of the times, he migrated to Trinity where he had congenial friends, and in particular William Hodge Mill. Mill was a born scholar who became a Fellow of Trinity in 1814 and in 1820 the first Principal of Bishop's College, Calcutta. He was an orientalist; he published works in Arabic, translated the Gospels into Sanskrit, and from 1848 until his death in 1853 was Regius Professor of Hebrew at Cambridge. From his friendship and example Samuel Roffey learned the meaning of research and imbibed a taste for oriental literature.

In 1811 Samuel Roffey left Cambridge. Though his doctrinal views would not now have satisfied a Scottish minister, he still felt scruples which prevented his subscription to the Thirty-nine Articles, and he could not proceed to a degree. For the next four years he lived with his parents at Peckham, reading—with intervals of wider literature—for the Bar. But, as he had not kept enough University terms, the Inner Temple was unwilling to call him. To meet the emergency he returned to Cambridge, and to St. John's College, until in the Easter Term of 1816 he became a barrister. According to Dr. Augustus Jessopp, who wrote his life for the *Dictionary of National Biography*, "in his chambers in the Temple he studied seriously, with music as his only diversion." His serious call to the law may be doubted. Scholarship, if not music, competed too strenuously for his attention, and within a year he had abandoned the attempt to practice.

On November 29, 1816, he married Selina, daughter of the Rev. Christopher Stephenson, Vicar of Olney. He had designed the event to coincide with "a great Solar Eclipse," but, through a misprint in his pocket book, he had chosen the wrong date. He was now moving from dissent to the Established Church. In 1823 he was ordained priest and became perpetual curate of the recently built Christ Church, Gloucester. But, if he had found the law distasteful, his mind was at once too sharp and too far-ranging to suffer the routine of parish work. By 1828 he had resigned his incumbency and had embarked on a journey through Germany to Poland. His immediate object was to study the work of the Society for the Conversion of the Jews, but the by-products of his tour were more refreshing. A journal, fragments of which survive with attractive sketches, reflects a lively eye engaged in the observation of custom and character. He enlarged the acquaintance with Hebrew to which he had been introduced by his friend Mill, and he strove to master German which, like Dr. Pusey, he realized was vital to the study of the Scriptures—though he proposed to put it to more dispassionate use than Pusey would have approved. When he returned to England he went to live in Gloucester where his father had built a house.[7] He had found his true vocation—the life of an independent historian with an appetite for theological controversy. Not only his ideas but his style and expression were his own, the outcome of desultory and eccentric reading before, during, and after his apparently aimless years at Cambridge and in London. As a Christian his faith was unshaken; as a scholar he accepted the duty of doubt.

He showed his quality in a number of pamphlets, whose cumbrous titles might seem, to later generations, unlikely to excite interest or to sow dissension. But the detachment with which accepted views were scrutinized disturbed the Evangelicals, and their uneasiness deepened when in 1832 Samuel Roffey published his first major work, *Facts and Documents Illustrative of the History, Doctrine and Rites of the Ancient Albigenses and Waldenses*. The ultimate origin of the book is to be found in the fifty-fourth chapter of the *Decline and Fall of the Roman Empire* where Gibbon indulged, or contrived, a diversion upon the story of the Paulicians, a sect whose name he identified with the devotees of St. Paul and who in the seventh century spread over the provinces of Asia Minor to the west of the Euphrates and especially Armenia. They disdained miraculous relics, denied the immaculate conception and the intercession of saints, rejected all ecclesiastical hierarchies, proclaimed the New Testament and abhorred the Old. For two hundred years they lived and multiplied under the shadow of persecution; but in the reign of Basil the Macedonian (867–886) they were defeated and dispersed. Gibbon insinuated rather than asserted that their disciples found their way to Western Europe. "It was in the country of the Albigeois in the southern provinces of France that the Paulicians were most deeply implanted"; and their success in the eleventh and twelfth centuries "must be imputed to the strong, though secret, discontent which armed the most pious Christians against the Church of Rome." In the thirteenth century they succumbed to the severity of the Inquisition reinforced by the secular sword. Having played their part on his stage, they were dismissed by Gibbon with a characteristic valediction. "The invincible spirit which they had kindled still lived and breathed in the Western world. In the state, in the church and even in the cloister a latent succession was preserved of the disciples of St. Paul; who protested against the tyranny of Rome, embraced the bible as the rule of faith and purified their creed from all the visions of the gnostic theology. The struggles of Wycliff in England, of Huss in Bohemia, were premature and ineffectual; but the names of Zuinglius, Luther and Calvin are pronounced with gratitude as the deliverers of nations."

The history of the Paulicians and of their successors and supposed descendants, the Albigenses and Waldenses, fired the imagination of two Evangelicals, George Stanley Faber and Joseph Milner, who engaged Samuel Roffey's critical attention. Faber was a Fellow of Lincoln College, Oxford, from 1793 to 1804 and afterwards Prebendary of Salisbury.[8] As early as 1801 he had revealed in his Bampton Lectures on the Pentateuch a devotion to the prophetical books of the Old Testament which survived fifty years of hard writing and culminated in 1852 in "The Revival of the French Emperorship Anticipated from the Necessity of Prophecy." He saw in the sufferings of the Paulicians a tribute to the continuity of Protestantism, and he was determined to identify them not only with the Albigenses but with the witnesses predicted in the Apocalypse. He who wills the end must will the means; and Faber felt instinctively that in so good a cause inspired conjecture might supply the deficiencies of evidence. In his *Facts and Documents* Samuel Roffey exposed the range of these defects. Faber had cited a number of "Testimonies," the most imposing of which were drawn from the records of the Inquisition. Two examples may suffice. The first testimony was that of "an ancient contemporaneous Inquisitor." Samuel Roffey proved that the Inquisitor lived more than two hundred years after the Albigenses had been suppressed and that Faber's conclusions contradicted the evidence offered in their support. A second testimony was that of the "Inquisitor-General Reinerius, once himself a Waldensian." From his own account Reinerius was not a Waldensian, and many passages showed that Faber "had never seen the book itself and only carelessly copied other writers." So loose an approach to learning was too common in compilers of ecclesiastical, and perhaps of other, history. "It is a sad thing that error and falsehood should be handed down from one to another till, after frequent repetition, they assume a tone of dogmatism and authority which seems to preclude all doubt."

The second writer who offered himself for dissection was Joseph Milner (1744–1797), at one time Headmaster of Hull Grammar School and later Vicar of North Ferriby. In the last years of his life he had published three volumes of a *History of the Church of Christ,* which was continued in two more volumes by his brother Isaac. A sound classicist and an ardent Evangelical, he could not approve of Gibbon, who had failed conspicuously to associate the Pope with the initial persecution of the Paulicians and, throughout the *Decline and Fall,* had portrayed the Christian life with unmerited gloom. Milner set himself to retrieve these errors and to "bring into prominence the bright side of Church history." His scholarship was, perhaps, not equal to his piety, and it wilted, like Faber's, under Samuel Roffey's penetrating eye. It was abundantly clear that Milner had not stooped to original sources, and he had not observed that Gibbon, gratified indeed to attack the Papacy, was ready to mock, if he could not undermine, the faith of all Christians, Protestant and Catholic alike. "Let Milner, or let any man, read this fifty-fourth chapter of Gibbon. I think he must see that all this talk about the Paulicians was only intended to introduce an invective against Christianity; and that the artful infidel dilated through twenty quarto pages on a subject which might have been dispatched in one, merely because it gave him an opportunity for sneer and sarcasm against the religion which both the Paulicians and their persecutors professed."

One more passage from *Facts and Documents* is not out of place. In it Samuel Roffey described the conditions which the medieval historian must expect and accept if he is to be worthy of his task. "He must be out at nights, creeping under the hedge and beside the ditch, in darkness and dirt, to catch the glow-worm . . . He must toil through much that is useless, worthless and repulsive; much offence to taste, logic and common sense; much ignorance and much superstition. He must be strong in mind, in body and in purpose. His daily task must be 'the reading that was never read', and half his books what were not thought worth printing. He must tuck up his sleeves and bid defiance to dirt and dog-Latin and all the tricks of monkish penmanship. He must have free access to old and large libraries—and he must *not* (however useful and honourable these employments may be, *he* must not) write basketfuls of sermons or spend six hours a day in teaching Greek or Latin."

The erudition no less than the uncompromising frankness of the book alarmed and angered the Evangelical leaders, and they were not softened when presented with a critical study of Fox's *Book of Martyrs.* Not unnaturally Samuel Roffey turned toward the Tractarians. He corresponded with Newman and Keble, and was especially the friend of Hugh James Rose who, though a son of Cambridge, was one of the fathers of the Oxford Movement and who founded in 1832 the *British Magazine of Ecclesiastical Information.* To this magazine Samuel Roffey contributed many papers, and on Rose's death in 1838 he became its editor. But as by his doubts he had alienated the Evangelicals, so he was driven to examine the justification, in history or in theology, for the later *Tracts for the Times.* When in 1841 he published a "Letter to a Friend on Tract 89," he became as suspect to High as to Low churchmen. The man of integrity, seeking for historical truth, is not always a comfortable colleague in the politics of church or state.

Meanwhile, in 1838, Samuel Roffey had been appointed Librarian at Lambeth by Archbishop Howley. When, in 1891,

Dr Jessopp was preparing his contribution to the *Dictionary of National Biography,* he asked Bishop Stubbs, himself Lambeth Librarian from 1862 to 1866, for reminiscences of his predecessor. Stubbs replied:[9] "I can really tell you hardly anything about Dr. Maitland's doings at Lambeth. I went and stayed with him at Gloucester just after I was appointed Librarian, with an idea of getting from him some notion of what his plan of management was. He was very kind but very sleepy, and told me very little. He did, however, give me a box full of slips prepared for an improved Catalogue, which I left in the Library in 1867 and which were (possibly) used in making the Catalogue (Interleaved Bodleian) now used in the Library. This, with the two volumes of Catalogue and Description of early printed books[10] and the collecting of a quantity of fragments taken from the bindings of the older volumes, comprises pretty nearly all the Librarian work which he did in the Library itself. He contemplated, I think, a classified Catalogue, but did not alter materially the existing shelf arrangements."

If it is not unfair to read between these lines, Stubbs seems to have written with less than his usual generosity. The post carried a nominal stipend; but there is no need to suppose that Samuel Roffey adjusted his work to his pay. Nor, in the spacious years of the mid-nineteenth century, were a librarian's duties considered incompatible with the pursuit, or even with the achievement, of scholarship. Stubbs himself thought it enough to attend the Library twice a week and found time not only to carry the responsibilities of a country living but also to edit three volumes of the Rolls Series. Samuel Roffey, throughout his years at Lambeth, remained editor of the *British Magazine* and its most constant contributor. It was in this period, indeed, that some of his most striking papers were written. One series was collected and published in 1844 under the title of *The Dark Ages,* and a second in 1849 as *Essays on Subjects Connected with the Reformation in England.*

The Dark Ages, if more popular in form than the earlier *Facts and Documents,* is equally penetrating and was directed against a more formidable antagonist. Robertson's *History of Charles V,* published in 1769, had brought him European fame, but its Introduction, offered as an estimate of the Dark Ages, invited and awaited criticism. That Robertson could have not only contemplated but completed his work without knowing German is not surprising; Gibbon himself, indefatigable in the pursuit of learning, thought it useless or unnecessary to attempt so uncouth a tongue. But Samuel Roffey had no difficulty in showing that of the Latin documents cited by Robertson some had been studied at second hand and others were misrepresented or misunderstood. Exposure, however, was only part of his aim. He was more concerned to examine for himself the state of religion and literature from the ninth to the twelfth centuries and to rescue these unfortunate years from the "ignorant disdain" with which Robertson had dismissed them. In this design he largely succeeded. He drew from his sources a sympathetic picture of monastic life, the libraries, and the scriptoria. Learning, sacred and profane, was richer and more widely diffused than Robertson had imagined. There was sufficient evidence that "the scriptures were more accessible to those who could use them and were in fact more used, and by a greater number of persons, than some modern writers would lead us to suppose." The book, read as a whole, was an advance, at once bold and careful, into territory from which, through prejudice or timidity, historians had hitherto recoiled.

In 1848 Samuel Roffey ceased to be Librarian. In his letter to Dr. Jessopp, Stubbs wrote: "The exact circumstances of his leaving the Library I never could hear. In all probability, however, it would be that Abp. Sumner did not ask him to continue his work, and, the appointment being regarded as a personal chaplaincy, the Archbishop nominated his son John Thomas, whose appointment, I suppose, lapsed when Abp. Longley nominated me. In the condition of things in 1848 the Archbishop, knowing Maitland principally as a critic of Milner and Fox, would scarcely be likely to give him the option of remaining—but he certainly ought to have done something complimentary, and as he did not I have no doubt that Dr. Maitland was a little disgusted." It is idle to inquire whether Archbishop Sumner's motive in failing or refusing to renew the appointment was the indulgence of a pardonable nepotism or a disrelish of inconvenient controversy. Samuel Roffey retired and lived for the rest of his life in Gloucester. He continued, at rarer intervals, to publish papers, such as the essay on Thomas Chatterton in which he supported the authenticity of the Rowley poems on the ground that Chatterton's avowed works were so poor that he could never have invented Rowley. "He was much to be pitied. He was placed by circumstances in a false position. He thought he was to write poetry: he did his best, but it was very bad." Versatile interests helped him to endure or mitigate old age. He contributed freely to *Notes and Queries,* founded in 1849 by a fellow antiquarian, William John Thomas. He was a musician, installing an organ in his house and studying the works of Tallis, Marbeck, and other sixteenth-century composers. He worked a small press and not only printed but bound books. A friend once sought to take from a shelf in his library a book entitled *Maitland's Works* and found that he was trying his strength upon one of the uprights of the bookcase, all of which was backed and lettered by its owner.

When ephemera are set aside, his scholarship remains at once sure and original. Two assessments may be offered. Written by very different men at different times, their agreement commands respect. The first is by Augustus de Morgan, who wrote Samuel Roffey's obituary in the *Proceedings* of the Royal Society.[11] "He was not a popular writer; his subjects are too recondite and his learning too profound. But he is one of a class of whose writings it must be said that whenever they take they bite. They are imbued, but not in excess, with a kind of humour which seems almost their own. It has more likeness to the peculiar humour of Pascal than is seen in any other writer of our day . . . The character of his learning is that of the man who reads books which he has always by him as distinguished from that of the man who knows how to go to the library and find by references. He had nothing to do with libraries except his own and that of which he was for ten years *in loco possidentis.*"

The second assessment is by Frederic William Maitland in a

letter to his sister in 1891.[12] "Judging him merely as I should judge any other literary man I think him great. It seems to me that he did what was wanted just at the moment when it was wanted and so has a distinct place in the history of England. The *Facts and Documents* is the book that I admire most. Of course it is a book for the few, but then those few will be just the next generation of historians. It is a book which 'renders impossible' a whole class of existing books. I don't mean physically impossible—men will go on writing books of that class—but henceforth they will not be mistaken for great historians. One still has to do for legal history something like the work that S.R.M. did for ecclesiastical history—to teach them, e.g. that some statement about the 13th century does not become true because it has been constantly repeated, that a 'chain of testimony' is never stronger than its first link. It is the 'method' that I admire in S.R.M. more even than the style or the matter—the application to remote events of those canons of evidence which we should all use about affairs of the present day, e.g. of the rule which excludes hearsay."

Samuel Roffey had one son, John Gorham Maitland, born on October 27, 1817. He went up to Trinity College, Cambridge, and had a distinguished university career: third classic of his year, second Chancellor's medallist, seventh wrangler, and a member of the Apostles. Writing in the year after his death, a contemporary described him as one "the extent of whose powers and attainments his great modesty veiled from the world . . . His mind embraced all subjects and was as fitted for the work of life as for speculation."[13] A further sentence records a gift peculiarly calculated to excite undergraduate admiration. Despite his academic success "he seemed never to have any work to do." Even when the warmth of young friendship is discounted such words seem extravagant; but it is perhaps severe to judge promise by performance.

When he left Cambridge he was, like his father, called to the Bar and, like him, found it uncongenial. Whether he attempted to practice is unknown; it is certain that if he did he failed. Of his occupations over the years in Lincoln's Inn little survives save a number of pamphlets, mostly on income tax.

These would not seem to offer much refreshment. But the subject, if dry, is not barren, and a reader will not find his venture wholly unprofitable. The pamphlets raise questions which, after more than a century, are still alive. The arguments are clear and pungent, and they are relieved by a sufficient command of irony. Disraeli, in his abortive budget of 1852, had sought to levy more tax from unearned than from "precarious" or earned incomes, and a supporter had urged the further refinement of distinguishing two classes of earnings, the commercial and the professional. John Gorham rebuked these eccentricities in *Property and Income Tax,* published in 1853. "There seems," he wrote, "considerable ingenuity in this view; but I need not discuss it, my only object being to show that, if instinct ought to satisfy us on the meaning of the positive 'precarious,' inquiry leaves us doubtful as to the comparative 'more precarious'." Upon the basic proposal to differentiate earned and unearned income he was resolute. "There is a class who by past labour and toil of their own, by past wear and tear, have realised property. Why, and for whom, do they save? They save for their children. They do not anticipate a time when even women, lunatics or cabinet ministers will be considered as legitimate subjects of fiscal oppression. It cannot be wise, for the sake of a temporary benefit to a class, to establish a distinction in principle between the right to income which is being earned and the right to property which has been earned and is now inherited." To an opponent who dismissed practical objections to a proposal as easy to circumvent if the theory is sound, he replied: "One way of overcoming (theoretically) a practical difficulty is simply to ignore it."

From fiscal questions he turned for recreation to German literature. He admired both form and content; but admiration stopped short of worship and allowed the indulgence of wit. The contemporary air was thick with translations of Goethe, and John Gorham was provoked by the intrusion of Abraham Hayward, a writer whose tastes were catholic and ranged from *The Art of Dining* to a version of Savigny's *Vocation of Our Age for Legislation and Jurisprudence.* Hayward had given to the world a prose rendering of *Faust,* with notes and a critical introduction. John Gorham in retaliation prepared, but forbore to publish, a metrical translation, warranted to be less intelligible than any rival version.

Pamphlets, even when relieved by *jeux d'esprit,* are not a satisfying diet for middle age. Samuel Roffey had left the Bar to pursue independent and controversial interests; John Gorham sought security. His chance came in 1855. Two years earlier a commission, of which Sir Charles Trevelyan was the moving spirit, recommended the selection of civil servants in the higher grades by a form of examination. The existing method of appointment was condemned with more force than taste. It allowed, in Trevelyan's words, "those whose abilities do not warrant an expectation that they will succeed in the open professions . . . and those whom indolence of temperament or physical infirmities render unfit for active exertions to be placed in the Civil Service, where they may obtain an honourable livelihood with little labour and with no risk." The proposal angered Anthony Trollope, already one of the ablest and most energetic of civil servants, who attacked the commission and its leader in *The Three Clerks.* But it was accepted, and three commissioners were chosen in 1855 to control the conduct of examinations. They were empowered to engage assistant examiners on a full-time or part-time basis. Among the latter was John Gorham, whose name appears in the minute books for the summer and autumn of 1855.[14] The work was not without its embarrassments. On one occasion he was summoned to explain to the Commissioners why a candidate had misunderstood his instructions and thus failed to attempt certain questions. But he impressed his superiors; and when James Spedding, the Secretary of the Civil Service Commission, decided, after a taste of office, that he preferred to devote his life to a study of Francis Bacon, John Gorham was recommended as his successor. For a short but anxious time his appointment hung in the balance. Gladstone, then Chancellor of the Exchequer, approved: he had read the income tax pamphlets. But Lord Palmerston, as Prime Minister, was disposed to be awkward. Spedding, who was a friend and fellow Apostle of John Gorham, wrote to comfort him. "I dare say the great Pam only makes the difficulty in order to keep up the tradition of a check on the Service."[15] Spedding was right. Palmerston relented, and John Gorham was appointed Secretary.

In this office he revealed a taste and a capacity for administration. He was in large measure responsible for the success of the new system, and, when in 1863 he died at the age of forty-six, the Commissioners paid him a tribute whose sincerity not even official language can disguise. But with all his talents he remains, at the distance of a century, a little colorless. Perhaps the life that he chose, or into which he drifted, confirmed, instead of relaxing, a natural reticence. Perhaps, once the warmth of youth had cooled, his personality, and more certainly his vitality, proved unequal to his gifts. But it is hard to see him in detachment. He stands in the shadows of a remarkable father and of a great son.

In 1847 he had married Emma Daniell, who brought a new strain into the family. She was the daughter of John Frederic Daniell, the son and grandson of lawyers but himself a versatile scientist. He was elected a Fellow of the Royal Society at the age of twenty-three and became Professor of Chemistry at King's College, London, in 1831. He was a meteorologist and organized the annual reports of the Horticultural Society from which the Greenwich reports were developed. He pursued eager research into the problems and possibilities of electricity and invented a "constant battery." Daniell's energies were too soon exhausted. On March 13, 1845, he gave a lecture at King's College, went to a council meeting of the Royal Society, and died suddenly on the same day.

There were three children of the marriage: Selina Caroline, born on April 4, 1849, Frederic William, born on May 28, 1850, and Emma Katherine, born on November 21, 1851. Their mother never recovered from the birth of her third child and died on December 26, 1851. John Gorham himself died on April 27, 1863, three years before Samuel Roffey, and the Gloucestershire property passed in 1866 from grandfather to grandson. It comprised at this date Brookthorpe Court, let to a working farmer, two farms, a small holding, eight cottages, surrounding land, and a wood then called Stockend but since given to the National Trust and known as Maitland's. The rent roll was not large, and, after the collapse of English agriculture in 1880, barely met the expenses. But it was happily buttressed by other capital left by Samuel Roffey and by John Gorham which, after providing for his two sisters, sufficed to give Frederic William Maitland both a good education and the sense of stability and independence which in itself justifies private income. But he inherited from his paternal grandfather more than land and money: a keen and original vision, intellectual powers both wide and deep, moral courage, and a resolve never to do less than his best. His was a rich inheritance.

Chapter II

Early Years

Frederic was nineteen months old, Selina (Sela) two and a half years, and Emma Katherine (Kate) barely a month when their mother died. Her place was taken by her sister, Charlotte Louisa Daniell, and no children could have had a better foster mother. Sensible but sympathetic, at once calm and warm-hearted, she deserved and won their affection; and in the background, if occasion demanded a knowledge of the world, stood a bachelor uncle, Frederic William Daniell, comfortable and comforting. Maitland had been born at 53 Guildford Street, London, but the family soon moved to 39 Woburn Place—the first home he remembered—and thence to a house in Rutland Gate. In 1864 they moved again to Durham Villas, Argyll Road, Kensington, and in 1874 to 19 Southwell Road. Through all these changes Aunt Louisa, until her death in 1880, gave the family the feeling of comfort and security which makes a house a home.

Diaries kept by Sela from 1863 to 1871 enable us to see

something of Maitland's boyhood. Almost the first entry records the death of their father in April 1863. Maitland was then at Mr. Peters' preparatory school in Brighton, whence, on July 23, "Fred came home for his holidays, bringing three prizes with him." On September 23 Uncle Fred took him for the first time to Eton. He entered the Rev. George Frewer's house; but in 1864 Mr. Frewer retired and was succeeded by the Rev. Edward Daniel Stone who became both Maitland's housemaster and his classical tutor. The available evidence suggests that relations between master and boy were happy throughout Maitland's years at Eton.

The diaries attest the fidelity with which the family kept the festivals ordained in the school calendar. Each year saw the ritual of the Lord's match and the visit to Eton for the Fourth of June. In 1864 "Aunt Louisa and I went to the fête at Eton and came home quite late with Uncle Fred after seeing the fire-works which were beautiful." In 1867, 1868, and 1869 Sela recorded that she had spent the day "with Fred and had luncheon and tea in his rooms." On July 28, 1866, she "went with Uncle Fred to Maidenhead and then rowed to Eton to see the Election Saturday procession. Fred dined with us and we saw the fireworks later." Election Saturday was the day appointed for the Provost of King's College, Cambridge, to visit Eton and take part in the examination for the election of King's College scholarships. A Sixth-Form Colleger delivered an oration known as Cloisters Speech; and in the evening the Boats proceeded to Surly and followed the Eton and Westminster Eights to Eton Eyot. According to the Eton College Chronicle of August 8, 1866, "Election Saturday passed off with its usual dullness." It is consoling to read that the customary fireworks were "better than usual."[1]

Neither in work nor in play was Maitland prominent at Eton. His sole recorded scholastic success was the award of the Newcastle prize for an essay on Chaucer, a paper that seems not to have survived. It is probably fanciful to see here a foreshadowing of his future interest in the Middle Ages. The theme is one which had attracted his grandfather and to which he may have been introduced on his visits to Gloucester. He played football with tepid interest, but enjoyed the river, on which he was a keen if not outstanding oarsman. In May 1868 he wrote to Sela: "I was tried for an oar in the 'Dreadnought' but of course I did not get in, which was no disappointment. I have still just the chance of being in the 'Thetis'."[2] In 1869 —his last year at school—he rowed in the Monarch, a boat whose crew, while it included such magnates as the Captain of the School and the Keeper of the Field, owed their places to activities off rather than on the river. His one vivid interest was in music. On many Sunday afternoons he ran to St. George's Chapel, Windsor, to hear the anthem; and it was a common love of music which brought him the lifelong friendship of Gerald Balfour who, while a less successful politician than his brother Arthur, was—if the epithet may properly be applied to either of them—the more professional philosopher. Gerald had his full share of the charm with which his family was graced. Maitland felt it early and affirmed it late, and when Gerald was a young Fellow of Trinity, the ladies of Cambridge sighed over him in vain. "He is just what you would imagine an English lord to look and be like . . . He is so beautiful."[3] The names of three other boys appear in Sela's diaries as Maitland's friends. "Mr. Young" visits them in the holidays; "Mr. Dent and Mr. Loder" have luncheon with them at Eton; and all three are met again at Cambridge. Charles Edward Baring Young (1850–1928) was called to the Bar in 1876 and was the Member of Parliament for Christchurch from 1885 to 1892. Mr. Loder (1849–1920) was afterwards Sir Edmund Loder of Leonardslee, Horsham, and Maitland stayed with him in August 1869. Clinton Dent (1850–1912) became a distinguished surgeon; but it was by his tastes and recreations that Maitland was attracted. He was an explorer of the Caucasus, a mountaineer, and from 1886 to 1889 President of the Alpine Club.[4]

Maitland's years at Eton, reflected in the light of his later life, may seem disappointing. More than one effort has been made to explain or excuse his failure to become a distinguished schoolboy. Professor Hollond, in his sympathetic memorial address, observed that Maitland "had none of the aptitudes which made Victorian schoolmasters interested in boys, and no one seems to have discovered what a remarkable person he was." It would rather have been strange had the discovery been made. Intellect, character, faculties, and interests ripen in different persons at different ages; precocity is not an inevitable or sure symptom of genius. H. A. L. Fisher, not content with surprise or regret, essayed a reconstruction. "We imagine a shy, awkward, delicate boy, bursting into jets of wittiness at the least provocation, caring for things which other boys did not care for, misliking the classics, especially Greek . . . To the masters Maitland presented none of the obvious points of interest . . . the boy was not a Hellenist and his deficiencies in Greek and Latin prosody put him outside the intellectual pale. He was whimsical, full of eccentric interests, of puns and paradox and original humour. His closest school friend thought that he would possibly develop into 'a kind of philosophic Charles Lamb'."[5] "Shy and awkward": these are epithets which "surprise by themselves." Maitland was modest, but there is no evidence that at any period of his life he was shy; and "awkward" is the last word to come to mind in evoking his characteristics, physical or intellectual.[6] Even "delicate," unless it means delicacy of frame, is a word suggested by knowledge of the man rather than of the boy. Maitland rowed vigorously and relished so much to stretch his limbs that at the end of more than one term he walked home from Eton. Nor is it clear what things it could have been for which other boys did not care. Music, reading outside the standard texts, "puns and paradox and original humour"—such tastes and qualities do not affront the more civilized boys in any school.

Fisher was on surer ground in stressing distaste for the classics and especially for Greek, and the consequent indifference of the more orthodox masters. When, at the other end of his life, Maitland asked Henry Jackson to correct the Greek accents in a proof of Leslie Stephen's *Hobbes,* he said that "the little Greek I ever had was of the compulsory kind and has long since flown."[7] A year after Maitland's death his old housemaster wrote to Sela, lamenting his own share in the inordinate sacrifices offered to the classics. "As regards education I consider my own to have been scandalous, but your brother had too much originality to submit to the grind and he escaped comparatively unscathed. I have been severely singed and have felt the effects ever since. The dreadful thing is that I should have helped to perpetuate the scandal."[8]

It is interesting, and may not be uninstructive, to compare Maitland's school days with those of his seniors, the two Stephens and Frederick Pollock. FitzJames and Leslie Stephen both entered Eton in 1842, FitzJames at the age of thirteen and Leslie as a little boy of nine and a half. They were "up-town" boys: their father, with doubtful kindness, had taken a house in Windsor, and they went daily to school. In later life FitzJames said: "I was on the whole very unhappy at Eton, and I deserved it; for I was shy, timid and I must own cowardly. I was like a sensible grown-up woman among a crowd of rough boys." When he was sixteen, his father, who had discovered his unhappiness, removed him. In retrospect he was able to discern some merits in Eton, chiefly from "the neglect of discipline and of teaching." The first omission taught him "that to be weak is to be wretched, that the state of nature is a state of war and *Vae Victis* the great law of Nature." The second drove him to learn for himself whatever he wanted. But he could never condone the pedantic and extravagant emphasis on Greek and Latin. "Balston, our tutor, was a good scholar after the fashion of the day and famous for Latin verse; but he was essentially a commonplace don." To FitzJames he once said: "Stephen major, if you do not take more pains, how can you expect to write good longs and shorts? If you do not write good longs and shorts, how can you ever be a man of taste? If you are not a man of taste, how can you ever hope to be of use in the world?"[9]

Leslie Stephen did all that a little boy could be expected to do who was in poor health and whose place in school was dictated exclusively by the classics. He won a prize for mathematics which, though outside the curriculum, was allowed to be taught. But when he was fourteen, his father "received a note from Mr. Balston in which, though praising Leslie for his conduct, diligence, etc., he spoke strongly of his want of success in composition, and his not having the power of perceiving beauty and the necessity of cultivating his taste." His father at once took him away from Eton. "If five years had been spent without success in learning to make Latin verses, it was no use to go on longer." Thereafter, said Maitland, "the Stephen whom I knew never talked of his school-days . . . One of the most Cantabrigian of Cambridge men, he was the least Etonian of Eton men. I do not think that he had any dislike for the school; his two step-sons went there; but he had left it while he was very young, and there was little about it that he cared to remember."[10]

In mitigation of their experiences it may be pleaded that, as "uptown boys," they were not truly a part of the foundation to which they were attached. Of Frederick Pollock, even as a boy, it is impossible to conceive such an indignity. As he looked back in old age he could see no cloud on the sunshine of school life. He took naturally to the classics, and among a happy band of masters one was *primus inter pares*. "My particular good fortune was to be one of William Johnson's pupils . . . My Greek and Latin, and my permanent interest in those tongues, are mostly of his planting. Moreover, he taught us, in the informal classes outside school hours called 'private', many things that were not in the regular lessons . . . History came into the school work only so far as necessary for understanding the classical texts, and then for the most part in a bare and dry fashion: William Johnson taught us its living interest and its importance in forming a wide and rational outlook on public affairs."[11] William Johnson was a master at Eton from 1845 until 1872, when he assumed the name of Cory, retired from teaching, and pursued literature. His attractive and elusive personality pervades many reminiscences of Eton, and in a wider world he lives as the author of *Heraclitus*. His poems are charged with the spirit of Greece; but that he should have indulged a taste for history, modern as well as ancient, and that he should have invited boys to share his indulgence is unexpected. Maitland was not a member of so esoteric a circle. Perhaps unless a boy was a classicist he was not given the key to the inner chamber of Johnson's interests.

The Eton of 1863, when Pollock left and Maitland came, had

altered little since the earlier years of the century: mathematics was still a work of supererogation and history still the handmaid of the classics. In his sentiments and impressions Maitland stood between Pollock and the Stephens. While he was no devotee like the former, there is no evidence that he shared the unhappiness of the latter. He was a boy who, without inspiring the worship which is the hallowed if ephemeral tribute paid to the athlete, would be liked by his contemporaries. He was neither opinionated nor unduly reserved; he was mentally eager and could use his wits in the sort of commentary on the scene around him which boys enjoy. His first publication was a "squib" in a school magazine on the opening of a new observatory.[12] Garnished with the puns which were then popular, it belongs to a fashion which has passed away. But at least it reveals Maitland as an amused and indulgent spectator of Eton life and school politics.

Leslie Stephen was wont to explain that when one of our great schools is said to have produced a famous man, the word produced means "failed to extinguish."[13] If Eton did not produce Maitland, neither did it extinguish him. The only positive burden he was made to bear was the dead weight of Greek and Latin. Negatively he may have sensed, half consciously, the frustration of missing what his own imperfectly realized powers demanded. It was perhaps for this reason that his daughter wrote of him as "one who felt that Eton had wasted so much of his time."[14] But even this feeling may have been retrospective. Though the inner sentiments of youth are unfathomable, he would seem to have derived as much happiness from school as the average reasonable boy can expect to enjoy.

To one master Maitland owed much. Oscar Browning, that remarkable figure who—not always fortunately for himself—became a legend in his own lifetime, had, as a boy, failed to relish Eton; but in 1860 he was tempted to return as a master. H. E. Wortham speaks of "the vitality, the enormous fund of good-humour, the frankness of speech, the idiosyncrasies of vanity, the enthusiasm, the magnanimity, the vindictiveness, all the strange jumble which went to lift Oscar Browning into a personality with that touch of absurdity which constitutes a character."[15] This chaos of qualities was, for the next fifteen years, yoked to the task of saving Eton from the pedants and the philistines. William Johnson, from Pollock's account of him, might have seemed a natural ally. So long, indeed, as "O.B." was content to recommend modern languages and history as school subjects, he could count upon Johnson's discreet support. But when he suggested that "construing in pupil-room should be abolished," Johnson felt his reforming zeal to be too destructive. When he went so far as to make his classes learn English poetry, Johnson protested, and Dr. Balston, now headmaster, vetoed the dangerous innovation. "The learning of English poetry I do not wish to encourage." At length in 1868, due to the pressure of a Royal Commission rather than to the pertinacity of Browning, changes were forced upon the "Old Eton Party." Maitland reported the revolution to Sela.[16] "Tomorrow morning I shall arise a reformed Etonian—My, ain't it terrible, what shall we du? We are going to learn all manner of abominations, have all manner of extra schools and be turned wholesale into Radicals. Today the 10th of May, 1868—the fourth Sunday after Easter, the festival of the blessed Antoninus, bishop and confessor—is our last day of unreformed bliss. The old masters are furious (bless their dear old conservative souls), the young ones jubilant (like a lot of nasty radicals that they are). I have got my choice of five subjects—French, German, Italian, Logic or Political Economy. The choice lies between German and Johnson on Political Economy."

The victory came late in Maitland's school days, and for Browning it was Pyrrhic. The outworks of classical domination had been reduced, but the citadel was held. Dr. Hornby, who had now succeeded Balston as Headmaster, timidly welcomed the changes, but as an end and not a beginning. O.B., baulked in his desire for drastic reforms in school work, consoled himself by making his own house a focus of taste. "Life in Browning's house was a pleasant combination of high thinking and good living. Artists and men of letters, actors and musicians, Ruskin and Solomon, George Eliot and Walter Pater, Dannreuther, the brilliant pianist who was the friend of Wagner, Sullivan, Sir George Grove, were more or less frequent visitors and brought with them the atmosphere of the intelligent and civilised society to which Oscar Browning liked to think that he belonged in spite of being a schoolmaster. Theatricals used to be given by the boys in the dining-room. Concerts were held periodically on Saturdays at which professionals from London performed chamber music . . . Arundel prints hung on his walls. Morris curtains framed the windows. Bronzes and marbles and plaster casts, especially the fragile plaster casts, helped to inculcate sobriety of demeanour. To play football in such corridors was as unthinkable as rough-housing in the corridors of the Vatican."[17] To this oasis Maitland was welcomed.

Browning, moreover, sought to temper the aesthetic life with water parties far beyond the environs of Eton, and Maitland was again invited. "Last week," he wrote to Sela on June 30, 1869,[18] "Browning took me and some other fellows by train to Goring, the station on this side and next to Didcot, and thence we rowed down in a 'gig'—the whole distance was 42 miles. We took from 11.30 a.m. to midnight getting over it, including stoppages for dinner etcetera. I was dreadfully 'beat' after it but it was a right jolly expedition—we passed Pangbourne, with its lovely woods, and Reading which is not particularly picturesque, on to Henley by the Fuller-Maitlands' place (which is about the prettiest spot I ever saw), over the regatta course, past the celebrated Medenham Abbey, to Marlow, where we dined at the inn famous for the bargees' feast off the 'puppy-pie'—past Cookham, Cliefden and Maidenhead in the moonlight to our couches, right sore as you may guess. I fell asleep in every school the next day but was not sorry that I went as the scenery was perfect—besides Browning, though he does make you do all the rowing, gave us lots to drink—not to mention ducks and peas such as the banks of the Thames alone produce."

Dr. Hornby distrusted culture and was not appeased by the water parties. Though he had in his time rowed both well and wisely, he resented the thought of the river as a source of pleasure. The breach widened between him and Browning; and in 1875, after a quarrel advertised and fanned by the press, Browning was dismissed and returned to Cambridge as a Fellow of King's. Maitland's sympathies were undivided. "The conduct of the Head Master," he wrote to Browning,[19] "is to me inexplicable. He surely must be able to see that a man may be a good schoolmaster, though he be neither an athlete nor a pedant. However, happily it is not my place to make excuses for him. I will only say (what I never should have said to you except in such circumstances as the present) that you were one of the very few masters who attempted to give me an interest in reading as opposed to cramming, and that is a debt which I cannot forget."

The education of the Maitland children reflected the disparate treatment of boys and girls in the middle years of the nineteenth century. For boys there were sufficient preparatory and public schools, however limited their scope. For girls few schools existed. They might be sent abroad to such institutions as the Pensionnat Heger immortalized by Charlotte Brontë, or to the school in Paris kept by Mrs. Bray until, like Louis Philippe, it fell a victim to the Revolution of 1848. Their English counterparts were not very palatable. Mrs. Humphrey Ward, who as the granddaughter of Thomas Arnold was a connoisseur of education, thought her own school years from 1858 to 1867 to have been "practically wasted." She recalled "poor teaching, poor school-books, indifferent food and ignorance as to the physical care of girls."[20] The pioneers of a new era were Miss Buss and Miss Beale—names inseparably coupled in the verse of an anonymous pupil.[21] Frances Mary Buss founded in 1850 the North London Collegiate School for Ladies;[22] Dorothea Beale became Principal of Cheltenham Ladies' College in 1858. But prejudice lingered until the end of the century. "The upper classes did not approve of day schools, though boarding schools for older girls might sometimes be allowed. The Aristocracy, however, did not even hold with boarding schools, for a peeress of our acquaintance once roused my mother to fury by snubbing her with the words, '*We* do not send our daughters away to school.' "[23]

While their brother was at Eton, Sela and Kate were supplied at home with a succession of governesses, sometimes French but, in deference to a learned race and to their father's predilection, more often German. Sela entered in her diary from 1866 to 1869 the books prescribed for her by these ladies:[24] Ranke, *History of the Popes;* Molière (unspecified plays); Sainte-Beuve, *Causeries de Lundi;* Schiller (unspecified plays); Macaulay, *History of England;* Sir W. Hamilton, *Lectures on Metaphysics and Logic;* Lessing (titles unspecified); Taine, *Essais de critique et d'histoire;* Dante, *Inferno;* Coleridge, *Biographia Literaria;* Lamartine (titles unspecified); *A Life of Aristotle* (J. W. Blakesley); Montalembert, *Mélanges d'art et de litterature;* F. D. Maurice, *Lectures on the Conscience;* Sir James Stephen, *Essays in Ecclesiastical Biography;* Milman, *History of Christianity.* The set tasks were relieved by more general reading: Shakespeare (many plays); Browning and Wordsworth (unspecified poems); Tennyson, *In Memoriam, Maud* (the Christmas gift of Aunt Louisa), *The Princess,* and *Lucretius;* Keats, *Endymion;* William Morris, *Life and Death of Jason* and *The Earthly Paradise;* Ruskin, *Modern Painters;* Thackeray, *The Newcomes* and *Esmond;* Disraeli, *Coningsby;* Jane Austen, *Pride and Prejudice;* Mrs. Gaskell, *Cranford, North and South* and *Wives and Daughters;* George Eliot, *Romola* and *Felix Holt;* Henry Kingsley, *Ravenshoe* and *Silcote.* The whole family shared the Victorian pastime of reading aloud; their favorites were Scott and Trollope.

Maitland's home was thus a second and more congenial source of learning. Many years later, in his speech on compulsory Greek,[25] he "reserved the greater part of his gratitude for a certain German governess," and a letter to Sela added a new beatitude: "Blessed be all your German governesses." Summer holidays were spent at Malvern, in Gloucestershire or in North Devon, where Maitland could indulge at will his passion for walking, sometimes with Sela and sometimes in strenuous but happy solitude. Christmas brought a round of London parties and dances, and Sela records many visits to Covent Garden, where Wagner had not yet displaced Meyerbeer and where

Gounod's *Faust,* with Mario in the title role, had won immediate popularity. But, save for the annual ritual of the pantomime, she saw no play until, at the age of twenty, she was escorted by her brother to the popular melodrama *Belphegor* at Drury Lane. The moral or physical atmosphere of the gaslit and unsanitary playhouse was deemed unfit for nice young girls. Other amusements were happily free from contamination. No harm could attend a visit to the Christy Minstrels at St. James's Hall or to the German Reeds in their Gallery of Illustrations. These assuredly were no flaunting actors or actresses but just an honest family party. The opéra bouffes of Offenbach were notoriously corrupt, but the German Reeds, as the name of their house proclaimed, presented not operettas but "illustrations": charming little pieces like Sullivan's *Cox and Box,* scintillating but innocent.

Of all recreations music was the most enjoyed and the most frequent. Family piety as well as its own attractions drew them to the Three Choirs Festival at Gloucester, and London offered a rich choice of music. They attended each year the winter concerts of the Civil Service Musical Society, which had been formed in 1864 "for the practice of vocal and instrumental music among the civil servants and excise servants of the Crown." The forte of the society, whose first conductor was Sullivan, was its male voice choir; and it endured until 1880 when, despite the fact that its president was the Chairman of the Board of Inland Revenue, it succumbed to financial difficulties. At Exeter Hall in the Strand the Sacred Harmonic Society, seven hundred strong, justified its title by performing the oratorios of Handel and Mendelssohn, relieved by the contrasting Masses of Beethoven and Gounod. Their conductor was Sir Michael Costa, a formidable figure who long dominated music in England. In 1889, five years after Costa's death, Bernard Shaw recalled him as one "who had no respect for the past, no help for the present and no aspiration towards the future—equally ready to murder anything old with 'additional accompaniments' and cuts, or to strangle anything new by refusing to have anything to do with it." But even so confident a critic had to admit his merits as a martinet. The London orchestras "feared nobody but Sir Michael Costa."[26] At the Crystal Palace August Manns was conductor from 1855 to 1901. He was a disciple of Schubert and of Schumann and he introduced Brahms to England. Sela records many visits with her brother and sister and notes especially performances of Beethoven's Ninth Symphony and of the Emperor Concerto, played by Charles Hallé, the founder of the Manchester orchestra. They were eager and regular attendants at the Monday and Saturday Popular Concerts, above all when Madame Schumann played. When in 1886 Maitland wrote to Sela of his engagement to Florence Fisher, he stressed her love of music and recalled past days. "We went last night to the last of the Pops. and heard some of the good old tunes that you and I have so often heard together—Schumann's quintet, Brahms' sextet, Hungarian dances, etc."[27]

The Maitlands were self-contained; but if they sought diversion they could find it in a wide range of cousins. One name recurs in Sela's diary. "Cousin William Rogers came to dinner"; "Cousin Rogers took me to the Lord Mayor's Banquet"; "Fred dined with William Rogers"; "Fred and I helped with an exhibition in Cousin Rogers' parish"; "Fred and I to an evening party in Cousin Rogers' schoolroom—six Christmas trees." William Rogers' mother had been Mrs. Maitland's aunt. He went to Eton and Balliol and rowed for Oxford in 1840. In 1843 he became Curate of Fulham, where he at once made friends with the watermen. "One of them was almost a religious man. 'Oh, Sir,' he said to me one day, looking at the Thames, 'I often think of old Peter rowing on this 'ere water.' "[28] In 1845 he was "promoted" to the living of St. Thomas, Charterhouse, at a stipend of £150 a year. The custom of the parish was one family to one room, where "half a dozen men, women and children steamed oranges, boiled winkles, fried fish, polished apples, smoked sprats, and lived and moved and slept and had their being. It was not to be expected that a man who lived in such conditions should—though he were soaked in a warm bath on Saturday nights—be sufficiently deodorised by Sunday morning to make him a welcome worshipper." Rogers did not despair of civilizing the parents, but he decided to start with the children for whom no schools existed. Within ten years he had opened four schools with places for seventeen hundred children. The parents were charged sixpence a child, and every place was filled and every fee paid. Attendance was gratifying save in the presence of so strong a counterattraction as an execution at Newgate, when "gone to the 'anging" was the recognized answer to inquiries after absentees. In 1863 Rogers became Rector of St. Botolph, Bishopsgate. There he supplied a new need: "middle-class schools for the children of clerks and small tradesmen at fees of £4 a year." In three years a thousand children were being taught.

Rogers himself paid for the earlier schools and their teachers, but even his generosity could not meet the cost of his later ventures. He became a successful mendicant, levying toll on family and friends, on Eton and Balliol, on the National Society, on the City Companies, and on the Educational Committee of the Privy Council. Throughout his efforts he met and welcomed strenuous opposition. The Ecclesiastical Commissioners objected to his first school, built against the walls of the church: "it would desecrate the church." In Bishopsgate he found the churchyard "a dirty, unwholesome spot and a receptacle for all the dead cats and dogs of the neighborhood." When he made it into a garden there was an immediate outcry. "People waxed indignant at the violence done to the bones of their ancestors, and the Rectory was besieged by heartbroken descendants." The middle-class schools aroused special resentment. Rogers insisted that they must be open to people of any or of no church: "distinctive doctrinal teaching should be left to parents and to those ministers of religion whom they might select." He was charged with the promotion of "godless education" and with the more dangerous sin of profligate finance. His reply was characteristic. "Hang economy, hang theology, let us begin." He believed also that recreation must temper instruction; and here the Maitlands, with many others, were pressed into service. The school chapel was used for dances, for concerts, for lectures, for exhibitions of pictures, and in later years "for the annual performance by the school children of one or other of Messrs. Gilbert and Sullivan's operas." If he had strength of purpose, he also had charm. So unexpected a witness as Henry James evoked the memory of intimate dinners given in his rectory by "this much-doing, much-enduring and all-beneficent and delightful man."[29]

So remarkable a cousin may be allowed a digression. Through him Maitland caught a glimpse of lives lived in conditions whose reality beggared description. He saw that something could be done, not only for children who lacked guides and standards, but also for their elders whose youth had passed without opportunity. He was strengthened in an innate distrust of a doctrinaire hierarchy, in or out of church. He wrote of Leslie Stephen that "the best of what he learnt at this time of life he learnt in the holidays." To apply the words to Maitland himself would not be wholly just. But it is clear that his holidays gave him questions to answer as well as comforts to enjoy. Life was both pleasant and fruitful as it radiated from the home of which Aunt Louisa was the center.

Chapter III

Undergraduate

In October 1869 Maitland went up to Trinity College, Cambridge, as a "pensioner" or commoner. He accepted at once the carefree and yet ordered living which Cambridge (and indeed Oxford) can offer to her fortunate sons, and perhaps with the greater assurance a hundred years ago. On the river he rowed with the same pleasure and with more success than at Eton. On the running track he distinguished himself and was awarded his Blue. Kate, who now shared with Sela the corvée of the diary, entered for April 7, 1870: "Oxford and Cambridge Athletic Sports. Fred ran in the 3 mile race. Oxford won." Maitland, more than thirty years later, wrote of the young Leslie Stephen as a "rowing rough," imbued with the "fanatical enthusiasm" of the towing path.[1] These phrases, strangely attached as they seem to the father of Virginia Woolf, ring true because Maitland himself shared the physical urge which exercise at once strenuous and rhythmical alone can satisfy. "The nature of the sports he preferred," wrote Buckland,[2] "give an indication of the character of the man. They both involve long and continuous effort. Even in Rugby football there are moments of rest; and it would not appeal to him, though I do not think it was much played here in those days. It was the same with cricket. I remember sitting with him once in the Downing grounds watching for a time the progress of a match. He looked at it with some curiosity, as if he had not seen it before, and then, turning away, said: 'Not much of a game, cricket—too much sitting about.' In the same way in later life he took up cycling, not so much for amusement as for exercise; and I have always thought that its main attraction for him was that you could not loiter—if you did not keep moving you fell off."

At the end of his freshman's year his family paid him a visit in state. Kate's diary offers a pleasing if ingenuous picture of Cambridge *en fête*.

May 28. "Aunt Louisa, Sela, Evans[3] and I went to stay at Cambridge. Mr. Loder and Mr. Dent (Fred's friends) came to luncheon. We went to see Fred's lodgings in Malcolm St., and then to see the boats row. Fred rowed in the Third Trinity second boat. We stayed at 10 Green St."

May 29. "Fred came to breakfast. Morning service, St. John's College Chapel: Evening Service, King's College. In the evening walked along the backs of the colleges which were lovely."

May 30. "Saw more colleges and the Fitzwilliam. Band played in Christ's College gardens. Saw boats again."

May 31. "Luncheon at Mr. Dent's in Trinity, where we met Mr. Pelham, Mr. Loder and Fred. Fred took us round Trinity. Boat race again."

June 1. "More colleges—luncheon at Mr. Loder's. Concert in Downing gardens."

June 2. "More colleges. We all, including Fred, dined at Mr. Maurice's."

June 3. "We went to stay at Mr. Maurice's. Evans back to London."

June 4. "Mr. Maurice took us to the University Library, Trinity Library and Queens' College. Saw Procession of Boats."

June 5. (Whit Sunday). "Morning Service, St. Mary the Less: Evening Service, Trinity Chapel."

F. D. Maurice had been a friend of John Gorham Maitland and was still a friend of William Rogers, whose zeal for education he shared. He wielded great contemporary influence as preacher and as writer. After suffering more vicissitudes than might have been expected of so gentle a soul, he had recently become the incumbent of St. Edward's, Cambridge. Leslie Stephen left an impression of him which, if not unkind, is scarcely sympathetic.[4] "Maurice," he wrote, "undoubtedly was one of the most attractive and saint-like of men. His very weakness and excess of sensibility gave to his friends the sense that they were the bodyguard of an unworldly teacher, whom they could relieve from practical difficulties and screen from the harsh censures of the ordinary controversialist and the religious newspaper. I always remember a photograph in which he appeared taking the arm of 'Tom' Hughes. Hughes was turning a reverential glance to his master and, at the same time, looking from the corner of his eye with an obvious wish that some caviller would try to punch the prophet's eye and require a lesson from a practical expert in the art of fisticuffs. The loyalty of the disciples was most natural and intelligible. Maurice in the pulpit was the very incarnation of earnestness, reverence and deep human feeling. But he did not strike me as an incarnation of clear-headedness."

A rowing man, and even a Blue, must sometimes work. At Cambridge, then as now, each undergraduate was allotted to to a tutor, who stood *in loco parentis* to his pupils and whose function was not so much to teach them as to watch over their welfare. Maitland's tutor was Robert Burn, a classic with a special gift for the writing of Latin hexameter verse. This talent was unlikely to recommend him to Maitland; but he had other and more congenial interests. He was persistent in the cause of University reform, ready even to remodel the Classical Tripos so as to find more room for the study of history.[5] In his earlier days, moreover, he had been a determined runner. Maitland, in his *Life of Leslie Stephen,*[6] quotes the story, as related by Dr.

H. A. Morgan, Master of Jesus College, of an epic race between Burn and Stephen when both were young dons. The course was "from the Railway Bridge to Baitsbite": Burn was to run along the towing path and Stephen along the more difficult Ditton side. "At last Burn, a good runner, came in sight, trotting steadily round the obtuse corner of the towing-path. Soon afterwards we saw Stephen tearing at full speed like a hunted stag through bushes and over ditches along the other bank; but to no purpose, for Burn won by a short distance."

As Maitland, *faute de mieux,* was studying mathematics, he read not with Burn but with H. M. Taylor, who lives still in Gwen Raverat's inimitable account of his earnest but hapless wooing of her mother.[7] His fellow pupil was A. W. Verrall with whom he formed a lifelong friendship. G. M. Trevelyan coupled them as "the most brilliant of all the sons of Alma Mater: their talk was like the play of lightning, rendered innocuous by their kindliness and good sense."[8] Verrall was to become a distinguished exponent of both Greek and English literature, and his idiosyncrasies, intellectual and physical, were as endearing as his gifts. Like his beloved Athenians, he rejoiced either to tell or to hear some new thing, and the novelty of a theory was apt to provide its own justification. Henry Jackson once wrote to Maitland: "Have you heard that Verrall gave a lecture in which he maintained that the *Birds* is a satire on that Palestinian religion now best represented in England and that what is satirised appears in the chapels of Jesus, John's and Trinity? . . . The lecture was set up for publication in the *Cambridge Review* when Verrall, the evening before the *Review* appeared, withdrew it. The editor revenged himself by publishing the facts and commenting upon the lecture—'si non e vero, e Verrall'."[9] Verrall had a vocal mannerism, recounted by different hearers in similar terms. Trevelyan wrote of his voice as "rising into a crow of delight at the end of some outburst of his wit." Buckland spoke of his "habit of prefacing and concluding his observations by a continuous noise which can best be described as a crow." Maitland claimed to have discovered, on a visit to the Verrall family home, the explanation of this curiosity. "All the younger Verralls were great talkers, better talkers than listeners, and when any one of them had completed his observations on any point, it was his practice to follow them at once with this crow in order to prevent any of the others from intervening until he was prepared with his next observations."[10]

Maitland's pursuit of mathematics, while it brought friendship, brought him little else. The quest, indeed, was not arduous. Taylor, learned and kindly as he was, may not have been an inspiring teacher; but Maitland was not very ready to be inspired. For whatever reason his performance in the annual college examination, it has been said, "was so poor that he refused to go to Eton with some friends rather than face his tutor with a request for an exeat."[11] The examination result is undeniable; the sequel it is permissible to doubt. Maitland's devotion to Eton, as to mathematics, was strictly limited.

Academically Maitland's first year had been wasted. Long afterwards, in words which have often been quoted but which must be repeated here, he told the story of his awakening. Henry Sidgwick, the man to whom he owed it, died in August 1900, and on November 26, 1900, a meeting was held in Trinity College to consider a suitable memorial. Maitland spoke, as he said, "to express the opinion of some of Sidgwick's pupils, who, for one reason or another, were not fitted or not destined to be philosophers."[12]

> It is now thirty years ago since some chance—I think it was the idle whim of an idle undergraduate—took me to Sidgwick's lecture room, there to find teaching the like of which had never come in my way before . . . I believe that he was a supremely great teacher. In the first place, I remember the admirable patience which could never be outworn by stupidity and which nothing but pretentiousness could disturb. Then there was the sympathetic and kindly endeavour to overcome our shyness, to make us talk and to make us think. Then there was that marked dislike for any mere reproduction of his own opinions, which made it impossible for Sidgwick to be in the bad sense the founder of a school. I sometimes think that the one and only prejudice

> that Sidgwick had was a prejudice against his own results. All this was far more impressive and far more inspiring to us than any dogmatism could have been. Then the boldest thinking was set forth in words which seemed to carry candour and sobriety and circumspection to their furthest limit . . . I believe that no more truthful man than Sidgwick ever lived. I am speaking of a rare intellectual virtue. However small the class might be, Sidgwick always gave us his very best; not what might be good enough for undergraduates or what might serve for temporary purposes, but the complex truth just as he saw it, with all those reservations and qualifications, exceptions and distinctions which suggested themselves to a mind that was indeed marvellously subtle, but was showing us its wonderful power simply because even in a lecture room it could be content with nothing less than the maximum of attainable and communicable truth.

In Sidgwick's lecture room Maitland had chanced upon a course of reading which, if not wholly attuned to his gifts, was alive for him where mathematics had been dead, and whose attractions were doubled by devotion to the lecturer. The next two years were full and varied: rich in intellectual stimulus, rich in social life, and rich in friendship. Of the many friends whom he now found four may be mentioned. Their names attest the wide range of Maitland's interests.

Edmund Gurney, three years older than Maitland, became a Fellow of Trinity in 1872. Handsome, brilliant, and restless, he toyed in turn with music, medicine, and law. He completed in 1880 a book on "The Power of Sound," but drifted into psychical research. In these shadowy regions he was the companion of Sidgwick himself and for a moment of Verrall. Verrall's curiosity waned when the spirits were tested with a line of Euripides and found allergic to Greek;[13] Sidgwick, faint but pursuing, endured to the end. Such mysteries could not tempt Maitland; but he was drawn to Gurney by charm of personality, by play of wit, by the love of walking and of music. Gurney would seem to have been one of those young men of talent and fascination, like Arthur Hallam and John Sterling and

Hurrell Froude, who die before age can test them and who find their memorial in the remembrance of friends: they prevail, if indeed they are still prevalent, by faith and not by works. Fourteen years after his death Maitland still thought of him. "I walked with Gurney in the Tyrol. What moods he had! On a good day it was a joy to hear him laugh."[14]

Walter Leaf, who came up to Trinity in 1870, recorded the impression made by Maitland on his Cambridge contemporaries.[15] "One of the bonds between us," he wrote, "was a love of music combined with a very inadequate technical power of expression." But his most vivid recollection was of Maitland as "beyond comparison the wittiest man I have known . . . His wit bubbled out spontaneously, whether in writing, in speeches or in private talk, and was always of the same high quality . . . With all this intellectual equipment went all that could attract affection as well as admiration." Edmund Gurney, he thought, was "for wit and humour a good second to Maitland, and he shared with him a love of speculative inquiry which made him a master of subtle dialectic." This assessment, if heightened by the warmth of remembered youth, is the mature judgment of one whose career the nineteenth but not the twentieth century could afford. Like Grote before him, Leaf was both banker and scholar. But, unlike Grote, he retained his commercial interests to the end of his life: he was chairman of the London and Westminster Bank and of the Institute of Bankers, and President of the International Chamber of Commerce. His publications attest his double life: an edition of the *Iliad* in 1888, *Homer and History* in 1915, *Strabo on the Troad* in 1923, *Banking* in 1926.

Cyprian Williams, the youngest of Maitland's Cambridge friends, admired him as a senior and came to know him as an oarsman. It was through Williams that Fisher drew the picture of Maitland's farewell to the river: "how on the final day of the Lent races of 1872 the Third Trinity second boat after a successful week made a crowning bump, how in the moment of victory the crew were tipped over into the cold and dirty waters of the Cam, and how in the evening the boat dined in Maitland's lodgings over Palmer's bootshop and kept up its festivity well into the morning."[16] Cyprian Williams, who had to grow up beneath the heavy shade of his father Joshua Williams, the author of standard books on the Law of Property, was not the intellectual peer of Gurney or of Leaf. Yet Maitland, when he was driven into winter exile, thought of him as fit to act as a deputy Professor. Friendship between the two men ripened and endured, and more than one holiday was spent together at Williams' house in Taynton, near Burford.[17]

William Cunningham and Maitland sat together at the feet of Sidgwick. They are said to have "devised a co-operative system of note-taking at lectures."[18] The tactics—not always exploited by the abler or more industrious pupils—are well known to the sophisticated tutor. Cunningham chose later to diverge into economics and, on the publication of his *Growth of English Industry and Commerce,* was hailed as a pioneer in economic history. Once again a community of interests, in music and travel as well as in the tripos, cemented friendship. In 1907 Cunningham wrote to Sela: "We had been so intimately associated in our undergraduate time and his friendship has been so well proved in recent years that it has been a terrible pain to have him go out of my life."[19] Cunningham ended his days as Archdeacon of Ely. G. M. Trevelyan left a vignette of him: "When his heavy, bearded figure moved majestically across the Great Court under the shadow of his huge Archdeacon's hat, he seemed to have walked into our world out of Trollope's Barchester. He could have met Archdeacon Grantley on equal terms."[20] Maitland, if put to the question, would surely have striven to return a hopeful answer to the most famous of medieval interrogatories: *An possit archidiaconus salvari?*

With such friends Maitland enjoyed the clubs and dinners of undergraduate society. Walter Leaf and Oscar Browning, opposed in temperament, agreed in rating him as the most brilliant after-dinner speaker they had known. Eminence in this art, when artist and connoisseur have passed away, must rest rather on reputation than on evidence. Few sensations are harder to recapture than the relish of a dead speech. The voice, the look, the set of the mouth, hinting at a smile or ironically grave, the phrase chosen to meet the need of the moment and the taste of a fastidious audience—all are withered and the husk remains. Maitland seems to have had, and to have kept in later life, an acute sense of the occasion. A. J. Butler, Dante scholar and mountaineer, remembered him as he returned thanks for the visitors at the annual dinner of the Alpine Club. "He had climbed several big peaks in the Eastern Alps; but with characteristic *eironeia* he chose to pose as the man who had scarcely seen a mountain. The effect was always heightened by the solemn tones of the speaker, just—but only just—enough exaggerated to betray the underlying banter. His face remained perfectly grave." Oscar Browning recalled another instance of happy irony when, at a club dinner, Maitland defended the pleasures of solitude by saying that the best thing he knew about heaven was that there were many mansions there and that he only hoped we should have one apiece.[21]

These were the very gifts to ensure success in undergraduate debates; and Maitland became Secretary of the Cambridge Union Society in Michaelmas Term, 1872, and President in Lent Term, 1873. According to Walter Leaf, he once "carried the Union off its feet by a speech which consisted of one long and elaborate sentence and which can hardly have lasted two minutes. It was one which was so nicely adapted to its audience and which touched so surely upon the small tricks of thought which stirred the undergraduate of the day that its effect was simply electrical."[22] At another time he exclaimed, stretching out his hands to the President, "Oh, Sir, I would I were a vested nuisance! Then I should be sure of being protected by the whole British Public."[23] He was roused by anything, national or local, which smacked of ecclestiastical intolerance, and fragments of epigram survive. "There are two things which we have learnt by costly experience that the law cannot control—religious belief and the rate of interest." "At the Reformation the English state put an end to its Roman bride but married its deceased wife's sister." A debate on the opening of the Union on Sundays lingered in Henry Jackson's memory for more than thirty years. "Of course," he wrote to Maitland, "I remember all about the Committee of the Whole House and your speech, which I can still repeat, and the smoking party at

Moulton's afterwards."[24] Of this speech Oscar Browning remembered the first words: "Sir, this is not a question of religion. It is a question of arithmetic." C. S. Kenny, who succeeded Maitland as Downing Professor, told Fisher of a debate on a motion to erase passages in the annual report of the Union's proceedings which had been compiled during the long vacation by a devoted but illiterate servant of the Society. The motion was moved by an undergraduate whose name was James, and the debate was held on November 4, 1872. Maitland, as Secretary, rose to defend his subordinate. "Tomorrow," he said, "is the Feast of the Blessed Saint Guy. Appropriately enough, the House appears to be under search this evening for indications of a new plot. Enter King James the Third, surrounded by his minions, with a loud flourish of his own trumpet. He produces the dark lantern of his intellect and discovers —not a conspirator but a mare's nest . . . We are attacked for bad grammar; a great crime, no doubt, in some men's eyes. For at times I have met men to whom words were everything and whose everything was words—men undistinguished by any other capacity and unknown outside this House, but reigning here in self-satisfaction, lords of the realm of Tautology."[25]

Many undergraduates make their mark at the Union. To become an Apostle was a more precious honor. The Cambridge Conversazione Society came into existence in 1820, and it soon won such prestige that its members were called, in awe or envy, The Apostles. All subjects were fit for discussion provided only that they could be termed serious, and the fathers of the little flock sought to spread culture among the Philistines. Missionaries were sent to Oxford (spelled disdainfully with a small o) to preach the message of Shelley. The evangelical fever soon abated, but the rolls of the Society continued to record some great and many interesting names. In 1830, recommended by his prize poem *Timbuctoo,* Tennyson was elected. It must be added that, when asked to read a paper on "Ghosts," he destroyed what he had written rather than submit it to critical minds, and thereafter kept silence.[26] In 1837 John Gorham Maitland became a member and ten years later FitzJames Stephen. Leslie Stephen, though he himself failed to be chosen, gave in the biography of his brother samples of the questions discussed.[27] FitzJames defended the biblical account of the creation "so far as it can be reconciled with geological facts" and approved the "strict observance of the Sabbath in England" so long as it was not confounded with the Jewish Sabbath. He doubted whether "the spirit of the age demanded a reconstruction of society," but, if it did, "no elements of socialism should be admitted." He thought poorly of Byron as man or poet, denied that Satan was the hero of *Paradise Lost,* and preferred Miss Austen's *Emma* to Miss Brontë's *Jane Eyre.* In 1859 Henry Jackson and Henry Sidgwick were both elected, and Sidgwick sketched a vignette of a cosy little coterie. "The meetings were held every Saturday at 8.30 in the rooms of the Moderator, that is to say, the man who was to read the essay. The business began with tea, to which anchovy toast was an indispensable and perhaps symbolic adjunct; and then the essay was read, the 'brethren' sitting round the fire, the reader usually at the table. Next came the discussion. Everyone who was there stood up in turn before the fire and gave his view on the subject or on the essay or on the arguments used by previous speakers or, indeed, on anything which he was pleased to consider relevant to any one of these."[28]

In 1860 there had been founded a Chitchat Club, which seems to have become—at least in the minds of those who were not admitted to it—a nursery for the Apostles, a training ground on which promising colts might show their paces. To this club Maitland was elected. The minutes record a meeting held on May 25, 1872, "in Mr. Maitland's rooms at 54 Sidney Street," when "Mr. Maitland read a paper on Walter Mapes." The subject shows at least that the taste for medieval literature apparent in the Chaucer essay at Eton had not evaporated. After his probationary period at the Chitchat Club Maitland was elected to the Apostles.[29]

Walter Leaf described the Society when he and Verrall and Maitland all belonged to it.[30] "Membership of the *Apostles* as we were known *sub rosa,* of 'The Society' as we named ourselves to the outer world, was the closest of all the bonds of fellowship. We not only called ourselves, but felt and acted like brothers. It was a point of honour not to reveal to outsiders the names of the members or even to admit the existence of such a body; and, though the fact of the meetings was no more than a secret de *Polichinelle,* yet the obligation of secrecy gave us the sense that we were in a way cut off from the outer world, and we were taught to regard our election as a passing into a world of real existence out of that of phenomena . . . The number of active members of the Society was always small—rarely more than six or seven and always far below the Apostolic twelve with which public opinion credited us. Soon after taking a degree and going out of residence, the active member was entitled and expected to apply for honorary membership and his attendance at meetings became purely voluntary. Thus there was established a continuous apostolic succession." The honorary members were known as angels; and at this period the most formidable of these visitants from another world was Frederick Pollock. He at least did all that longevity could do to deserve the name. Elected into the Society in 1865, he remained, a brooding presence, until his death in 1937, spanning the generations of Cambridge men from Henry Maine to Lytton Strachey.[31]

The aims and methods and the paraphernalia of the Society might seem calculated to make its members superior persons. But it is impossible to think of Maitland as prim, and difficult to believe that he would not clear the atmosphere of any meeting in which he took a part. There is no doubt that among the Apostles he found and gave pleasure; as an undergraduate and active member, as an "angel" when the customary diet of anchovy toast was varied by a descent upon the Star and Garter Hotel at Richmond, and as a don when he tasted once more the austere delights of college rooms.[32]

Social success did not distract Maitland. He was made a Scholar of his College and in 1872, with William Cunningham, was bracketed senior in the first class of the Moral Sciences Tripos. The subjects of the Tripos were four: moral and political philosophy, mental philosophy, logic, and political economy. History and Jurisprudence, previously included in the examination, had recently been yoked in uneasy union in a

Law and History Tripos.[33] It was the custom of the period for candidates to be entered on the Class Lists simply by surname and college. There chanced to be two undergraduates at Trinity named Maitland. The one appeared as "Maitland, Trinity" at the head of the list in the Moral Sciences Tripos, 1872; the other by the same designation in the middle of the First Class of the Law and History Tripos, 1873. Confusion was invited. Even the editors of the University Calendar succumbed, and for some time the annotation "Downing Professor of Law" was attached to the wrong man. Many years later, when the name of Frederic William Maitland was becoming famous, W. J. Whittaker, his former pupil and faithful friend, met a lawyer who had been classed above the "Maitland, Trinity" of the Law and History Tripos but whose subsequent career had been disappointing. "After all," the lawyer consoled himself, "it will always be a feather in my cap that I once beat Professor Maitland in examination." Whittaker was kind and left him to nurse his delusion.[34]

Chapter IV

London Years

The three years that follow Maitland's success in the Tripos offer only desultory evidence of his activities. In 1873 he remained in Cambridge. In the Lent Term he took his Degree and was President of the Union. Of the Easter Term nothing is known. In the Long Vacation he went to Munich and spent solitary happy days at the opera. In August he joined Aunt Louisa, Sela, and Kate in Bonn for the Schumann Commemoration Festival of which Clara Schumann was the tutelary genius. The four then went up the Rhine and into Switzerland before returning to England. In the Michaelmas Term he won the Whewell Scholarship in International Law.

Too much should not be read into this new success. The scholarship had been founded in 1867 by a bequest of William Whewell, Master of Trinity College, to attract and reward young men of promise. It was at the winner's discretion to pursue or to abandon the subject of the examination, and it need not be assumed that Maitland had already resolved to be a lawyer. He was not venturing into new fields. International Law fell within the scope of Political Philosophy as prescribed for the Tripos, and Henry Sidgwick lectured on it for twenty years.[1] Nor should any firm inference be drawn from the fact that Maitland had been admitted on June 6, 1872, as a student of Lincoln's Inn. Now that he was no longer an undergraduate he must decide what life he was to live, and the decision was not easy. Was he to be a scholar or—if the antithesis is not unkind—a practitioner? If he was to practice, the only obvious professions were the Bar and the Civil Service. If he preferred academic life, the range was equally limited. He was not a classic or a mathematician, and if he essayed to be a philosopher his preference for the concrete rather than the abstract was always in danger of breaking through. To keep terms at Lincoln's Inn committed him to little; and while he ate his dinners, he could digest his prospects.

In 1874 he went down from Cambridge and joined his family at 19 Southwell Gardens where they were now living, a tall narrow house with a basement and four stories which was to be his home until his marriage. In the summer he spent a holiday in Germany with William Cunningham, walking in the Black Forest. At Mannheim he was introduced to Wagnerian opera. "Tannhäuser," wrote Cunningham, "carried us both away completely."[2] In London he took some part in adult education. Toward this end, dear to the more generous minds of the nineteenth century, two movements converged. The first owed its impetus to Brougham, who had planned a network of "mechanics institutes," where, surrounded by good books, working men might meet for lectures and discussion. The London Institute was opened in 1824 and soon had many branches. But these tended to fall into the hands of the lower middle class, clerks and shopkeepers, unimpressed by the importance of being earnest, and seeking enjoyment rather than learning. A new start had to be made. In 1854 F. D. Maurice and "Tom" Hughes founded the Working Men's College. William Rogers, though the founders were disturbed by his flippancy, was its ardent and irrepressible supporter.[3] A second approach came from the universities and especially from Cambridge. In 1872

Henry Sidgwick wrote to his sister that he was "considering a scheme for educating the whole country, at least as far as it is willing to be educated and has left school."[4] The project might seem ambitious even when tempered by the condition characteristically introduced at the end of the sentence. But it was in part realized by the development of the University Extension Lectures which were begun in the autumn of 1873. Under the double pressure of Rogers and of Sidgwick it was difficult for Maitland to avoid some share in this work. He gave in 1874 a course of Political Economy, seductively entitled "On the Cause of High and Low Wages," to a class of twenty workmen in the Artisans' Institute, Upper St. Martin's Lane, which provoked the audience to ask and the lecturer to answer "many knotty questions."[5] He may not wholly have enjoyed the experience, but, with whatever reluctance, he continued from time to time to answer similar calls upon him. In the last summer of his life he wrote to Sela that a "horrid lecture looms in the foreground. I wish that I had never promised it." Entitled *The Making of the German Civil Code,* the lecture was duly delivered to the Social and Political Education League of which he was then President.[6]

In 1875 he entered for a Fellowship in Philosophy offered by his College. His competitors were William Cunningham; A. T. Lyttleton, later Master of Selwyn College, Cambridge, and Suffragan Bishop of Southampton; and James Ward. Ward submitted a thesis on "The Relation of Philosophy to Psychology" and was elected. He was seven years older than Maitland and, before he became a scholar of Trinity, had studied in Germany and had thought to become a Congregational minister. He had eminent claims to a Fellowship, and his subsequent work, both as psychologist and as philosopher, showed how proper had been his choice of a subject and his success. Maitland's thesis was cumbrously entitled "A Historical Sketch of Liberty and Equality as Ideals of English Political Philosophy from the Time of Hobbes to the Time of Coleridge." It was printed in 1875 by Macmillan and described as by F. W. Maitland, B.A., Scholar of Trinity College, Cambridge.

It is possible to detect in the thesis some hints of the maturer Maitland. He doubted the purity of political economy as a science. "Even Ricardo breaks off his almost algebraic speculations to tell us what is the only justification for the poor laws." "We cannot say that *laisser faire* should be our rule until we are agreed upon subjects which are quite alien to the science of wealth. Our economists must make their choice; either they must give up talking about what ought to be or they must take into consideration ethical and political doctrines on which the methods of the science of wealth throw no light." Such inconsistencies, distilled into popular manuals, "go far to justify Coleridge's opinion that Political Economy is solemn humbug." He was not bemused by accredited reputations. Locke's premise that men are "promiscuously born to all the same advantages of nature and the use of the same faculties" is the cornerstone of his politics. But he does not attempt to justify it; "he quietly assumes it." Locke was indeed troubled by the paternal right of coercion which seemed to menace the doctrine of equality. But Herbert Spencer had got rid of this difficulty. "We are to have a free nursery. In that complete democracy which he thinks the one possible form of government, lunatics, idiots, babies in arms are apparently to have the suffrage. Coleridge said that this was a legitimate deduction from the politics of pure reason. Perhaps he thought it a *reductio ad absurdum.*" Bentham was naïve to imbecility. He sought to be simple: but "the love of simplicity has done vast harm to English political philosophy. The question of how far the interests of all men are harmonious is of fundamental importance, and yet our philosophers have failed to find a satisfactory answer because they have assumed that the answer must be simple." When Bentham wrote on international law, he admitted that a statesman might be perplexed between the interests of his own country and those of others; but on reflection "every statesman will find that the line of action which aims at the happiness of all nations is the line of least resistance." Maitland derided this phrase. "Sometimes our line of least resistance leads to the public good, sometimes it does not. But Bentham had a hankering after mathematics and vagueness was an abomination; so he makes now one simple (and therefore improbable) supposition about human nature, and now another. On the whole, the longer he lived the less well he thought of mankind." Austin, like Bentham, was open to serious criticism; and the value of his analysis was vitiated by his indifference to history. This judgment, at least, Maitland never reversed.[7]

Such passages reflect the confidence if not the infallibility of youth. They are disarmed by an introductory note prefixed to the printed thesis. "Even from the following sketch it will be apparent that a complete account of what our philosophers have said of Liberty and Equality as ideals for State action would not be an inadequate history of English political philosophy so far as it has been concerned with the discussion of first principles. Had I sooner realised this fact I should have hesitated before making so wide a subject the theme of an occasional piece." The note reveals a scholar's integrity. The exercise itself is attractive and well conducted, but such as more than one of his contemporaries could have produced. Sidgwick, who was one of the examiners, thought well of it. "I was so impressed by Maitland's thesis," he said, "that this in itself rendered me cautious. I found myself so often saying, 'this is just what I should have written myself if only I could have put it half so well', that I suspected a hidden snare of partiality for a pupil whose ideas agreed so exactly with my own." Coulton, who recorded these words, capped them with a story told by H. M. Butler, Master of Trinity, of three tutors in his own undergraduate days. "There was the good Dean Peacock, so sensitively conscientious that nothing could ever tempt him to vote a scholarship to one of his own pupils. Next, there was X, so devoted to his pupils that he could never bring himself to vote for anyone else. And lastly, there was Dr. Whewell, who voted with the utmost impartiality, because he did not know his own pupils by sight."[8] Sidgwick was as sensitive as good Dean Peacock; but as both Ward and Maitland were his pupils, his scruples had to be thrown into the balance against each of them. Today it is difficult to read the thesis without feeling it to be derivative rather than individual, and its rejection is less surprising than Sidgwick's praise. Maitland himself, when he looked back upon it after a quarter of a century, recoiled as he did from most juvenilia. He wrote from the Canaries to F. J. H. Jenkinson, the University Librarian: "I think that somehow or another you must have come upon a copy of an unsuccessful dissertation composed by one who would have accepted a fellowship had it been pressed upon him. If so, it is not published and should have been 'wiped up' like the products of the infant Grotius."[9] Professor Hollond's judgment is just: James Ward "had found the field wherein his particular genius lay, while Maitland had not." Maitland, to adapt his own words at the Sidgwick Memorial meeting, was not destined because not fitted to be a philosopher.[10]

He had now to turn seriously to the Bar. Until 1852 the Inns of Court had for two centuries offered no instruction to their students. In that year a Council of Legal Education was created, dominated by the acid personality of Lord Westbury. Lectures were at once instituted, but it was not until 1872 that an examination was made compulsory. If there were lecturers there were no tutors, and students were left to read as they thought fit. When in 1889 Maitland, as Downing Professor, advised undergraduates how to prepare for the Law Tripos, he recalled his own tribulations as a Bar student. "I began my reading of law with *Williams on Real Property,* and though *Williams on Real Property* was then a much easier book than it is now I had a very bad time with it.[11] I have always regretted that I did not begin with Blackstone; this would have saved me a great deal of labour. But unfortunately I had read Austin and was inclined to think of Blackstone as a muddle-headed fogey long since annihilated by our analytical jurists . . . Were I a second year man required to learn Property Law for the Tripos, I would begin by reading Blackstone's second volume." Williams, once he were understood, would reveal the current law. Blackstone, so easy to understand, would through the past explain, if not excuse, the present. "I would not," said Maitland, "make a burden of my reading. I would only read two or three chapters at a time in a leisurely way, in an armchair—not attempting to remember details, for probably the details are no longer law—but trying to get a general notion of the law as a whole, trying to accustom myself to the technical terms, trying to grasp the great elementary ideas and distinctions . . . After all the book is not a very big one—thirty-two chapters; 500 pages. One might read it easily and profitably in a fortnight and do a great many things besides. If any law book can be a book for the May Term, that book is Blackstone's Commentaries." As a student at Lincoln's Inn Maitland had disdained or neglected this agreeable mentor and had plunged *in medias res.* It was a consolation that he could read with his friend Verrall, who at this time had thought to become a barrister; and in the Easter Term 1876 both took the Pass Examination in Real and Personal Property, Equity, and Constitutional Law.[12] Verrall was called to the bar in May and Maitland on November 17.

Maitland is said to have been for a time the pupil of Charles Upton at 11 New Square; but, unless he went into Upton's chambers before his call, the time must have been short. There is no doubt that in 1877 he was the pupil of Benjamin Bickley Rogers. Rogers, a Fellow of Wadham College, Oxford, had been called to the Bar in 1856 and in the next twenty years had secured a substantial Chancery practice. He was also a devoted student of Aristophanes and for more than half a century published annotated verse translations of the plays, from the *Clouds* in 1852 to the *Acharnians* in 1910. Writing to Fisher in 1907 he explained how he came to know Maitland. He had agreed to take as a pupil "a very distinguished young Cambridge scholar," who insisted that he should also take his friend. The young scholar was Verrall, whose love of the Greek drama atoned for his importunity. Rogers accepted Maitland as an extra pupil. "He had not been with me a week before I found that I had in my chambers such a lawyer as I had never met before. I have forgotten, if I ever knew, where and how he acquired his mastery of the law. He certainly did not acquire it in my chambers; he was a consummate lawyer when he entered them. Every opinion that he gave was a complete legal essay, starting from first principles, showing how the question agreed with one, and disagreed with another, series of decisions, and finally coming to a conclusion with the clearest grasp of legal points and the utmost lucidity of expression."[13] It is obvious that Maitland made an immediate and lasting impact upon Rogers, but it seems excessive to describe as a consummate lawyer and a master of law a young man with little or no experience of chambers, who had made his own painful way through the elementary books. Rogers, when he wrote these words, doubtless recalled the bright promise of a pupil afterwards distinguished and lately dead; and in any approach to elegy or epitaph latitude has been traditionally permitted. "Allowance must be made," said Dr. Johnson, "for some degree of exaggerated praise. In lapidary inscriptions a man is not upon oath."

After his year as a pupil Verrall returned to Cambridge. He had found that his heart was in classical scholarship or he feared that he lacked the physical gifts required for forensic success. In after years Maitland wrote: "I have often thought that with another voice Verrall would have been one of the greatest of advocates, would have won hopeless cases and have saved all sorts of rogues from their due punishment."[14] Maitland also left Rogers and went into chambers at 2 New Square. Here he helped Bradley Dyne and began to get work for himself. But at the end of 1879 Rogers was in poor health and becoming increasingly deaf. He appealed to Maitland; and for the next three years, though Maitland kept his address at 2 New Square, he worked in Rogers' chambers in 3 Stone Buildings. In Rogers' words, "he superintended the whole of my business, managed my pupils, saw my clients and, in case of necessity, held my briefs in Court." In 1883 and 1884 he returned to Bradley Dyne, now at 6 New Square. In 1901 W. J. Whittaker, after teaching law at Cambridge, went into Dyne's chambers and found that Maitland was still a vivid memory. The clerk described a ritual observed from time to time. "When Maitland had been digging into conveyancing papers till he thought he had done enough, he would get up and ring the bell. When the clerk appeared, he would say, 'George, bring me Equity 2.' George, after a moment's hesitation to make it certain that he had grasped the true purport of the order, would retire and return in a minute or two with the morning's *Times*, with which Maitland spent the next hour."[15] No man who was not at once attractive, capable, and willing would remain for seventeen years the hero of such a story.

Maitland's name is rarely to be found in the Law Reports. As he was deviling either for Rogers or for Bradley Dyne, his arguments would for the most part remain anonymous. He was, moreover, in conveyancing chambers, and the bulk of his work, for himself or for others, would not take him into Court. Two cases reported in 1880 may be mentioned. *In re Morton v. Hallett*[16] concerned the powers of a customary heir under a trust for sale of copyhold lands. Maitland, led by Chitty, Q.C., argued the case and lost it, both before Sir George Jessel, Master of the Rolls, and before the Court of Appeal. *In re Cope*[17] is of more particular interest. It was of this case that Rogers wrote to Fisher, "A long and learned argument is put into the mouth of Chitty, Q.C. and myself, not one word of which was ever spoken by either of us. It was an opinion of Maitland's on the case laid before us which I gave to Chitty to assist him in his argument."[18] A doubt had been raised by opposing counsel upon the power of an administrator, during the heir's infancy, to sell the assets of the deceased to pay his debts. The doubt was based upon a case in Coke's Reports; and Maitland, in the opinion he gave to Rogers, had sought to dispel it by analyzing this case and tracing its fortunes through the reports and abridgments of the seventeenth and eighteenth centuries. Chitty and Rogers won their case without difficulty and without requiring Maitland's historical analysis. Sir George Jessel, before whom the case came, was the last man to seek subtle dissection when he was minded to bludgeon an unpalatable decision. Half a page sufficed for the whole of his judgment. "The question in this case," he began, "is raised by some obscure dicta in some musty old law books about the power of an administrator *durante minore aetate*." In a few energetic sentences he then dismissed the case as occult and obsolete rubbish.[19]

With intervals for such refreshment as the *Times* might afford, Maitland gave his mind to the demands of the bar while he was faced with them. But, unlike the harassed practitioner overwhelmed by professional success, he could indulge other pursuits. One day he found William Stubbs's *Constitutional History* in a London club and "read it because it was interesting."[20] He discovered Savigny and was captivated. It is tempting to recall the "accident" of finding in a country house library the *Continuation of Echard's Roman History* which led Gibbon to his life's work and provoked the immortal sentence: "I was immersed in the passage of the Goths over the Danube, when the summons of the dinner-bell reluctantly dragged me from my intellectual feast." Such chance discoveries are less casual and more significant than they seem. They reveal to the finder needs and powers which before were latent within him. Maitland thought at first to translate Savigny's *Geschichte des Römischen Rechts.* But one German led to another; and he read Brunner's *Das Anglo-normannische Erbfolgesystem* and Grimm's *Deutsche Rechts-Alterthümer*. These books and his own experience of conveyancing turned him from Savigny to the insular task of analyzing the English Law of Property. Already in his Fellowship essay he had derided the attempts—as varied as they were fanciful—made by Locke and Ricardo, Spencer and Coleridge, to sustain the distinction drawn between land and other property. Sidgwick, himself embarrassed by the dichotomy, urged him to examine the possibility of reform. In 1879 Maitland wrote some chapters of a projected explanation of Property Law; but in January 1880 he told Sidgwick that he must abandon the attempt. "I have found it practically impossible to continue the work except by making it a prolonged attack on the distinction between real and personal property. I was therefore beginning afresh, but now it is said that the government is going to abolish the law of inheritance, and though I fear that they will not cut deep enough to do all the good that might be done, it becomes necessary to wait and see whether they are in earnest."[21] As an alternative he thought of a book on the law of marital property. "The law of Husband and Wife is in an awful mess (I don't think that a layman would readily believe how bad it is), and I would willingly write something which should be useful." This in turn came to nothing.

But his efforts had not been in vain. He had been able in

1879 to publish anonymously in the *Westminster Review* a sustained onslaught upon the English Law of Property. The antiquary, if he were not fastidious, could hope to find, and possibly to reconstruct, the many relicts of the past, dusty and distorted, preserved among its lumber. But antiquarianism, and even history, were not substitutes for contemporary law, and curiosity must not frustrate reform. "If we want barbarism at its best, we can turn to the *Lex Salica;* if we want scholasticism at its best, we prefer Thomas Aquinas to Lord Coke."[22] Halfhearted and spasmodic attempts had been made to rid the law of anachronism: "accidents will happen in the best regulated museums." But nothing short of revolution would avail. Primogeniture must be abolished, the heir at law disestablished and disendowed, and everything converted into personal property.

These London years were thus years of divided allegiance, or of divided aspiration, between practice and learning. But throughout he kept his friendships in repair and added to their number. He was certainly not "unclubable." Rogers, after writing to Fisher about him as a lawyer, spoke of him as a man: "wholly without conceit or affectation, simple, generous and courteous to everybody, he was the pleasantest companion that anybody could ever wish for." A glimpse is caught of him as a member of the Rabelais Club, "that most delectable of dining clubs."[23] George Saintsbury, in his *Last Scrap-Book,* gave a list of its members. They included, beside Maitland and himself, Sir Walter Besant, George du Maurier, Thomas Hardy, W. E. Henley, Henry Irving, Henry James, Andrew Lang, George Meredith, Fletcher Moulton, and three Pollocks: Sir Frederick, the reigning baronet, and his two sons, the second Frederick who was to succeed him in 1888 and Walter Herries, the editor of the *Saturday Review.* The club was to be a declaration of faith in intellectual virility. Thomas Hardy had been elected as the most virile of contemporary novelists; Henry James was at first rejected as the least. Hardy described the inaugural dinner at the Tavistock Hotel in December 1879, in a "large, empty, dimly-lit cheerless apartment, with a gloomy crimson screen hiding what remained of the only cheerful object there

—the fire. There was a fog in the room as in the streets, and one man only came in evening dress who, Walter Pollock said, looked like the skull at the banquet, but who really looked like a conjuror dying of the cold among a common set of thick-jacketed men who could stand it . . . There were also Fred Pollock, girlish-looking, and genial Walter Besant with his West-of-England sailor face and silent pantomimic laughter. Sir Patrick Colquhoun[24] was as if he didn't know what he was there for, how he had arrived or how he was going to get home again . . . Du Maurier, now as always, made himself the clown of our court, privileged to say anything by virtue of his office. Hence, when we rose to drink the health of absent members, he stayed firmly sitting, saying he would not drink it because they ought to have been there and afterwards lapsing into Spanish on the strength of his going some day to publish a translation of Don Quixote. Altogether we were as Rabelaisian as it was possible to be in the foggy circumstances."[25] The club may have become more "delectable" when it exchanged the dim precincts of the Tavistock Hotel for the more aesthetic background of the Grosvenor Gallery where, at least in 1883, its dinners took place.[26]

Maitland continued to indulge his love of music. The concerts which Hans Richter started in 1876 to acclimatize Wagner in England confirmed him in the admiration he had felt at Mannheim, though *Meistersinger* supplanted *Tannhäuser* as the most popular opera. To these and to other concerts he went regularly, either with his sisters or with Cyprian Williams who was now at the Bar. But the recreation which both body and spirit required and which running and rowing had once supplied he now found in walking. He was sometimes able, with such friends as A. J. Butler and Edmund Gurney, to walk and climb in Bavaria and the Tyrol. Butler remembered that they climbed together the Gross Venediger:[27] "as we were going down the long hot Tauern Thal in the afternoon, silent for the most part for dryness of mouth, he turned to me and said solemnly, 'What would we not give for this thirst a month hence?' " These were holiday escapades. At home and to meet the needs of everyday life he was happy, during the last four of his London years, to be enrolled in the Sunday Tramps, a goodly fellowship fit to be numbered with the glorious company of the Apostles. *Beati omnes qui ambulant.*[28]

Of the origin and progress of the Sunday Tramps Maitland wrote in his *Life of Leslie Stephen.*[29] Late in 1879 a few friends, led by Stephen, joined together in Sunday walks; and a practice soon became an association. Stephen kept in a notebook the records of the society. Each member as he joined was given a number. The first ten members included Frederick and Walter Pollock and A. J. Butler; Maitland was number 14. "First and last the total number of names in the book was 60; but at any one time there were not more than twenty effective members, and if ten actually appeared that was a good assembly." Two walks were engraved on Maitland's memory. On Sunday, April 4, 1880, he was initiated into the society and first met Stephen. On Sunday, October 10, 1880, the venue was Harrow. "I was the only tramp who had obeyed the writ of summons, which took the form of a post-card. When the 'guide' (we had no president, certainly no chairman, only, so to speak, a 'preambulator') and his one follower arrived at Harrow Station, the weather was so bad that there was nothing for it but to walk back to London through drenching rain; but that day, faithful alone among the faithless found, I learnt something of Stephen, and now I bless the downpour which kept less virtuous men indoors."

The rule of the society was to walk on every other Sunday for eight months in the year, and it was kept loyally until 1891. Stephen had then, through ill health, to resign the leadership. "The deceitfulness of golf and the vanity of bicycles distracted some of those who had been consistent members"; the last walk, the 252nd, was taken in March 1895. "The form of government was unlimited paternal despotism. Stephen would never have granted us a charter or have admitted that we knew the way . . . When he was collecting his flock at the railway station, his face had something of the solicitous look of a schoolmaster. 'Come, I must sweep these creatures away!'—that was the manner in which a lady heard him speak of us in a house in which we were being entertained; and 'swept away' we were accordingly.

Not that his rule was 'sanctioned' by any pains or penalties, except such as he could prove to be the natural and inevitable consequences of our own disobedience and self-will. If we missed a train or had to break into a run, it was demonstrably our fault." The patron saint of the society was George Meredith, and Stephen was the original of Vernon Whitford in *The Egoist.* In a letter to Robert Louis Stevenson in 1880 Meredith told him that, armed with a sack of cold sausages, hock, and Apollinaris, he met the Tramps at Dorking Station.[30] They walked to Leith Hill, where they "consumed the soul of the sack" and then went "by Friday Street into the sloping meadows each side the Tillingbourne, leaping through Evelyn's Wotton, along under Ranmore to our cottage and dinner."

There was also, said Maitland, an inner circle of the society. "Eight of the Tramps, calling themselves the Scratch Eight, used to dine together and talk philosophy.[31] Unfortunately it is the least philosophic member of the crew who here records its existence. A phrase from an essay on rowing, about 'delightful intimacies' formed in the process of 'talking nonsense and mistaking it for philosophy', comes back to my mind at this inopportune moment." One of the Scratch Eight, and number 3 on the list of the Tramps, was George Croom Robertson, Professor of Mental Philosophy and Logic at University College, London, and the editor of *Mind.* Maitland, though "the least philosophic member of the crew," was goaded, or suffered, by Robertson to contribute three papers to *Mind:* one in 1880 on "The Relation of Punishment to Temptation" and two in 1883 on "Mr. Herbert Spencer's Theory of Society." It was perhaps impossible to mistake them for philosophy, and Maitland henceforth eschewed metaphysics.

Number 2 on Stephen's list, and also a member of the Scratch Eight, was Frederick Pollock. He acted, if need be, as deputy guide, though, as Maitland was careful to insist, de facto and not de jure. On one occasion, when summoned by him to a Sunday walk, Maitland replied on a postcard, pleading an essoin.[32] "Fredericus de Cantebrigia essoniavit se de malo lecti . . . Predictus Fredericus seisitus fuit de uno frigore valde damnando." Lest such an essoin should be inadmissible *in brevi de trampagio,* he added a demurrer. "Et dicit quod non debet ad hoc breve respondere quia non tenetur ire in trampagio nisi tantum quando dominus capitalis suus eat in persona sua propria." Pollock was the inventor of a formula to be used by the Tramps when they trespassed. "I give you to notice that I claim no right of way or other easement over this your land, and I hereby tender you the sum of sixpence by way of amends." According to his son,[33] the formula was developed into an anthem, which Pollock "would execute by himself, enacting and chanting the part of the priest as he intoned the first words, then to be taken up and repeated by the trebles, the tenors and the basses in the choir, until the whole swelled into a majestic unison on the word Amen."

One "corresponding member" appeared on the list of the Tramps: Paul Vinogradoff of Moscow. He was four years younger than Maitland and was born with the gift of tongues. At the age of thirteen he could read English, French, and German; his first English author was Macaulay. After graduating as a historian from the University of Moscow he was admitted to the seminars of Mommsen and Brunner in Berlin and published in German a paper on the legal aspect of manumission. In 1877 he lectured in Moscow on medieval history, and spent the next year in Florence seeking material for a treatise on the origin of feudalism in Italy. In 1883 he came to England for research into the feudal land system. He stayed for fifteen months, working in the Public Record Office and the British Museum, in the Bodleian and the Cambridge University Library, and in Sir Thomas Phillips' library at Cheltenham.[34] Neither Stephen nor Maitland knew him until the following year, and only then could his name have been numbered among the Sunday Tramps, even *in partibus.*

Maitland was becoming unsettled. He was feeling ever more strongly the bias away from the practice and toward the history of the law which had been imparted by Stubbs and Savigny and Brunner. Pollock "had done a little to put him on the scent" when they talked together in Lincoln's Inn;[35] and in March 1883 he added example to precept by his election as Corpus Professor of Jurisprudence at Oxford. Maitland congratulated him.[36] "To F. Pollock, Professor of All Laws in all Universes and Universities and reputed Universities. May it please your Enormity to accept the congratulations of your sincere votary and humble brother over the fact brought to his notice by the *Times* that you have become more vested than ever and, having had the animus to profess the law in Oxford, have now the Corpus also. Ave Verum Corpus Juris." In an earlier postcard to Pollock[37] Maitland had shown himself acquainted with medieval pleading; and in three successive papers he advanced along the path to legal history. In 1881 he published a study of the kindred and the blood feud in the ancient laws of Wales; in 1882 he discussed the criminal liability of the hundred; in 1883, with some examination of the Year Books, he wrote *The Early History of Malice Aforethought.*[38]

He was further disturbed by the disruption of the family life whose stability had meant so much to him. Aunt Louisa had died in 1880; and on June 19, 1883, Sela married the Rev. Vincent Charles Reynell Reynell. Writing to her on her honeymoon, Maitland said that he was "working at my Liverpool lectures and deep in the difference between larceny and embezzlement." These were twelve lectures on "The Ownership and Possession of Chattels" which he had been asked to give at the University College, Liverpool.[39] Later in the year he offered himself as a candidate for the Readership in English Law at Oxford, but was defeated by Thomas Raleigh, a Fellow of All Souls. As with his earlier failure at Cambridge, it is easy, in retrospect, to regret the choice of the electors. But on the evidence available in 1883 Raleigh was at least as eligible a candidate, and he showed power and independence in his *Outlines of the Law of Property,* published in 1890. Six years later he left Oxford to become in turn Registrar of the Judicial Committee of the Privy Council and Legal Member of the Viceroy's Council in India.[40]

If in 1883 Maitland was both unsettled and disappointed, 1884 was a year of opportunity and decision. In January he met Vinogradoff; either, as Vinogradoff thought in 1907, at Pollock's house or, as Maitland remembered in 1891, on a "Sunday Tramp." Fisher, following Maitland, gives January 20 as the date.[41] During the next three months the two men may have met again, and they certainly corresponded. On April 28 Maitland wrote to Vinogradoff that he hoped to see him in Oxford on Sunday, May 11.[42] Fisher described their meeting in epic vein.[43] "The day was fine and the two scholars strolled into the Parks, and lying full length on the grass took up the thread of their historical discourse. Maitland has spoken to me of that Sunday talk; how from the lips of a foreigner he first received a full consciousness of that matchless collection of documents for the legal and social history of the middle ages, which England had continuously preserved and consistently neglected, of an unbroken stream of authentic testimony flowing for seven hundred years, of tons of plea rolls from which it would be possible to restore an image of long-vanished life with a degree of fidelity which could never be won from chronicles and professed histories. His vivid mind was instantly made up: on the following day he returned to London, drove to the Record Office, and, being a Gloucestershire man and the inheritor of some pleasant acres in that fruitful shire, asked for the earliest plea-roll of the County of Gloucester. He was supplied with a roll for the year 1221, and without any formal training in paleography proceeded to puzzle it out and to transcribe it."

This stirring story has been severely criticized and is chronologically incredible.[44] Maitland, in his inaugural lecture, said that it was seven years after his call to the Bar when he first realized the treasures to be found in the Record Office. The date of his call was November 17, 1876. It need not be supposed that he celebrated the anniversary by invading the Office; his name appears for the first time in the literary search room register on February 25, 1884. In his letter to Vinogradoff on April 28 he wrote: "I am indeed glad that you are working at Bracton and settling the relation between the MSS. I wish that you would stay here and teach us something about our old books. Pollock is looking forward to your paper and I am diligently reading Bracton in order that I may understand it. I have written for Pollock a paper about seisin and had occasion to deal with a bit of Bracton which, as printed, is utter rubbish. I therefore looked at some of the MSS and found that the blunder was an old one. I shall not have occasion to say any more than that there are manuscripts which make good sense of the passage—but I have made a note about the matter which I send to you thinking it just possible that you may care to see it, as it goes some little way (a very little way) to show that certain MSS are closely related." The paper by Vinogradoff to which Pollock, as editor of the *Law Quarterly Review,* was looking forward was "The Text of Bracton." The paper which Maitland had written was "The Seisin of Chattels";[45] he had already "looked at some of the MSS" and he added a note about them as a postscript.

He undoubtedly went to the Record Office on May 13, after his sunny day in the parks. But after his first visit on February 25 he had also been there on April 30 and again on May 5. On August 28 he told Vinogradoff that he had "just finished the last proofs of the Eyre Roll."[46] If Fisher's story is to be accepted, Maitland must have begun and ended the whole of the work on *Pleas of the Crown for the County of Gloucester* in three and a half months. As Plucknett pointed out, two rolls, comprising 155 large pages, had to be collated, an introduction of fifty pages to be written, a publisher found, type set up, and the proofs corrected. Maitland was a fast worker and, as a conveyancer, accustomed to gut documents and "come to the charging part." It was an achievement to have done so much between February 25 and August 28; had nothing been done before May 13 it would have been impossible. When he wrote to Vinogradoff seven years later, he said: "I often think what an extraordinary piece of luck for me it was that you and I met on a 'Sunday Tramp'. That day determined the rest of my life." Vinogradoff, for his part, remembered that on this first meeting in January 1884 Maitland had spoken of his wish to "devote his life to the historical study of English law";[47] and Vinogradoff's enthusiasm, then expressed, may well have turned the wish into a resolution. Maitland may also have been ashamed, when he visited the Record Office in February, that he should have neglected what a foreigner had found and recognized. He himself said to Bigelow in the following year that he lived "in constant fear that some German or Russian or even Turk will edit Bracton and shame the nation which produced a certain six volumes of rubbish."[48] It is possible that Fisher confused the memories of the meetings in January and in May, and that on the Sunday in Oxford Maitland told Vinogradoff that he was already at work on the plea rolls and was encouraged to complete them.

Pleas of the Crown for the County of Gloucester before the Abbot of Reading, 1221 was published in the second half of November. Maitland dedicated the book to Vinogradoff and thanked Pollock from whom he had received encouragement and a ready help out of difficulties. He described in the Preface his aim and his method.

> It is a picture, or rather, since little imaginative art went to its making, a photograph of English life as it was early in the thirteenth century, and a photograph taken from a point of view at which chroniclers too seldom place themselves. What is thence visible in the foreground is crime, and crime of a vulgar kind—murder and rape and robbery. This would be worth seeing even were there no more to be seen, for crime is a fact of which history must take note, but the political life of England is in a near background. We have here, as it were, a section of the body politic which shows just those most vital parts of which, because they were deep-seated, the soul politic was hardly conscious, the system of local government and police, the organisation of county, hundred and township.
>
> It is not indeed supposed that there is anything in the roll which should startle anyone who has learnt the story of our constitution and the story of our criminal law from the best modern books, still less any one versed in Bracton's treatise *De Corona* . . . but it is believed that a large stock of examples, given with all their concrete details, may serve to provide a body of flesh and blood for the ancient rules which, whether in the pages of Bracton or in those of modern historians, are apt to seem abstract, unreal, impracticable.

Despite Maitland's disclaimer, "picture" rather than "photograph" would have been the appropriate simile. If the past is to be revived, not only must detail be observed with a discerning eye but it must be quickened into life by the force of personality. Like other writers who look back upon their first book, the mature Maitland was amazed at the temerity with which he had ventured into unknown territory. Later research has revealed limitations and disproved conjecture.[49] But he had entered ready armed upon the field of legal history. He knew what he wanted to do; he knew how to do it; and anyone but himself would have said that he had done it well.

Maitland's return to Cambridge was the result of a generous act. In 1878 the Senate was asked to approve a recommendation made by the Teaching Syndicate for the appointment of Readers. Approval was given, "though one speaker, going on the principle that it is never too late to learn, suggested that they should be appointed in high and difficult subjects only, so that their work might be useful to members of the Senate as well as to persons *in statu pupillari.*" The number of Readers was to be twenty, and they were to be appointed "as soon as sufficient funds can be provided conveniently for the purpose."[50] In 1883 the Board of Legal Studies, upon this somewhat tepid encouragement, urged that two of the twenty should be chosen to advance the teaching of English Law. In academic circles it is often dangerous to reduce a principle to a particular proposition; and nothing might have been done but for the offer of Henry Sidgwick to provide £300 a year for four years if a Readership were established. The offer was accepted, and on November 14, 1884, a few days before the *Pleas of the Crown* was published, Maitland was elected to be Reader in English Law.

The inquest upon Maitland's demise at the bar has produced varying verdicts. Despite his abilities, Rogers was not sure of his future: he lacked confidence in his own powers. Sir Cecil Carr would not accept the diagnosis. A man could not become President of the Union at Cambridge without believing in himself as well as being believed in by others. Vinogradoff recalled the impatience with which the young counsel "watched in his chambers for the footsteps [sic] of the client who never comes." Such words are "common form." Maitland was accumulating a practice and, if he kept his health, might anticipate reasonable success. Fisher suggested a dilemma. While Maitland was making enough for his needs, a barrister's income is uncertain and he might still fail; but if he succeeded he would have made "an intellectual sacrifice which he was not prepared to face."[51] He did not wish to be buried in a career of professional eminence. Such thoughts may have been in Maitland's mind. But the vital cause lay deeper and took time to rise to the surface. Fisher said of him that "he loved the law and all its ways."[52] Such pervasive affection may be doubted. Maitland was not one to relish—unless enjoyed *coram* Chief Justice Bereford—what Sir Thomas Overbury in his *Characters* called "the nice snapperadoes of Practice." His heart was not in the profession of the law but in its history. Had he lingered in chambers with doubtful loyalty he would have courted defeat. The law is a jealous god and will not give its rewards to any acolyte who strays from the strait and narrow path. Sir Cecil Carr observed that his father and his grandfather had both been called to the Bar and had eventually made careers elsewhere. But these are not analogies. In each generation the man and the motive differed. His grandfather abandoned the Bar because his aggressively independent mind demanded lone if not eccentric satisfaction; his father because diffidence did indeed preclude success. Maitland left it because he had come to know that, to be true to himself, he must try to be a scholar and a historian.

Henry James in *William Wetmore Story and His Friends,*[53] the tenderest and most revealing of his books, sought to explain why Story, born in the purple of the law and himself a successful practitioner and writer, should have abandoned his profession to become a sculptor. His life thereafter, said James, was "of the simplest as the lives of men of distinction go; simplest because it unfolded itself altogether from within . . . He had no adventure beyond *the* adventure of having given way to his inspiration; and this is the great sign of good fortune. Ill fortune, for the man conscious of gifts, is *not* to have been able to unfold from within; there is no other that in comparison with it matters." Maitland, ever eager to explore the countries of the mind, subtle of thought, rich and daring in expression, was yet in essence a simple man—unwarped by prejudice, uninhibited by frustration. Like Story his crucial adventure, his great good fortune, was at the crisis of his life to have become at once conscious of his gifts and able to give way to his inspiration. Henceforth, though illness might cast shadows upon his path, he was a happy and single-hearted man, resolute to fulfil his inner self.

Chapter V

Return to Cambridge

Glimpses of Maitland's work as Reader in English Law are afforded by contemporary lecture lists and by his own letters. From 1885 to 1888 he advertised the following courses.[1]

Mich. 1885	Tort
Lent 1886	Real Property
Easter 1886	Real Property
Mich. 1886	Rise and Progress of the laws of England
Lent 1887	Stephen's Commentaries
Easter 1887	Real Property
Mich. 1887	Stephen's Commentaries
Lent 1888	Constitutional History
Easter 1888	Constitutional History: Real Property

University lectures may be grouped into two classes. Some

seek to meet the supposed needs of the syllabus. These, unless touched into life by the vitality of the lecturer, are apt to be patronized by undergraduates who like the sensation of thinking without the trouble of thought. Other lectures offer points of view not to be found in books or only in books which invite criticism; and these stand apart as rare and refreshing. The lectures which Maitland had to give as Reader fell for the most part into the first of these classes. Upon such efforts Dr. Johnson had pronounced a century earlier. "Lectures were once useful; but now, when all can read and books are so numerous, lectures are unnecessary. If your attention fails and you miss part of the lecture, it is lost; you cannot go back as you do upon a book."[2] Maitland had his own opinion of their value. In 1889 he was advising second-year undergraduates on their course of study for the Second Part of the Law Tripos.[3]

> I cannot help saying that some subjects require more study than others, that some are pre-eminently subjects about which you ought to have lectures, while the necessity of hearing lectures about others is not so obvious . . . I must not say much about this matter, but I do think that among the most industrious men in this University there is some little superstition about the virtue of attending lectures. I speak particularly of lectures on law. From the nature of the case a lecture on law can seldom be so good as a book on law. From the nature of the case lectures must be composed far more hurriedly than books are composed. I will just mention my own case. In six months I wrote a set of some fifty lectures on Constitutional History and Constitutional Law. Had I been writing a book of the same length on the same subject, I should have taken at least six years over the task; and of course the result was that about many things I could only say very briefly and meagrely what is to be found at length in very accessible books. All that I really could do was to make a more or less intelligent abstract of these books with perhaps a few remarks of my own about parts that for one reason or another happened to be familiar to me. Now do you want a

> course of lectures of that kind? Let us for a moment put matters at their very best. The lecturer delivered a highly intelligent abstract of Stubbs' *History;* his hearers took highly intelligent notes and so wrote out an excellent abstract of an excellent abstract. Was this worth all the labour that it cost them? Might they not have made the abstract for themselves? I ask these questions; I do not answer them. I don't think that they have any answer which should come from all men. Some men will get good out of the ordinary expository lectures because they have not yet learnt to read books; some will get good because words they hear stick in their memories better than words they read. But you are not without experience; I am not talking to freshmen; and I want you to ask yourselves whether you want many lectures or few.

In April 1886 Maxwell Lyte, Deputy Keeper of the Public Records, consulted Maitland on a proposal for a new edition of the Year Books. The proposal came to nothing; but Maitland's letter in reply is astonishing in its immediate perception of the whole project—questions and answers—as if he had thought of it for years.[4] The letter is interesting for another reason. Maxwell Lyte had asked him to take part in the design if it materialized. Maitland welcomed the invitation but thought it proper to explain the time at his disposal. "I consider," he wrote, "that the readership I hold at Cambridge ought to require of me half my working time. The other half I would very willingly devote to work on the Year Books." Even when allowance is made for the progressive debasement of the currency since 1914, any university might think itself lucky to be able, for £300, to command the services for six months each year of so able, so quick, and so devoted a worker. Nor were his duties confined to teaching and lecturing. He had to examine as rotation or necessity dictated, and he had to take his share of administration.[5]

That Maitland, fresh from conveyancing chambers, should have lectured on real property was to be expected. But his first course was on tort, and this initiated a fruitful correspondence with Melville Madison Bigelow, Professor of Law at Boston University. "It is my duty," Maitland wrote in his first letter,[6] "to attempt to teach the law of torts. You therefore are no stranger to me for your books are constantly in my hands and your name in my mouth." In October 1886 he thanked Bigelow for the third edition of his *Elements of the Law of Torts* and hoped that "in a very short while it will be a text book in our law school. There is a faint prejudice against American books among those who do not know how closely the courts on your side of the water have kept to 'the common law', but this is fading." In May 1887 he was able to report that it was "definitely established at the head of the books which we recommend to law students." Bigelow was meditating an English edition; and Maitland discussed the conditions of its success with R. T. Wright, Fellow of Christ's College, who had now taken over the responsibility for the teaching of torts. "We want, if possible," he wrote to Bigelow, "to induce our students to look beyond the text books to the reports. This is at best a difficult task, for our students are I believe much younger and much less instructed than those whom you have to teach. But difficult as it is to persuade them to study English reports, it is more difficult to send them to American cases. For one thing, the only library at their command, our University Library, is—I regret to say it—by no means wealthy in American Reports. In the second place, it is of course desirable that the few cases which they master and remember should be cases which are of the very highest authority in our own courts."[7] He added that the Cambridge University Press, which had as yet "done nothing for the study of law," might be persuaded to publish the book. Wright, who was one of the Syndics of the Press, laid the proposal before his board, and in January 1889 it was duly published. The English edition was dedicated to Maitland and Wright and was described as "a book of the law of England instead of the law of America."[8]

While Bigelow and Maitland exchanged letters, Pollock completed a book on the law of torts which suggested the possibility of rivalry. Maitland, indeed, on Pollock's invitation, was preparing for him a historical appendix on the "Forms of Personal Action." In his letter of May 13, 1887, he wrote to Bigelow: "I have lately had occasion to use your Placita Anglo-Normannica and your History of Procedure and see that when writing the Appendix for Pollock's Torts I ought to have referred to what you have said about the check put to the invention of writs by the Provisions of Oxford."[9] The point was noted in the Appendix. The situation was made the more piquant by the fact that, when Pollock's book was published in November 1887, it contained a prefatory letter to Mr. Justice Holmes, and Holmes thought little of Bigelow. "He is a man," he had written to Pollock,[10] "whom I greatly respect for his sincere love of learning which he has proved in spite of poverty, etc., but there is nothing incisive or masterly about him—so that whatever he does will have to be done over again." But Maitland avoided embarrassment by distinguishing the aims and characters of the two books. "There would be no competition between your book and Pollock's," he told Bigelow, "for the two are laid out on different lines and his is a decidedly hard book for undergraduates who yesterday were schoolboys." Bigelow had "supplied just what is wanted as an elementary text-book. Pollock is a little too philosophical for beginners" and must be reserved for "the best of the undergraduates."[11]

On November 12, 1887, Maitland wrote to Pollock: "For weeks I have been in horrible bondage to my lectures. Stephen's Chapters about the Royal Prerogative and so forth—I speak of the Stephen of the Commentaries—are a terrible struggle; when one is set to lecture on them three days a week one practically has to write a book on constitutional law against time."[12] That he should have taken Stephen as a framework and not Blackstone is surprising. When he recommended the *Commentaries* to undergraduates he insisted that they must be Blackstone's and not some later version.[13] But he seems to have been preparing for a course of lectures which he delivered in 1888 and which he developed in the two following years under the title of Constitutional Law and History. These lectures were published posthumously by Fisher as *The Constitutional History of England.* Fisher in his preface admitted that he was defying Maitland's own decision. "I have written a course of lectures in six months on Constitutional History. Do I publish it? No."[14] The book has been a commercial, and presumably an educational, success—reprinted twelve times in fifty years and allowed in 1961 the dignity of a paperback edition. Maitland had certainly brought a fresh mind to a well-worn subject, illuminating history by law and law by history. But it lacks the life which he gave to the books he designed and wrote, and he would not have been amused at its publication.

Some words in a letter to Bigelow show Maitland's reaction to the Law Tripos as he surveyed it in 1887. "I am sorry to say that at present we have a great deal of Roman Law and of what is called General Jurisprudence in our scheme."[15] Of the comparative value of Roman Law for senior students he had no doubt, though undergraduates could have too much of it. Jurisprudence, so far as it meant thinking about law, was to be encouraged, provided that knowledge preceded reflection. In the current syllabus it was unduly analytical: "the formal jurisprudent sits heavy upon us."[16] Austin, even when diluted by lectures, was not delightful, and to the young analysis meant little more than learning by rote. But Maitland hoped that a projected alteration might "give English law a fairer chance." The project materialized in 1889. In the new syllabus Part II of the Law Tripos contained two papers on Real and Personal Property, with the equitable principles applicable; two papers on Contract and Tort, with the same provision; one paper on Criminal Law and Procedure and on Evidence; and a sixth paper of Essays. The pattern remained unchanged until 1922.[17]

To turn from the routine of the Tripos to his individual interests was a relief. While still in chambers, he had become interested in seisin. Seisin had led him to Bracton, and Bracton was to lead him deep into the heart of medieval law. His first paper on "The Seisin of Chattels" was printed in 1885; in 1886 he published "The Mystery of Seisin" and in 1888 "The Beatitude of Seisin." But during these years he was engaged, whenever he could find or borrow time, upon a major task. The story begins with Vinogradoff's discovery of a manuscript in the British Museum containing a "collection of cases written about the middle of the thirteenth century, with a good many notes on the margin. The first leaves and the last quires are missing, and there is no direct evidence as to the person who compiled and used the book, but the contents make it very probable indeed, if not certain, that it was drawn up for Bracton and annotated by him or under his dictation." Vinogradoff announced his discovery in a letter printed in the *Athenaeum* for July 19, 1884, and persuaded Maitland to edit the manuscript.[18]

Scarcely had Maitland begun the work than he had to put it aside. He must "grub away and make a dreary book about petty sessions and policemen."[19] Macmillan, with the recurrent optimism with which publishers hope to persuade the common reader to pay for his further education, had started a series with the depressing title of The English Citizen: His Rights and Responsibilities. Pollock had already written *The Land Laws* for this series and had induced Maitland to undertake a book of similar aim and length to be called *Justice and Police*. Maitland was not happy with it; and his own valuation when he sent it to Pollock in 1885 is not unjust. "I had at one time a thought of dedicating it to you. This I have not done because I don't like it well enough. I began writing on much too large a scale and at the end had to sacrifice whatever interested me most. This I hope is a wholesome lesson."[20]

Once he had ejected this tiresome trespasser upon his time, he returned eagerly to the manuscript. His progress may be traced through the letters. On October 31, 1885, he told Bigelow of the discovery and of his own work upon it. As the Readership obliged him to live in Cambridge during term time, he was driven to transcribe by fits and starts. "Also I am trying to verify the extracts from the plea rolls by collating them with such of the said rolls as are still to be found, and this is rather a long job. You will understand that the mass of the book consists of cases extracted from the rolls; they were transcribed by divers clerks who obviously did their work in a mechanical and sometimes stupid fashion. Then there are marginal notes written by another hand and these notes I think may come from Bracton himself." He summarized the evidence for connecting the manuscript with Bracton's text, but he was not yet prepared to say in public that the note book was made by Bracton. "I am endeavouring to keep an open mind until the whole is legible in type and shall be quite ready to say that Bracton cannot be the annotator." On April 24, 1886, he told Maxwell Lyte that he had been copying the cases and getting them into print "for a year and a half," and hoped that "by the end of the year the really laborious part of it will be accomplished." By October 1886 more than three quarters of the text was in print; "but there is still much to be done, an introduction to be written and indexes made. There will be three stout volumes and I fear that the look of them will frighten readers." He would not yet use the name of "Bracton's Note Book," but had "not much doubt that when my investigations are at an end I shall be entitled to do so." On December 12, 1886, he told Thayer that he had finished the copying and that he hoped to publish the book in the following year. On June 12, 1887, the book was completed but the printers lagged behind. It was published in late October at Maitland's expense.[21]

The cost was considerable, the toil heavy, and the achievement astonishing. In three years, amid all his other work, he had transcribed material filling nearly one thousand four hundred printed pages, had written a long introduction and compiled an intricate set of indexes and tables. The *Pleas of the Crown for the County of Gloucester* had been inevitably an experiment; the introduction to the *Note Book* revealed Maitland as a master of his craft. He presented his arguments with a clarity which his years at the Bar had helped him to develop. He made his hero live by bold experiments in time and space. "We take the train to Barnstaple; Bracton was archdeacon of Barnstaple. The next morning we may stroll easily to Raleigh, the cradle of the great house, and so on through Heanton Punchardon and Braunton Gorges to Staunton, the manor which Bracton held . . . The way lies straight across Dartmoor; it is a wild way but (*teste meipso*) there is none pleasanter in England."[22] The weight of material did not lie heavy upon him; it seems indeed to have raised his spirits. The whole introduction is infused with a joie de vivre which can be sensed across the gulf of years.

He ended his preface with an apology which proved, if proof were needed, both his integrity and his courage. It is a don's disease to defer, or even to abandon, a publication because it does not realize a fastidious ideal or because the author dreads the judgment of his peers. Maitland was ready to do his best in the time and on the evidence available and to let his work take its chance of success or failure. If the fates were kind, it would contribute to learning, and at the worst it would incite others to do better.

> When I say I am not satisfied with it, this is no common protestation. Down to the last moment I have found so many faults in my own work that I cannot but believe that there are many yet to be found. Down to the last moment I have been learning many things about the law of the thirteenth century which I ought to have known at the outset. For sins of omission no excuse should be offered, for none should be accepted. But before I am blamed for having done less than might have been done in the way of collating rolls, giving various readings, making indexes and notes, it will, I hope, be remembered that this has been a private enterprise. I have often had to count the cost; also to reflect that another day in the Record Office or the British Museum would mean another hundred miles in the train . . . I am sure there must be more to be learned about Bracton's life than I have been able to discover; at this eleventh nay, thirteenth hour I find what I believe to be his marks on a roll of King John's reign . . . But it seemed that the *Note Book* would remain unprinted for many years unless some one would make an edition of it such as could be made at his own cost. Perhaps I was not the man for the work, but I have liked it well.

While he was engaged upon the manuscript, he had been

scrupulous not to prejudge its connection with Bracton. When he published the work, he arrayed the evidence and presented his case, but he still refused to be dogmatic. "I am of course happy in believing that Bracton's work was in my hands; and my eyes may have been shut to facts which make against this pleasant belief; let some one else now go through the book to disprove me."[23] Others have since "gone through the book" only to confirm his conclusion. Lady Stenton planned Volume 53 of the Selden Society as a supplement to his work. She recalled his suggestion that the whole of the Note Book had not survived and that it once contained cases from other rolls. There was, he had said, "nothing to be said against this supposition . . . but then there is nothing to be said for it." There was in truth much to be said for it, and Lady Stenton has said it. But she has also pointed out that, though both Vinogradoff and Maitland described the manuscript as a Note Book and the name is now inseparably connected with it, it was not properly a book at all. "When Bracton used it, it was probably a collection of loose quires. The present binding is a modern one and Maitland notes that the first folio was at one time 'lying loose from the rest and suffered ill usage.' Nothing is more probable than that several quires containing cases from other Assize rolls were lost before the book came into the hands of Chief Justice Sir Anthony Fitzherbert in the early sixteenth century."[24]

Among those to whom Maitland sent complimentary copies of the *Note Book* were Brunner in Berlin, Tardif in Paris, Thayer and Bigelow in the United States. Thayer had already received from the *Nation* a copy for review; Maitland's gift he transferred at once to Ames, who had been eagerly awaiting it and who was "better able to appreciate it than any of our people." Thayer also sent to Maitland notes which Ames had made upon the book and thus initiated between the two men a "pleasant gossip about legal history."[25] Bigelow wrote: "Your work will help us here very much. None of our Law Schools has a chair of legal history, and what we do in teaching we must smuggle in or get in as best we may in connection with other work. Not that legal history is looked upon with distrust or even with indifference, but that no funds have as yet been provided for professorships or lectureships of the kind. I believe your book will help greatly the growing feeling here in favour of attending seriously to our wants." Maitland had made a sudden and deep impact upon the American lawyers, who had already done more than the English to cultivate a common heritage, and with whom he was to keep in touch throughout his life.

While Maitland was still at work on *Bracton's Note Book,* the Selden Society came into existence. It is impossible to say if he may properly be termed its originator. Fisher called it the creature of his enthusiasm; B. F. Lock, in the *Dictionary of National Biography* but not in the memoir in Selden Society Volume 22, wrote of him as its founder; Pollock in old age thought him its "chief promotor."[26] It may be guessed that the idea of a society devoted to legal history had been discussed between Pollock and Maitland and that, while the driving force came from Maitland, Pollock was the better equipped to recommend it to the Inns of Court. Pollock may also have suggested its name. Selden's *Table Talk* was already one of his congenial books, and Selden's prolific erudition made him a likely godfather. A third man, P.E. Dove, was concerned with the promotion of the Society. Dove, while struggling to gather a practice at the Bar, dabbled in legal history and at this time was editing *Domesday Studies,* parts of which, contributed by J. H. Round, are excellent. Whatever his qualifications or motives—scholarly yearning, doubt of professional success, a wish to make a name—he passes, a fitful and unhappy figure, across the early records of the Society.

It was in Dove's chambers that twelve members of the Bar met on November 26, 1886: Sir Richard Webster, Montague Cookson, Q.C., J. Fletcher Moulton, Q.C., P. Meadows White, Q.C., W. Paley Baildon, R. Campbell, P. Edward Dove, E. Macrory, F. W. Maitland, H. S. Milman, Stuart Moore, and Frederick Pollock. Sir Richard Webster was the Attorney General. The Solicitor General, Sir Edward Clarke, did not attend. He expressed "the most sweeping contempt for antiquity and did not see why any book or document more than forty years old should exist."[27] Fletcher Moulton had known Maitland at

Cambridge and was a fellow member of the Rabelais Club. Milman was Director of the Society of Antiquaries. Baildon was to become one of the Selden Society's editors, and Stuart Moore from 1913 to 1951 its secretary. Immediately after the meeting Dove placed a notice on the Boards of the Libraries and Common Rooms of the Inns of Court.

> A Meeting of Members of the Bar and of other persons interested will be held on an early day to consider the advisability of establishing a Society to encourage the study and advance the knowledge of the History of English Law. Lord Justice Fry[28] has kindly consented to preside. It is suggested that the name of the Society shall be the SELDEN SOCIETY and that its objects shall include:
>
> I. The printing of inedited MSS and the publication of new editions of works having an important bearing on English legal history;
>
> II. The collection of materials for a Dictionary of Anglo-French and of Law Terms;
>
> III. The collection of materials for a History of English Law;
>
> IV. The holding of meetings for the reading and discussion of papers;
>
> V. The publication of a selection of the papers read at the meetings and of other original communications.

A provisional committee of the Selden Society met on February 2, 1887. Lord Justice Fry was present, but the chair was taken by Lord Coleridge, the Lord Chief Justice, recommended by office rather than by learning. Maitland was absent but was appointed with Pollock, Stuart Moore, and Dove (acting both as Secretary and as Treasurer) to prepare a report for the committee at its next meeting. The report was in fact drafted by Maitland in a letter which, like his earlier letter to Maxwell Lyte on the Year Books, is a revelation of sudden mastery both of strategy and of tactics.[29] The Society was a private venture, dependent upon subscribers to whom legal history was a luxury. If they were to be captured at all, they must be enticed: austerity would frighten them away. Maitland suggested that a beginning might be made with select Pleas of the Crown to illustrate the medieval development of the criminal law.

> Were it certain that the Society's books would find many purchasers, there would be much to be said for working through the plea rolls in their chronological order and taking thence all cases of interest no matter what their subject-matter. I doubt however whether at the present time the first volumes of a series made on this principle would prove attractive. The extracts in any volume would be very miscellaneous, and some years would elapse before there would be a sufficient mass of matter about any one topic to make any inductions safe or profitable. Subscribers will naturally demand results of which they can at once take advantage. Besides it must be confessed that records of real actions would be found dull by many who would gladly read of matters for the understanding of which no great amount of obsolete technical knowledge is required. What is more, the selection of the records best worth copying will in the case of the real actions demand such a thorough knowledge of medieval procedure as is (to say the very least) extremely rare at the present day; it may come in time as editors are trained by lighter tasks, but it is hardly to be had at a moment's notice.

Several reasons recommended as a theme a selection of criminal cases. "The subject is well defined; the boundary will be no arbitrary line of the editor's drawing." Many of the cases were interesting and even entertaining. They were intelligible because criminal law had always been simpler than civil procedure and had left its legacies to later law. "The indictment we still have with us: the assize of novel disseisin is a thing of the past." There was still much to be learned about the history of the criminal law, and not least the development of the petty jury.

No detail escaped Maitland's attention. Like other scholars

and artists he was more businesslike than many businessmen. He thought that, at least in the early volumes, the extracts from the records should be accompanied by translations. "Of course if translations were not required the Society could at the same cost publish twice as many records; but probably there are many persons who will only begin to believe that records are interesting when they see them in English." He discussed the problems of printing and especially the difficulties involved in the expansion of contractions.

> There seem to be three courses open, namely (i) to use what is called "record type",[30] (ii) to represent by italic type those letters which in the original are represented by stenographic signs, (iii) to expand all contractions and to print the whole in ordinary type. It is fairly certain that, whichever course be adopted, some persons will be dissatisfied. I do not myself believe that many readers have been found or will be found for documents printed in record type, and in my opinion the number of mistakes which can be saved by its use is extremely small. Again, as to the use of italics—this tells the reader very little, while it must add to the cost of printing and must add very largely to the labour of transcribing documents and correcting proofs. The vocabulary of our law Latin is really very small, the grammatical structure of the records is in general very simple, and I much doubt whether an editor will transcribe correctly stenographic signs the meaning of which he does not understand.

Maitland emphasized that the Society should seek to print not essays but records. "What is wanted above all things is as much first-hand evidence as can be obtained." Finally, he offered, "if the services of a better editor are not to be had," to edit the first volume. He proposed as its subject "Select Pleas of the Crown from the Thirteenth Century" up to the accession of Edward I.[31] "I very much wish," he wrote, "that I could offer to do the work for nothing. This however I can not do, and that of course is a reason why the Society should if possible find another editor." He provisionally suggested payment at the rate of four guineas a sheet; but "if the Society is going to be very small and another editor is not forthcoming, I will try to make a better offer."

On July 2 the committee welcomed his offer. Dove, for his part, was able to report the names of eighty-five subscribers. They included twenty Americans, notably Ames, Bigelow, George Tucker Bispham of Pennsylvania, John Chipman Gray, Professor Clarke Hare of Philadelphia, Oliver Wendell Holmes, Professor W. A. Keener of Harvard, Langdell, and Thayer. The list of American subscribers steadily lengthened, and a year later Maitland wrote to Bigelow: "I can't tell why it is, but certainly you seem to care a deal more for legal history on your bank of the Atlantic than we do here. It is a malarrangement of the universe which puts the records in one continent and those who would care to read them in another."[32]

Immediately after the meeting of July 2 Maitland began to copy records for the *Pleas of the Crown*. In January 1888, despite the irritating distraction of lectures, he completed the transcript and was becoming interested in early manorial rolls.[33] On February 23 the executive committee, as it was now called, decided the format of volume 1 of the Society's new series: it was to be printed on crown quarto paper and bound in dark slate buckram. The committee also accepted Maitland's offer to edit, as volume 2 of the series, selected cases from thirteenth century manorial rolls. By the beginning of May volume 1 had been published and Maitland sought critical opinions which might help him with its successor. He had some fault to find with the printers. "They set up the type very accurately, but in striking off the copies they have allowed letters to slip from their places. I think that they must have done the actual printing somewhat roughly." He told Dove that he would "not take more than ten guineas *at most* for volume 1: this will very handsomely cover all expense to which it put me. I had originally dreams of a large and rich Society and they may yet be fulfilled—but at present we must give the subscribers as much as possible for as little as possible." He was also anxious that the Society should not depend upon a single editor. "Would not Mr. Round do something, or is he too busy with his charters?" Despite his insistence, the committee, when it met on May 8, refused to profit at his expense and paid him a fee of fifty guineas. He accepted it with anxious gratitude. "I hope and trust that I am not crippling the Society."[34]

If he failed to avoid an additional fee, he succeeded in finding another editor. Round either had not been approached or had declined. But W. P. Baildon was ready to edit, as a companion to the Pleas of the Crown, a volume of civil pleas. Maitland pressed on with the manorial rolls. He first transcribed in King's College, Cambridge, "a beautiful set which once belonged to the Norman Abbey of Bec,"[35] and then examined the records of six seignorial courts preserved in the Public Record Office. He wrote of his discoveries to Ames, Bigelow, Thayer, and Vinogradoff. Vinogradoff was especially interested: he was preparing an English version of his *Villainage in England* and was sending the manuscript for Maitland's comments. Maitland spoke to him of his own delight in the manorial records and wished that he "were allowed to make three Selden books this year." On October 14, 1888, he could say that the introduction was taking shape; he was restricting it to the powers and procedure of the courts. He assured Vinogradoff that he would not poach on his preserves. "You can, I think, trust me not to take an unfair advantage of our correspondence and your kindness—but if you had rather that I did not see the sheets of your book which deal with the courts, please say so."[36] In November he finished the introduction and had the unusual experience of being told by members of the Society that it was too interesting to be so short.[37] The only dissenter seems to have been Dove. Maitland, when he had reluctantly lengthened the introduction, wrote to Thayer: "Dove evidently is afraid that the book will be very dull and writes me many letters adjuring me to be lively. I do not see my way to satisfying him and yet I must own that I am giving our subscribers an unpalatable morsel."[38] In February 1889 he had finished the proofs, and in April the book was published.

Of Maitland's first two Selden volumes, so far as they illustrate his aims and methods, a little should be said. In his introduction to volume 1 he bore in mind his warning to the Society of the need—at least in the early years—to conciliate subscribers and other readers who might be led into the fold. Two passages must suffice as examples. In the first he described the Plea Rolls from which he had made extracts.[39]

> A Plea Roll, it may be well to explain, is not like one of the Chancery Rolls—for instance, a Patent or a Close Roll—a long continuous strip of parchment made by the sewing of the top of one membrane to the foot of another, but consists of membranes filed together by their tops. It is worth while to observe this, because it must be added that to determine the exact date of an early roll is not always easy, and the possibility must be had in mind that its membranes are not all of the same date, but have been bound together capriciously. Too often the scribe, while careful to note it is Hilary Term or the Octave of Trinity, has forgotten to say what year it is; too often the first membrane of the roll has perished, and the date of every particular membrane then becomes a serious problem. As may well be imagined, there are many signs that a uniform orderly method of making, arranging and preserving records was only attained by long practice; the earliest rolls are often very untidy and are disfigured by erasions, interlineations and clerical errors corrected and uncorrected; the work of one clerk differs widely from that of another, and this not only in externals but in substance also: in reporting the business done before justices in eyre this scribe will habitually give details that other scribes will omit. One gay clerk of John's reign, fonder, it would seem, of classical poetry than of legal drudgery, has finished off a list of essoins with *Omnia vincit amor et nos cedamus amori;* such an enrolment would hardly have been ventured in later days. On the whole, however, the art of recording grew apace; a roll from the middle of the thirteenth century is very unlike a roll from the beginning: far neater, fuller, more regular, more mechanical; the rapid development of common law is mirrored on the surface of the rolls.

In the second passage he explained the basis of his selection and offered tentative conclusions from his study of the rolls.[40]

> In order to illustrate the justice of the central court it has been necessary to copy records of which too many end without a judgment; there were no better to be had; the series of rolls is so broken that we often lose sight of a a case before it is decided. The main object kept in view has been the thorough illustration of the normal course of criminal justice. Cases of special interest have been copied, but the editor has not conceived it his duty to hunt for curiosities: the history of law is not a collection of curiosities; therefore many entries have been copied which may fairly be styled "common form entries."
>
> The worst of a mere selection of cases is that it cannot entitle its reader to negative conclusions; therefore a few inferences derived from a superficial perusal of all the rolls of John's reign may be acceptable. In the first place, criminal justice was extremely ineffectual; the punishment of a criminal was a rare event; the law may have been cruel, for, in our eyes, it was capricious—it made use of the irrational ordeal; but bloody it was not. In Henry the Third's time some satisfactory hanging was accomplished, but the number of presentments of undiscovered crime is very large. His father's reign may have been a bad time for honest folk; it seems to have been a holiday for robbers and murderers. Secondly, trial by battle in criminal cases had already become uncommon; the justices seem to have delighted in quashing appeals. Thirdly, success at the ordeal seems to have been far commoner than failure; indeed, only one single case of failure has been found. Lastly, the reader may be asked not to approach these records with the belief that criminal procedure necessarily involves the use of two juries; as yet the jury which presents the crime is, at least as a general rule, the only jury that there is.

Despite his own enjoyment of the manorial rolls and the committee's encouragement, Maitland feared that the second volume might prove indigestible. He repeated the statement made in volume 1 that cases had not been chosen because they were whimsical; readers were not being invited into an antique shop. But where the context allowed he still indulged his sense of the contemporary scene. When tracing the steady erosion of the lord's jurisdiction by the royal courts, he compared the situation in the middle and at the end of the thirteenth century.[41]

> We may note that even Bracton, a royal judge, though he holds that all temporal justice is in some sort derived from the king, has not attained the point of view from which it seems natural that every injury should be redressed in the royal courts. He gives reasons why this and the other action should be heard there—all disputes about advowsons, for example, must come there, *because* none but the king can force the bishop to say whether the church be empty; actions by a widow who has got no part of her dower must come there, *because* perchance the marriage may be denied, and none but the king can compel the bishop to say whether marriage there was; actions to try the question of free or villan status must come there, *because*—well, Bracton does not know exactly why this is, but perhaps it is in favour of liberty. A few years of civil strife followed by a few years of Edward's government make a wonderful change. Men are no longer clamoring about the multitude of new writs; parliament has to urge the chancery not to be too pedantic, but to grant new writs when new cases fall under old principles; the king's courts have triumphed all along the line, but triumphed by becoming the courts of a king who habitually legislates with the consent of a parliament . . . In course of time a feudal court becomes unimportant except in so far as it is a manorial court: a jurisdiction over freeholders is a mere adjunct to the jurisdiction over villans and customary tenants. But this latter jurisdiction is of the utmost importance, it is the very lifeblood of the agrarian and economic system. And, let the lawyers say what they will, it is a true jurisdiction, an administration of the custom of

> the manor; it is no mere exhibition of the will of a lord who is owner of the villan tenements and owner of the villans: —no decent lord treats it as such.

Of the seven sets of rolls used in the volume Maitland especially enjoyed those of the Fair of St. Ives in 1275. They had even "cheered the soul of the apprehensive Dove."[42] "The spot then as now known as St. Ives in Huntingdonshire seems to owe its town to its fair, and to owe its fair and its name to a miracle. In Domesday Book it is represented by the Abbot of Ramsey's manor of Slepe . . . But in 1002 or thereabouts there had been a lucky find of bones in Slepe and a dream proved that they were the bones of S. Ivo. Thus the place became of some note."[43] In 1110 the Abbot procured from Henry I the grant of a fair which became profitable. It was the focus of the traffic in wool, cloth, and hides, and its records reflect the busy commercial life of the thirteenth century: the *lex mercatoria,* the law of contract, the obligatory writings payable to bearer. A conspicuous feature was the presence of "communities" of merchants not only from English towns but from Ypres and Bordeaux. When, after Maitland's death, Charles Gross edited for the Selden Society further records of the Fair of St. Ives, he stressed its cosmopolitan character. In a case of 1312 complaint was made "in a plea of trespass" against a number of defendants that they sang *(carolaverunt)* to the terror of the fair and to the great damage of the merchants. Among the complainants were merchants of Louvain, Diest, St. Trond, Bruges, Ypres, Ghent, St. Omer, Caen, Dinant, and the Florentine society of the Bardi.[44]

In 1886 Maitland had met and married Florence Henrietta Fisher. Her father, Herbert Fisher, had been tutor to the Prince of Wales when the latter, after matriculating as a nobleman at Christ Church, was isolated with his governor in Frewen Hall, a house in Oxford, to protect him from the social contamination of ordinary undergraduates. In this seclusion the unfortunate Prince endured lectures on Political History from the

Regius Professor, Goldwin Smith, who complained that he was so far from appreciating the privilege of private tuition that he was scarcely able to enjoy the Waverley Novels. But Herbert Fisher, who taught him Constitutional Law and History, by tact and sympathy won his friendship; and in 1862, when the Prince married and had his own household, Fisher became his private secretary. In 1870 he was appointed Vice Warden of the Stannaries, an office of the Duchy of Cornwall. While still the Prince's secretary, Fisher had met a Dr. John Jackson and his wife Maria. Maria was one of the seven Pattle sisters famous for their beauty. Another of the sisters had married Henry Thoby Prinsep who lived at Little Holland House as a patron of art in general and of G. F. Watts in particular. A third sister married Charles Henry Cameron and was a pioneer in photography, taking portraits of such great contemporaries as Browning, Darwin and Tennyson. Maria's husband, Dr. Jackson, was, amid this galaxy, eminently without distinction. "Somehow," said Leslie Stephen, "he did not seem to count as fathers generally count in their families."[45]

Dr. Jackson and his wife had three daughters. The eldest, Adeline, married Henry Halford Vaughan, Professor of History at Oxford, who published three volumes of Shakespearian commentaries described by Stephen as "singular instances of misapplied ingenuity." The youngest daughter, Julia, had all the charm and beauty of her mother and her aunts. She was the model for Burne-Jones' *Annunciation;* she was painted brilliantly by Watts and in later years was drawn with less grace and more severity by William Rothenstein.[46] She was first married to Herbert Duckworth, by whom she had three children, George, Stella, and Gerald. Duckworth died suddenly in 1870, and eight years later Julia became Leslie Stephen's second wife.

Dr. Jackson's second daughter, Mary, married Herbert Fisher. They had eleven children. The eldest son, Herbert Albert Laurens, was to become a historian, a Cabinet Minister, and Warden of New College, Oxford. A younger son became Admiral Sir William Fisher. One daughter married Ralph Vaughan Williams, and it was the eldest daughter, Florence, whom Maitland met at Leslie Stephen's house. They became engaged in

April 1886. Maitland wrote to his sister Sela, now Mrs. Reynell, who was expecting a baby.[47]

I am sorry indeed that times and seasons have so fallen out that you will hardly know Florence Fisher as such. Still you will know her when she has changed her name and I make no doubt that you will like her. I shall not attempt a description, for naturally Kate will be more impartial than I can be and will tell you how *she* appears (bother! my grammar has broken down! 'she' ought to mean Kate but it doesn't) to one of her future sisters-in-law. I feel inclined to leave 'in law' out of the term, for I think that you will some day come to regard Florence as a sister, be the law what it may. To tell truth, for a fortnight past I have not thought very much of the law, for Florence and I have been singularly well treated. We have been allowed to go about together without a keeper and I have spent whole days in her company.

He added that Florence was "a splendid player"—on violin, viola and piano—but that he was glad that she "has really not heard very much music: there is much for her to hear for the first time along with me." Maitland was thirty-six and Florence twenty-two. They were married at Brockenhurst, where the Fishers then lived, on July 20. Three days earlier Maitland had written again to his sister.[48]

My own very dear Sela,

I know that your thoughts will be with me on Tuesday and that Florence and I will have your kindest wishes. Would that you could be there! I should like to see your dear old face at the great moment of my life. I dare say that you think that I am rushing into marriage in a rather haphazard way. I don't think it is so but can not quite explain it all; so believe the best—at least believe what is good, for I think it is good. Very likely I shall not be a very gay bridegroom or Florence a very gay bride—but we have thought it over, we love each other and are neither of us very sanguine of getting nothing but happiness. I believe that there is no illusion on her part—I have said all I could to dispel any; I am sure that there is none on mine. So if not gay, I am not gloomy but very hopeful of the life before us. I am going to give you a framed photograph of her; it seems to me the best thing I have to give you. It may not come to you for some little time as I shall be away and not able to see to the framing of it. But it makes me happy to think that she and I will be near you and Vincent[49] and that we need not rely on photographs—my own good sister. I too think of the days that we three had together when Aunt Louisa was with us—and I fear that Kate will be lonely now.

Goodbye my dearest

F.W.M.

After a holiday at Lustleigh in Devon Maitland and Florence went to live in Cambridge. Two daughters were born to them: Ermengard and Fredegond. Ermengard's name was found by Maitland while editing *Bracton's Note Book*. Of her sister he wrote to Vinogradoff on March 12, 1889, "Miss Maitland No. 2 is named Fredegond. After that, don't I belong to the Germanistic school?"[50]

Chapter VI

Downing Professor

The Years from 1888 to 1898 (I)

Sir George Downing, who died in 1749, devised property in Cambridgeshire, Bedfordshire, and Suffolk to four cousins in succession and ultimately to found a college in Cambridge. By a happy dispensation of Providence the first devisee died in 1764, the three others had predeceased him, and neither he nor they had issue. But legal vicissitudes intervened, and it was not until 1800 that Downing College was founded by royal charter. The foundation stone was laid in 1807, and William Wilkins was appointed architect. As well as other work in Cambridge, Wilkins was responsible in London for St. George's Hospital, University College, and the National Gallery. His design for Downing was grandiose: "one large stone-faced quadrangle, more spacious than that of Trinity College"; and only the east and west sides were built.[1]

The Charter provided not only for a Master and Fellows but

for two Professors, of Law and of Medicine. The first Professor of Law was Edward Christian.[2] He had lectured in Cambridge since 1785 and in 1788 had been granted the title of "Professor of the Laws of England until Downing College shall be founded." He was appointed Downing Professor in 1800 and held the chair until his death in 1823. He wrote books on the Game Laws and on Bankruptcy and increased his income, if not his burdens, as Chief Justice of the Isle of Ely. He prepared four editions of Blackstone's Commentaries on which he based his lectures. The pleasant informality of the time is reflected in an advertisement in the *Cambridge Chronicle* for November 5, 1813: "Professor Christian will begin his lectures on the Constitution and the Laws of England on Monday next. Inquire at Mr. Deighton's."

His successor was Thomas Starkie, a member of Lincoln's Inn with a busy practice on the Northern Circuit. He published in 1813 a "Treatise on the law of slander, libel, scandalum magnatum and false rumours"; in 1814 a "Treatise on criminal pleading"; in 1817 his Nisi Prius Reports; in 1824 "A practical treatise of the law of evidence." This last book made its way not only in England but, until superseded by Greenleaf, in America, and was cited by Thayer as late as 1898.

On Starkie's death in 1849 Andrew Amos was elected to the Chair. A member of the Middle Temple and of the Midland Circuit, he was Recorder of Oxford and had a large practice in arbitrations. In 1829 he became Professor of Law at University College, London; and the future Queen Victoria, as a child of eleven, was initiated by him into the mysteries of Constitutional Law. In 1837 he succeeded Macaulay as fourth member of the Governor General's Council in India, and, when his term expired in 1843, he became, with some danger of bathos, county court judge for Marylebone, Brentford, and Brompton. He was joint author of a treatise on the law of fixtures and wrote a book on the trial of the Earl of Somerset for the poisoning of Sir Thomas Overbury.

Amos died in 1860 and was succeeded by William Lloyd Birkbeck. His father had founded the Birkbeck Institution in Chancery Lane, and he himself became its President in 1841.

Until his election as Professor he practiced as a conveyancer, and in his lectures he concentrated on Real and Personal Property. In his first year at Cambridge he enjoyed an august experience. The Prince of Wales had been suffered to sample Oxford; but it was thought proper to buttress or to dispel the influence of the one university by a taste of the other. He migrated to Cambridge, still chaperoned by General Bruce and still consoled by the gentler presence of Herbert Fisher. On January 26, 1861, the Prince and Fisher attended at Downing the first of a course of lectures. Professor Birkbeck left a record of the occasion.[3] "The Prince shook hands cordially with me. I said 'I feel much honoured by seeing your Royal Highness in my house.' We sat down. He and his tutor, Mr. Herbert Fisher, took out their note-books, and I spoke a little lecture on the countries subject to the laws of England. When I was nearly *au bout de mon Latin,* I asked whether I should proceed to another subject; but Mr. Fisher requested that I should recapitulate. This I did. They then took their leave and are to come again on Tuesday." In April 1861 Birkbeck was received at Windsor and favored with the royal views upon the education of a future sovereign. "I am desirous," said the Prince Consort, "that he should study Constitutional Law. He should understand his position as Prince of Wales. He should understand that he is placed in an exceptional position, not for his own sake but for the benefit of the nation. There may be many things which other young men may do and which are quite innocent in themselves, but which would be injurious in him. The clergy are an example of men suddenly placed in an exceptional position. There are many things, innocent in themselves, such as dancing, which would be unbecoming in clergymen. This is because of the effect that might be produced on an auditor who remembered that the night before he had observed the preacher dancing." Whether the Prince of Wales danced at Cambridge is unknown; he certainly learned to appreciate the less severe aspects of dramatic art.

For the last three years of his life, while remaining Professor, Birkbeck was also Master of the College. He died on May 23, 1888, and Maitland became a candidate for the Chair. Maitland offered testimonials from the Lord Chief Justice, from Lord Justice Fry, from Mr. Justice Wills, and from Stubbs. Pollock was an elector and not to be approached. Lord Justice Fry put in evidence *Bracton's Note Book* and the first volume of the Selden Society's series. In a private note he told Maitland that he had "heard but one opinion about his work." Stubbs wrote: "I do most heartily wish you success in your candidature. I think that the work which you have done in legal history proves that you have the qualifications for it in good measure and proportion—I mean the patient industry of the historian, the grasp of principle which becomes the jurist, and the power of seeing the point and deciding upon it according to the weight of evidence which, I take it, is the mark of the good mere lawyer." Maitland wrote also to Thayer to ask if he might tell the electors that the review of the *Note Book* in the *Nation* was his work. "I want to send them the review in any case, because it explains the way in which I have been using my time since I was appointed reader, and I can not expect all of them to know anything at all about Bracton. But I should very much like to be able to add that you wrote it; it is so much more than favourable that I may be suspected of having written it myself."[4] At the end of July Maitland went with his family to Cornwall, and there on August 5 he heard from Pollock that he had been elected. "Your letter from Downing," he replied, "tells me what I expected, namely, that the struggle was severe. I can very well understand that there was much to be said against me—some part of it at all events I have said to myself day by day for the last month. My own belief to the last moment was that some Q.C. who was losing health or practice would ask for the place and get it. As it is, I am reflecting that in spite of all complaints the bar at large must still be doing a pretty profitable trade, otherwise this post would not have gone begging."[5]

On October 13, 1888, Maitland delivered his inaugural lecture: "Why the History of Law Is Not Written."[6] In the first half of the nineteenth century Ranke and Niebuhr had seen and proclaimed a new vision of history. In 1867 Stubbs, in his own inaugural lecture as Regius Professor at Oxford, had sought to found a historical school in England, based upon the documents "now being poured forth from the great storehouses of record throughout Europe"; and the publication in 1870 of his *Select Charters* was a tribute to German methods. With the same hope and upon the same basis Maitland approached English law. Its records had "no equal, no rival in the world." But the weaving of the raw material into history was a formidable process.

The crux of the problem lay in the contrasting outlook of the practicing lawyer and of the historian. Contemporary historians could make common assumptions upon the species and value of evidence; contemporary lawyers differed in different countries upon such an issue as the admissibility of secondary evidence to prove a fact or to interpret a document. The use of sources revealed a similar divergence. "What the lawyer wants is authority and the newer the better; what the historian wants is evidence and the older the better." Maitland had learned this truth at the feet of Sir George Jessel.[7] History, moreover, must be studied comparatively, and the English lawyer "had a traditionally consecrated ignorance of French and German law." Divergent methods sprang from divergent aims. The historian sought to show how people lived and had their being in any given place or time. To tear a record from its setting was a capital crime; but to give or withhold judgment was a matter of individual discretion. The lawyer at the Bar or on the Bench had to face a current and urgent issue demanding decision. He must therefore interpret the past in terms of the present. The analysis of old cases was an accident arising out of and in the course of his employment, to be faced only if precedents had to be evaded or deflected to strange uses.

The problem was more easily stated than solved. There were few aspirants to legal research. In 1888 law had scarcely come of age in English universities, and it was premature to assume a steady if slender succession of graduates eager to explore its history. Nor, in any generation, have there been many willing to accept the ideal of a university as a community dedicated to the disinterested development of intellectual powers. On the other hand, the practitioner who had achieved or who still courted success would have neither time nor inclination for scholarship. Maitland could see but one hope. "Where then lies our trust? Perhaps in failure." The barrister who despaired of clients might realize not only that a university post was vacant but that the history of English law had not been written. Even so he must not look for wealth or fame. "Let him at least know that within a quarter of a mile of the chambers in which he sits lies the most glorious store of material for legal history that has ever been collected in one place, and it is free to all like the air and the sunlight."

Few have found fault with Maitland's diagnosis. His reluctant remedy has found less acceptance. To Plucknett it was at once so dismal and so perverse that it could be explained only by sickness of body reacting on the mind.[8] Maitland had indeed been ill before the lecture, and six months after it his doctors gave him a grave warning. Its nature can now only be guessed; but it seems likely that it stressed the danger that cold or damp might cause recurrent pneumonia or pleurisy with serious injury to the lungs. This risk Maitland had to run for the rest of his life. But he needed no *aegrotat*. Few men were less morbid or more resilient. When he was ill he was *hors de combat;* once the attack was over he was eager for battle. The days of inaction were balanced by the exhilaration with which he threw himself once more upon his work. "When I am hurt I cry. When I am not crying I am happy."[9]

Maitland's recipe for the making of legal historians, however explained or excused, Plucknett felt bound to condemn. "The proposal that legal history must be annexed to the study of law," he wrote,[10] "is entirely misconceived. Maitland had himself just shown that their material, their method and their logic were incompatible, and that there was no necessity for a lawyer, *qua* lawyer, to bother with history. To make legal history the preserve of professional lawyers was indeed to condemn it to extinction. As for his requirement of legal training and experience of practice, what of Stubbs, whose handling of law Maitland admired so much that he almost wished he had been a judge? What too of Vinogradoff, who had never been a lawyer of any sort?" Plucknett's criticism need not pass unchallenged.

Maitland did not think of historical research as the handmaid of the lawyer whether in the university or in the courts. In his first essay on the reform of the land law he had been at pains to dispel such an illusion, and he repeated the lesson in his inaugural lecture. Nor did he seek to make legal history "the preserve of professional lawyers." He would have subscribed without reserve to Plucknett's dictum that "legal history is not law but history"; but it may reasonably be supposed that a man is the better equipped to write it who has either studied or practiced law. "The discipline and evolutions of a modern battalion," said Gibbon, "gave me a clearer notion of the phalanx and the legion, and the captain of the Hampshire grenadiers has not been useless to the historian of the Roman Empire." Maitland attested in his lecture the value of his own years in chambers. "Think for a moment what lies concealed within the hard rind of legal history. Legal documents are the best, often the only evidence we have for social and economic history, for the history of morality, for the history of practical religion. On such a point as village life the evidence is inexhaustible, but no one will extract its meaning who has not the patience to master an extremely formal system of pleading and procedure, who is not familiar with a whole scheme of actions with repulsive names. There are large and fertile tracts of history which the historian has to avoid because they are too legal for him." It is hard to deny the truth of Maitland's words, and it is ludicrous to suppose that they tempered his respect for Vinogradoff or for Stubbs. Of Vinogradoff it is enough to say that he admired him only less than he venerated Sidgwick and Stephen. To Stubbs he paid tribute in an obituary written in 1901 for the *English Historical Review*,[11] and he detected in him a latent appetite and aptitude for legal problems. "That he had a strong taste for law—and the history of institutions is the history of public law—cannot be denied. It has often seemed to me that if he had changed his profession he might have been a very great judge." But neither Stubbs nor Vinogradoff set himself to compose, on any sustained note, the history of legal rules and concepts—an exercise for which to have been a lawyer must be at least an added qualification.

That Maitland should seriously have sought to beat up recruits from men who had failed at the Bar may indeed seem a desperate remedy. He himself had not been a failure. He had a fair prospect of success and turned from it only when he knew that there was another life he preferred to live. He hoped that others might follow his example, and he may not have realized that a young man of scholarly tastes has rarely the insight, the will, or the means to make the right choice at the right time. Maitland's conclusion was frank and perhaps unpalatable. But the years to come showed that if those prepared to make sacrifices for legal history were worthy, they were few.

An inaugural lecture is an ordeal. Once he had passed through it, Maitland had to give a succession of courses appropriate to his Chair. It is convenient to name them as they spanned the years from 1888 to 1906.

Mich. 1888.	Parliament.
Lent 1889.	History of the English Manor.
Easter 1889.	Personal Property.
Mich. 1889.	Constitutional Law and History (I). Contract.
Lent 1890.	Constitutional Law and History (II). Advanced Real Property.
Mich. 1890.	History of the English Manor.
Lent 1891.	English Law in the Thirteenth Century.
Mich. 1891.	English land law in and before 1086.
Lent 1892.	Advanced Real Property.
Mich. 1892.	History of English Law, cents. XII and XIII, Introduction and Tenure.
Lent 1893.	History of English Law, cents. XII and XIII, Status and Jurisdiction.
Mich. 1893.	General Sketch of English Legal History. History of English land law.
Lent 1894.	History of English Law, cents. XII and XIII.
Mich. 1894.	General Sketch of English Legal History.
Easter 1895.	Some points in the law of Real Property.
Mich. 1895.	History of the Canon Law.

Mich. 1896.	The English Village Community.
Easter 1897.	Some points in the law of Real Property.
Lent 1898.	Agrarian Cambridge.
Mich. 1900.	Introduction to the study of English Law.
Vacation 1901.	Contract.
Mich. 1901.	Contract.
	Introduction to the study of English Law.
Vacation 1902.	Introduction to the study of English Law.
Vacation 1903–6.	Some points in the law of Real Property.

Two other courses of lectures need separate mention: "Equity" and "The Forms of Action at Common Law." Like *The Constitutional History of England* each was published after Maitland's death and each has found a ready market.[12] Both are free from the recondite allusion and the threads of argument too tightly woven which have sometimes troubled readers of the *Constitutional History*. If a book was to be made of any lectures offered to undergraduates, Maitland might, with the least reluctance, have sanctioned the course on Equity. It was given every year from 1892 to 1906. He was able to observe the reaction of his audience, to balance sense and sound, to add, amend, prune, and polish as he thought fit; in his own words, to "invent business for it."[13] The lectures on the Forms of Action are slighter—too slight for their theme. Though they bear the hallmark of their author, they dwindle at times into notes; and the long period from 1307 to 1833 is scantily sketched. Even in the pages on the earlier years there are passages which, as they stand, it is hard to believe Maitland would have printed. In Lecture III the Writ of Right is introduced with the words: "There is good reason to believe that Henry, in some ordinance lost to us, laid down the broad principle that no man need answer for his freehold without royal writ." In Lecture IV, with less confidence, clause 24 of the Statute of Westminster II is said to be regarded "as the statutory warrant for the variation of the writs of trespass so as to suit special cases." These statements may have been enlarged or qualified in the lecture room. Had they to be revised for publication, Maitland would not have been content with a bare assertion or have dismissed a controversial clause without analysis. As conjectures they have since been disproved, and the ubiquity of the writ, upon which the lectures as a whole are based, has been successfully challenged.[14] But even now such central problems as the origin of Trespass and of Case remain unsolved; and generations of students, neither tempted nor required to compare the value of Maitland's lectures with that of his books, have found in the *Forms of Action* as in *Equity* inimitable guides to intricate subjects.

In addition to the lectures Maitland conducted an occasional seminar in medieval handwriting. He made his first experiments in the Michaelmas Terms of 1893 and 1894. They met with little response, and he attempted no more for nine years. In 1903, full of the challenge of the Year Books, he tried again. In July of that year he asked R. L. Poole, "Have any examination papers been set at Oxford on Palaeography and Diplomatic? If so, could a man obtain copies for money or for love? In October I shall try to start a little scriptorium." He held his class and was sufficiently encouraged to repeat it in the Michaelmas Terms of 1904 and 1905. But he had to admit failure. On November 17, 1905, he apologized for his writing in a letter to Fisher. "I have been reading Merovingian documents with my one pupil and they seem to have spoilt my hand."[15]

Of Maitland as a lecturer some personal impressions remain. Sir Cecil Carr said: "In his lectures he spoke as he wrote. They were carefully prepared and indeed seemed ready for the printers; his pleasant voice delivered them deliberately so that one could take down what notes one wanted; there was the apt illustration, the arresting sentence that summed up the argument."[16] J. N. Figgis was more elaborate. "Maitland was not merely a writer; he was also an orator. Although as a lecturer he was extremely nervous and read nearly every word, he had the orator's power of thrilling his listeners both by his voice and his intense preoccupation with his subject . . . His style was like that of no one else, compact of extraordinary Biblical and other archaisms, intensely individual, vivid and striking, packed with allusion, sparkling with humour and suggesting even more than it stated . . . It had an extraordinary quality of reproducing the atmosphere of the time he was discussing. It was not descriptive or picturesque in the ordinary sense. There was neither the hardness nor the brilliance, still less the partisanship, of Macaulay in Maitland's mind. But, as he discoursed in his vibrating and nervous tones (for he was nervous to the last), he left his hearers under the impression that there was only one thing worth living for—the study of twelfth-century law."[17]

The words "extremely nervous" arrest attention. But it is a commonplace that in every orator or advocate mind and body are taut to take the strain. The convincing lecturer need not expect to escape contagion. To be glib is not to be persuasive. That Maitland "read nearly every word" is more surprising. Special addresses—the inaugural lecture, the Rede lecture, the Ford lectures—would inevitably be written with care. But it is strange that even advice offered to undergraduates embarking on the Second Part of the Tripos should have been meticulously prepared. Speaking of his lectures, Maitland said to Gross, "I *can not* improvise."[18] In debate he was never at a loss for words, and the idiosyncrasy in the lectures must have been caused by intense anxiety not to mislead by chance word or unhappy allusion. Learning was sacred and loose thinking a sin not to be forgiven. He was happily able, by intensity and force of personality, to avoid the deadening effect that too often attends the reading of a lecture. He had the power of keeping in the written the urgency of the spoken word. His daughter caught glimpses of him at work. "In dealing with words I believe he said them as he wrote, or at any rate heard them clearly, and that at times he walked up and down saying his lectures to himself. There was nothing of the actor in him, but I feel sure he never merely wrote or read—he taught by word of mouth."[19]

Heads have been shaken at the sad waste of genius in the delivery of lectures to young men. Pollock, condemning "the absurd sacrifice of our universities to the schoolboy grind and examinations," lamented that "when a teacher like Maitland comes once in two or three generations, we have nothing better to do with him than to set him serving the tables of triposes."[20] Maitland had his own opinion of a professor's duties and, indeed, of Pollock as a lecturer. Pollock, he wrote, had "no notion of adapting supply to demand; you must take what he thinks good for you or leave it alone, and the young gents with examinations before them left it alone." For himself he did not disdain the demands of the Tripos. But he sought to follow Sidgwick and to give his best, "not what might be good enough for undergraduates."[21] To make the dark ways light without oversimplification is a delicate mission. Yet to him who gives with a whole mind much is given; and words prepared for babes and sucklings may teach their author. Many a lecturer, in the moment of emitting a cherished phrase, has suddenly realized that it was ambiguous or exaggerated, that behind the facade of language a fallacy lurked, or that the phrase meant nothing at all.

But Maitland, while he did not shirk this obligation, realized that it was only part of his duty. Once he had met the needs of the Tripos he could try to stimulate the more mature or adventurous minds. H. E. Bell marked the close correspondence between Maitland's more advanced lectures and the progress of his books:[22] *Memoranda de Parliamento, Select Pleas in Manorial Courts, Township and Borough,* the *History of English Law.* The coincidence was not fortuitous. Maitland, despite the obstacles that he foresaw in his inaugural lecture, still hoped to excite eager young men and women to explore regions of legal history which, if not undiscovered, had certainly not been cultivated. At the worst he could test the value of his own experiments. In 1892 he told Round that he felt the challenge of Domesday Book the more that he read it. "I lectured on it for a whole term and wrote all that I said; but I have no intention of publishing anything, at any rate for a long time to come."[23]

The contrast between the two types of lecture explains the discrepant views expressed of their popularity. According to Oscar Browning, Maitland's lectures "were never numerously attended, at least not in my experience. More than half of the scanty audience were women; there was perhaps one undergraduate law student, then a few B.A.'s and four or five historians from King's." According to Sir Cecil Carr, "his lectures attracted an audience by no means exclusively legal; the seats were sometimes overfull. I remember one occasion when more chairs had to be brought in, the lecturer remarking with a playful pensiveness that he had never known the room he could not empty."[24] To dismiss Browning's recollection as one of his "little ways" is tempting but unfair. The lectures which catered for the undergraduate with his eye on the syllabus might well attract an audience which would melt when tougher fare was provided.

The evidence suggests that, whether he spoke to the few or to the many, Maitland was a successful lecturer. That he would have been equally successful in the weekly contact of don and pupil, with its reciprocal and repeated burden of essay and comment, is less certain. To an individual and promising undergraduate, indeed, he would give ungrudging help. In 1894 O. J. Charlton was being prepared for the Law Tripos by J. P. Bate of Peterhouse. Bate asked Maitland if he would take his pupil for special instruction in legal history, and Maitland consented. Charlton obtained a First Class in the Tripos, and Maitland sent him a copy of *Bracton's Note Book* "in memory of pleasant hours we passed together."[25] Such men of necessity were exceptions. The most dedicated tutor has to learn that the intelligent pupil may be idle and the earnest pupil dull, and has to steel himself to prod the one and leaven the other. Maitland at least was spared weary hours on such a treadmill.

To scholars embarking on advanced medieval studies in Cambridge or elsewhere Maitland gave lively encouragement and, if they sought it, constructive criticism. In 1889 George Neilson in Glasgow was wrestling with his first book, *Trial by Combat.* On June 30, he wrote to his fiancée: "I have sent the English part off to Professor Maitland. It was a very serious step. If he condemns it, it will take the heart out of me to no small extent, and as he knows more of the subject than any man alive it is very likely that he may cut the little infant's throat in the very first bloom of its innocence. I am waiting with very just anxiety for his letter which may come to-morrow or may not come for a week." Before Neilson had posted this letter he was able to add a postscript: "Much fear and trembling has been mine since I wrote to Prof. Maitland with the first part of the MS. So much depends on his opinion. What if he were to write back and say—'I greatly admire your work and think it excellent in every respect. I have never seen all this learning—some of which is quite new to me—set forth so well, and I venture to foretell a great success.' Wouldn't it be very gratifying? Yes it would. Well, my dear Jennie, these words are his in very truth. They have made me very, very proud . . . He has sent me half a dozen pages of notes for additions. One or two corrections he has also made—I almost wish they had been more."[26]

If a professor is required to lecture, he is also expected to engage in university business. Maitland, if he did not welcome, did not evade this duty. He examined five times in the Law Tripos, three times in the Moral Sciences Tripos, and twice in the History Tripos. The weary work was occasionally relieved by the gaucherie of candidates. A historian "finished a list of kings of England with George I. II. III. IV. Anne, William IV and Mary, Victoria." A budding lawyer defined a deed as "a document written on two pieces of paper and then torn in half."[27] He was a member not only of the Law Board (of which he was Secretary from 1886 to 1895), but also of the History Board. On the former he felt at home. Of the latter he thought little. "I never came upon any Board that had so little cohesion as this History Board . . . It consumes endless time."[28] He grew only too familiar with the recurrent call to "revise the syllabus," an academic pastime admirably designed, by the necessity of defending or attacking pet subjects, to encourage feline amenities. He was appointed to the General Board of Studies, created in 1879 to supervise the work of the faculties, and was at different times on the Press Syndicate, the Library Syndicate, and the Economics Syndicate.

Of these various bodies he enjoyed the work of the Library Syndicate. He redrafted the regulations, advised on books, and became a close friend of the Librarian, F. J. H. Jenkinson. In 1890 he welcomed on the Syndicate's behalf the members of a conference on the local lectures of the University. His speech was characteristic, seasoning counsel with the wit that delights at the time and preserves for the future.[29] His opening words set the tone of the speech. "It has been thought by those who have planned today's programme that the pleasant office of welcoming you to our Library could not prudently be entrusted to anyone whose deep knowledge of its history might tempt him to speak for many hours on a favourite theme. Thus it comes about that, as one who could not possibly pretend to any such temptation, I have been employed to collect from obvious sources a few main facts . . . and to string those facts together into a short discourse."

After a historical sketch he made three points. He first explained why a Library which, by the Copyright Act, had the privilege of claiming a copy of every book published in the United Kingdom, should still need money. The United Kingdom, unhappily, was not the world. "Imagine yourselves having to satisfy a greedy crowd of readers, of hungry students each of whom is apt to believe that his own special subject is of preeminent importance and singularly neglected by the mass of mankind; then think how large the world is, how large the world of letters is, how copious is the flow of ink in Germany, how new countries, new continents are becoming lettered, how new sciences are arising and subdividing themselves—then £1000 or £2000 a year will not seem so much to you, and maybe you will doubt whether in this matter the University is doing all that it ought to do. Should you go so far as to say that there should be more books and fewer professors I do not know that I could contradict you."

He then explained how the Library was used. Unlike the Bodleian, "we allow men to take books out of the library; we make exceedingly little provision for their reading books in the library. To put the rule briefly, every Master of Arts . . . may visit the library, inspect, ransack the shelves for himself and take out books. He may have ten out at one time. Four times a year the Library is shut for a few days, and before its shutting every book ought to be returned. The process of taking out a book is the simplest. You write its name and your name on a ticket and give that ticket to the porter, then you make off with your book and you keep it until you see fit to return it . . . So if you pass through our rooms don't suppose that all our books are there. Where are they? Scattered over the face of the globe. In a Swiss railway carriage I have seen produced from a knapsack a guide-book which bore the unmistakeable mark of the University Library."

Finally, he asked his hearers not to think of the manuscripts which they might see on display, "exquisitely written, exquisitely painted," as the toys of aesthetes or antiquarians. They, and the many more prosaic manuscripts in the Library, were the instruments of the scholar's trade. "I need not remind you how within the present century all history, I use that word in its very widest sense, has been re-written, or how first and foremost among the means that have enabled men to rewrite it have been the MSS stored in public libraries. The whole aspect of the world has been changed for us by the study of MSS. By and by you are to see our scientific museums and there you will see some of the tools and plant of modern physical science; it is here that we keep the tools and plant of modern historical learning. Whether physical science or historical learning has done more to change the aspect of the world, to give us new thoughts about men and things, is a question too deep for me—I take the humbler course of asking you to notice one difference between the two kinds of plant. If the scientific instrument is broken or lost, I suppose that its place can generally be filled by another; not so with MSS., for not only is the supply of ancient MSS strictly limited, but every MS is absolutely unique. One copy of a printed book may be as good for all practical purposes as any other copy of the same edition, but no two MSS ever were alike; every copyist puts something of himself into his work even though it be his own stupidity, and then his stupidest blunder may be the one really valuable thing that he has left behind him. And then one never dares to say that a MS has been used up, that everything that was in it has been got out of it. This has been said over and over again; but there has come the gifted man who knew what to look for, and he has seen for the first time what had indeed been under many eyes but had never been seen before."

In 1894 Maitland was elected to the Council of the Senate,

The Council is the channel through which all Graces to be submitted to the University must pass; it consists of the Chancellor (present only on ceremonial occasions), the Vice Chancellor, and sixteen graduates elected by the Regent House. An impression of Maitland at work on this body was given in 1907 by Armitage Robinson, then Dean of Westminster—the more convincing since the two men often differed on academic policy.[30] "It was my pleasure and privilege to sit next to Professor Maitland at the Council meetings for some time, and once or twice he and I were asked to draft regulations together. This brought me to close quarters with him, and it was a rare advantage to be set to make the first draft and then to be criticised by his kindly wisdom. His judgment in the interpretation of statutes impressed me again and again by their sagacity and courage. 'I always stretch a statute,' he whispered to me once, half-humourously. He seemed to be making the law grow under his hands."

The routine of Council business was sometimes shattered, or relieved, by perilous issues. Few were more likely to arouse passion than the place of women in the University. The first mutterings of the storm had been heard in 1868, when Sidgwick wrote to his sister: "Do you know that I am violently engaged in a scheme for improving female education? A Board is constituted of Oxford and Cambridge men (no end of swells, including the men who have refused Bishoprics, etc.) to examine governesses and schoolmistresses."[31] In June 1869 the first examination for women was held by the University. In 1870 lectures for women were started. These at first were restricted to local inhabitants; but in October 1871 five students, under the care of Miss Anne Clough, the sister of Arthur Hugh Clough, moved into a house in Regent Street, Cambridge, which Sidgwick had taken and furnished, and which was the germ of Newnham College. In 1873 Miss Emily Davies, who had previously organized a College for women at Hitchin, transferred it to Cambridge and inaugurated Girton College. Such an irruption might emotionally disturb individuals; the University, as a body, ignored it. Only by courtesy were women examined at the same time and in the same place as men. But in 1880 Miss C. A. Scott of Girton was informally adjudged equal to the Eighth Wrangler. Mrs. Sidgwick was now Vice Principal of Newnham, and she, with her husband and many friends, used Miss Scott's achievement to urge the formal admission of women students to the examinations of the University. To their surprise the Senate on February 24, 1881, accepted the proposal. Successful candidates were to be named in the lists, but they were not to be awarded degrees or given any role in the University constitution. In 1887 Miss Ramsay was placed at the head of the Classical Tripos list. Zealots sought to exploit her triumph by demanding that women should be given degrees. Sidgwick opposed the proposal. He feared, by moving too soon, to endanger what had already been won, and his caution prevailed. Not until 1895 did the Associates of Newnham College—a composite body of staff and former students—suggest a new approach to the Senate. Sidgwick still doubted the prudence or the success of such a step. But a quarter of a century had passed since women had been allowed to take the examinations, and the University could not be accused of recklessness if it now felt able to go further.

In May 1896 the Senate appointed a Syndicate "to consider what further rights or privileges, if any, should be granted to women students by the University, and whether women should be made admissible to degrees in the University, and if so, to what degrees, on what conditions and with what restrictions, if any." On this Syndicate Maitland reluctantly agreed to serve, and he drudged in the galley for a year. Like Sidgwick, he wished to do all that might be done for the women's cause without risk to their existing status; but the time consumed, if not wasted, was irksome. He ended a letter to Fisher on February 21, 1897: "Meanwhile there are these women—drat them. I have some hope that in another week I may have done my share of the work and may be able to think of other things." On February 23 he told Sidgwick that "our proposal, signed by 9 out of 14, is (in brief) to give the titles of the degrees of B.A., M.A., D.Sc., and D.Lit.—to do this and no more. The minority would wish alternative resolutions in favour of fancy titles." The Syndicate thus reported on March 1, and its proposals were debated on March 13, 15, and 16.[32]

Maitland's speech, made on the first day of the debate, lived in the memory of all who heard it. It was directed to two ends. He sought first to disarm opposition by recommending the report as a compromise. "If Cambridge is to be a place of learning, then we must jealously guard the little leisure that is left to us by Boards, Syndicates and Committees; and when to the Boards, Syndicates and Committees is added the pest of the fly-sheet and the caucus, then I think it behoves every man who has the interest of the University at heart to labour for the peace . . . Let us beat our swords into ploughshares, for the undergraduates have need of these." There was nobody on the Syndicate and nothing in its report to excite apprehension or indeed interest. It was "a Syndicate of peaceful men, not all logical men, but all peaceful men, dull men, perhaps the thirteen dullest men in the University." He had then to meet a counterproposal to found a women's university, to be called The Queen's University of the British Empire, to be patronized by both Oxford and Cambridge, and to be situated at a convenient distance from each. Here there was no room for compromise, and he killed the scheme by ridicule. "Having so grand a name as 'the Queen's', you might at first do with a humble home. But you would have to pay rent even for what I think would be the most suitable place—the waiting room at Bletchley Station. Again, you could not oblige the women to take the Bletchley degree. You would be waiting, waiting, waiting in the waiting room, and they would be waiting, waiting, waiting outside, and on whose side would public opinion be in that case? I see it is said here with some emphasis that the title of the University *shall* be the Queen's University. What! Whether the Queen likes it or no? Do not you think that the Queen may have an opinion about it? Do not you think that after sixty years of reign she might say that she did not choose that you should take her name in vain, in order to advertise your needy, seedy institution which will be banned and boycotted by the women from the first moment of its existence? No: I think the Bletchley Junction Academy—that is the name. You wait there; but you do not wait there always. You change for Oxford and Cambridge."

Buckland, who heard Maitland's speech, never forgot "the impression of his slight and graceful figure with, oddly enough, a habit of somewhat awkward gesture which passed entirely from observation as soon as he was in full tide of speech. All that one could then see was his wonderful face. He looked at that time a youngish man, though he was nearing fifty; but his face was covered with a network of minute lines, too fine and delicate to be called wrinkles, and contributing not a little to the general impression of intellectual power and intensity of purpose. No single feature of his face ever seemed to be still. Every emotion expressed in his speech was reflected equally clearly in his countenance—contempt followed enthusiasm; intense conviction succeeded persiflage; humour, sweet reasonableness, pity, detestation, were as plainly visible as they were audible. But after a little time even his features faded—at least from the notice of one observer—and all that one could see, or at any rate, note, was his wonderful eyes. All that one was conscious of was the flow of epigram, argument and even invective—and the eyes."[33]

The vote was not taken at the debate but postponed for two months. The delay enabled the leaders of the opposition to rally their forces, especially among nonresident voters. They did not confine their efforts to senior members of the University. Maitland told Sidgwick that he feared "an attempt to raise the undergraduates, i.e. to get from them some emphatic declaration." The voting took place on May 21, and the Syndicate's proposals were rejected by 1707 votes to 661. The undergraduates had certainly been raised. They threw rotten eggs and lighted crackers in the Senate-House Yard, and in the evening marched on Newnham College with the intention of burning on the lawn an effigy of a woman graduate. Maitland was hit by an egg, and during the night the Downing trees were wreathed with toilet rolls. "You can imagine," wrote Miss Maitland, "what a hero my father seemed in the nursery."[34]

Maitland in debate was a different man from Maitland at a lecture. He was ready to conciliate if conciliation would pay. But if he could not persuade he sought to destroy, and he would use without compunction all the weapons at his command. As a master of irony he was not innocent of the art of making enemies. Buckland once asked Henry Swete, Professor of Divinity and a colleague on the General Board of Studies, how he got on with him. Swete "lifted his two hands towards heaven and said: 'Oh, Maitland!' Then something prompted me to ask Maitland how he got along with my friend on the General Board. To my intense but carefully concealed amusement, he lifted both hands towards heaven and said: 'Oh, Swete!' "[35] Maitland's support of the women's cause indicates his political views. He took no part in public life and disdained the paraphernalia of state. "I have no use for modern kings," he told Pollock.[36] But in University affairs he was a convinced Liberal; and, faced with such national issues as the South African War and the alternatives of protection and free trade, he allowed himself no such deviation as his friends Sidgwick and Jackson indulged or tolerated.

As a Fellow of Downing, Maitland had to take his share of College business. Downing was small in number both of senior and of junior members, but there was enough work to make inroads on Maitland's time. He audited accounts, visited farms, advised on legal difficulties and made or avoided decisions on the perennial and exacerbating details of domestic economy. Downing, like other colleges, drew much of its revenue from its farms; and the last two decades of the nineteenth century were years of agricultural depression. In 1877 English wheat averaged 56s.9d. a quarter; by 1894 it had fallen to 19s.8d. The gross returns from rents throughout the country sank from £59 million in 1888 to £42 million in 1901. "True rent" had almost vanished, since landlords received too little to maintain their estates.[37] To mitigate its loss the College had either to sell some of its farms—if indeed they could be sold—or to sacrifice part of its demesne. At the turn of the century it was resolved to sell the northern part of its grounds to the University. The dilemma was urgent, the decision bitter; and the Master, Alex Hill, became the focus of controversy. In this and in later troubles Maitland was staunch in affection and support. He wrote from the Canaries to Henry Jackson: "I am hoping that there will be no great rumpus at Downing while I am away. If only A. H. would keep his fingers from the ink pot! But, mind you, that man is a saint and will go straight to heaven without questions asked."[38]

Pollock complained that Maitland had been set, not only to "serve the tables" of the Tripos, but also to "grind in the mills of boards and syndicates."[39] University and College business must needs be done. Yet a professor is elected because he is learned and seeks to pursue learning; and the cares of administration, if not incompatible, are still a tax imposed upon him for irrelevant ends. Maitland's discharge of his duty drained energies which could have been spared for less ephemeral purposes and for work which he alone could have done. But there was one form of activity to which he was always drawn. The Selden Society was a meeting place of business and pleasure, of law and history, of life and scholarship. To it Maitland remained constant until he died; and if on occasion he met with disappointment and anxiety, this was the price he had to pay for the unique chance to develop all his powers.

Baildon, the new editor enlisted for the Society, had been at work on its third volume since the beginning of 1889, and the book was published in the summer of 1890 as *Select Civil Pleas, A.D. 1200–1203*. Maitland thought well of the book and of the man, and he suggested that they should collaborate in the next volume. As a sequel to Volume 2 they would print further pleas in the manorial courts and accompany these with one of the tracts on procedure which appeared in the thirteenth and fourteenth centuries. But the book changed in the making. Maitland had been lent by Mr. Oliver Pell of Wilburton Manor, Ely, a manuscript of pleas tried in the court of the Bishop of Ely at Littleport between 1285 and 1327, and courtesy suggested an early printing.[40] The tracts on court procedure, moreover, had proved so fascinating that he could not content himself with a single specimen. "From one of these books I was led on to another, and so to a third, and to a fourth; for, having once opened this new vein of materials, one could not stop working it until it had been somewhat fully explored." Here, as elsewhere, he was caught by the lure of the chase. "I constantly find things that ought to be printed. I wish I were three men with three Selden Societies at my back."[41] In the result there was no room for the material which his partner had been preparing; and, though Maitland took care that Baildon should not suffer financially, it is difficult not to condole with a collaborator who is crowded out of the book.

Volume 4 was published in the early summer of 1891 under the title of *The Court Baron* and with Maitland and Baildon both named as editors. It was divided into two parts. The first comprised four of the tracts which had charmed Maitland. They had been written to help those who had business in the local courts: "to teach stewards how to preside, clerks how to enrol, pleaders how to count and defend." One of these "guides for court keeping" has a peculiar interest. It was apparently compiled in the last quarter of the thirteenth century by a certain Brother John of Oxford who became a monk in the Priory of Luffield twenty miles from the city and who also collected a series of conveyancing precedents of which Maitland had already written in the *Law Quarterly Review*.[42] Brother John wistfully recalled Oxford days. "He mentions the High Street (*magna strata*), the churches of S. Mary and of All Saints, and the *aqua que vocatur Charewelle;* and among his precedents is one well suited to the needs of an undergraduate, for it is a letter by a son studying at Oxford to his father, asking for money—*'Ne pro tali defectu scolas relinquere, tempus amittere, domumque redire compellar.'* "

The second part of the volume was devoted to the Littleport manuscript. Littleport in the thirteenth century "was surrounded on almost every side by unlimited and undrained fen. Its people must have been an amphibious race, largely employed in catching eels for the bishop. When they were 'attached by their chattels' to answer in court, boats, oars, nets and bundles of 'lesch' were taken; indeed 'lesch' seems to have fulfilled some of the uses of money amongst them; they are habitually owing and being owed so many hundreds or thousands of 'lesch'."[43] To a historian of the law of contract the most significant pleas in the Bishop's court are the actions brought on informal agreements. But the rolls are rich in local interest: actions of debt and detinue, trespass and defamation, orders for the removal of lepers, presentments of bakers and alewives for breach of the assize of bread and beer, fines for collecting bitterns' eggs and "exporting them out of the fen" and for building pigsties or putting dung heaps on common land.

The Selden Society secured three more editors: the Rev. William Hudson, R. G. Marsden, and Charles Gross. Hudson, with quiet competence, prepared a book on Leet Jurisdiction in his native city of Norwich. Marsden was to be responsible for two volumes of Admiralty Pleas. He had been introduced by Hubert Hall, a faithful friend of Maitland and of the Society. Hall became Assistant Keeper of the Public Record Office and Director of the Royal Historical Society. Warmhearted and single-minded, he was a devoted and, but for a certain ingenuousness, might have become a distinguished historian. Charles Gross, of Harvard, had already made his name by his work on *The Gild Merchant*. In January 1893 he sent Maitland a copy of his essay on the office of the coroner, and he was meditating a collection of coroners' rolls. Maitland asked him to entrust them to the Selden Society. "The pay that it can offer its editors is but small—but still it pays a little, while my own experience is that publishing records at one's own risk means less."[44] Gross accepted the offer.

Maitland was now in the midst of his *History of English Law*. But he made time to plan two books for the Society. In 1890 he had become interested in a manuscript in the library of Corpus Christi College, Cambridge, which in 1642 had been printed, anonymously and with many blunders, as *La Somme appelle Mirroir des Justices vel Speculum Justiciariorum, factam per Andream Horne*. It was a curious book, but it had been devoured by Coke "with uncritical voracity" and through Coke had influenced the common law. It offered intriguing problems to be solved. Maitland asked his former pupil W. J. Whittaker to prepare the text; he planned to write an introduction himself. Whittaker, eighteen years younger than his tutor, had won a Whewell Scholarship and the Chancellor's medal; and, until he went to the Bar in 1901, he taught and lectured in Cambridge. Maitland was won by his devotion, kindliness and innate simplicity, and relied on his help in routine work. In one long vacation he met with an accident; and Maitland wrote to R. L. Poole: "The dear Whittaker, who usually stands between me and 'elementary real property' has been ejected from a trap and has concussed his massive brain—so I am writing lectures for dear life."[45]

Of the second book Maitland had long felt the want. In "The Materials for English Legal History," which he wrote in 1889 for the *Political Science Quarterly,* he observed that Bracton's work was "profoundly influenced by Roman law" and added that "the part played by Roman and Canon law in this critical stage of the formation of the common law deserves a minuter examination than it has as yet received." In the summer of 1891 he offered suggestions for future Selden volumes. Among them was "Bracton's Roman Law: a good text of those portions of Bracton's work in which he was following Azo, printed in parallel columns with Azo—the texts cited from Code and Digest being printed in foot notes. This should be a good book. It wants a good man." The Council accepted the proposal and asked Maitland to carry it out. His immediate aim was "to enable readers to compare the most romanesque portions of Bracton's treatise with the texts from which they are derived"; but he hoped also to "advance, by however little, the day when a creditable edition of that treatise will have been produced."[46]

Work on these two books was interrupted by a catastrophe. Dove had acted as secretary and treasurer of the Society since its birth. He had sought success in scholarship as well as in practice, and he had failed in both. He had no money and no hope. In the small hours of Wednesday, November 21, 1894, he killed himself. Maitland wrote in agony to Bigelow and to Thayer.[47] "Dove has destroyed himself, and there can I fear be no doubt that the cause of his act is to be found in the affairs of the Selden Society. How bad the matter is I hardly yet know, but I dread the very worst, namely that the funds of the Society have totally disappeared . . . Poor Dove! I did not like some of his ways, but I never suspected this." He trusted only that the executive committee would "make the end of the Society as honourable as it can possibly be, but, as this will I fear involve the provision of a large sum of money out of purses some of which are not very full, I dare hope for no better than an issue of those volumes that are due in respect of subscriptions already received—and then my beloved Society will come to an end."

Maitland's worst fears were not realized. The affairs of the Society were certainly in confusion. Lord Coleridge, who had died earlier in the year, had been "an all too easy-going president."[48] No meetings had been held for two years and no books or accounts were kept, not even a current list of subscribers. Dove owed the Society £1,000, of which nothing could be recovered, and over £500 had long been due to the printers, Spottiswoode and Co. But within three months the crisis was past. Gifts from members amounted to £625, and the printers, with great generosity, halved their bill. At the annual general meeting on March 8, 1895, the Society was re-organized. The "executive committee" became a Council, with Lord Herschell as President and Lord Justice Lindley and Mr. Justice Romer as Vice Presidents. Maitland was appointed Literary Director "to supervise the editing of the Society's publications, to suggest suitable editors and generally to advise the Council on policy." The offices of Secretary and Treasurer were separated, and Benjamin Fossett Lock was elected to serve as Honorary Secretary. Lock, three years older than Maitland, was a barrister in good practice at Lincoln's Inn. He continued to act as Secretary until he became in 1913 a County Court Judge, and was as efficient, prudent, and precise as Dove had been desultory, reckless, and inaccurate. His eyes were on everyone: printers, editors, even the Honorary Treasurer. When I. S. Leadam, who edited *Select Cases in the Court of Requests,* fell ill at a critical stage, Lock saw the volume through the press. He and Maitland worked well together. They liked and respected each other; and Lock, watching but not worried by detail, protected Maitland from importunity.

Maitland and Lock had now to prepare a list of forthcoming volumes in order of priority. *The Mirror of Justices* and *Bracton and Azo* were nearly ready; the first was published as volume 7 in July 1895 and the second as volume 8 in October. They made little demand on the Society's funds. Maitland and Whittaker refused to take fees for volume 7, and the entire cost of volume 8 was met by Mr. Justice Stirling. In May 1895 Maitland received from Gross the manuscript of the *Coroners' Rolls*. Both he and Lock read the proofs, and to save time Maitland compiled the indexes. In February 1896 the book was published. The next volume to demand attention was the *Select Cases in the Court of Chancery* which Baildon had been editing before Dove's death. He was now urged to complete it; and, when he appeared to delay, Lock told him in August 1896 that it "would be a great disappointment to all persons interested in the Society if the book were not published before Christmas."

The *Mirror of Justices* in itself is not a rich source of legal history; but it led Maitland to write an introduction as self-revealing as it is delicious. The book was apparently composed in the reign of Edward I and probably about the time of the judicial scandal of 1289. Who wrote it and why was it written? These questions were intertwined. Andrew Horn, fishmonger of Bridge Street and Chamberlain of the City of London,[49] made his will on October 9, 1328. He bequeathed to the chamber of the Gildhall six books, of which one was *De Veteribus Legibus Angliae* and another *Speculum Justiciariorum*—the mirror of justices. On a page of the former was a legend in red ink adorned with the drawing of a fish: "Horn michi cognomen Andreas est michi nomen." The same legend appears on the first page of the *Mirror*, accompanied by four Latin verses which serve to thicken the mystery.[50] Was Horn not only the owner but also the author of this book?

Before attempting to answer this question, Maitland preferred to consider the book's purpose. "If we ask for [the author's] motives, we had better for a while use the word *motive* in the sense that Richard Wagner has made familiar. No other law-book is so like 'the art-work of the future.' It is constructed out of a few leading motives, each of which is frequently introduced with more or less ornament and embroidery. We might pick these out and label them as 'the false judge motive,' 'the Hebraic *talion* motive,' and so forth; but any reader will soon see that he can do this for himself and will find the task amusing . . . A strong religious strain runs through the work; indeed the whole book might be marked *Religioso*." But the author was no churchman, certainly no high churchman. "We seem to hear in advance the voice of the modern Nonconformist who objects to compulsory church-rates." Nor was he a lawyer. He knew Bracton, but any legal argument on which he ventured was fantastic or puerile. "His political theory is simple. He is strongly opposed to an unfettered monarchy and to a king who is above the law. But his ideal of the body which is, or ought to be, a check upon the king is quaint and impracticable . . . We must go back to 'the coming of the English.' Further back than that we need not go. He is as ardent a Teutonist as was the late Mr. Freeman; more ardent, for of the Norman Conquest he says no word. The strain that dominates the whole book is the dislike of the king's officers and their ways. Corrupt are they and become abominable in their doings; there is none that doeth good, no not one." These were dangerous sentiments; and the author sought to cloak them by talking not of contemporaries but of "the forty-four false judges whom Alfred hanged in the space of a year." To make the fable plausible the judges must be named—but not with names current in his own time. "So let them be Watling, Billing, Bermond and so forth. Watling Street, Billing's Gate and Bermond's eye give him useful suggestions." "What then shall we say of this book? and what shall we call its author? Is he lawyer, antiquary, preacher, agitator, pedant, faddist, lunatic, romancer, liar? A little of all, perhaps, but the romancer seems to predominate. He would like that some of his tales should be believed . . . But he is careful not to tell us when he is in earnest and when he is at play. So to do would not merely be an inartistic blunder; it might end in his being taken too seriously. He is making an attack on powerful persons, on the king's justices and officers. He is hinting that the royal court is a den of thieves. It is well for him that, if called to account for his words, he can say that he was but telling stories of Alfred and Arthur and ask you whether you cannot see a joke. That is what makes his work so puzzling to us nowadays. We guess that he wanted his readers to believe some things that he said. We can hardly suppose him hoping that they would believe all. We feel sure that in Paradise, or wherever else he may be, he was pleasantly surprised when Coke repeated his fictions as gospel truth and erudite men spoke of him in the same breath with Glanvill and Bracton."

At length Maitland returned to the crucial question: did Horn write the book? His summary of the evidence was impartial but, like that of many judges, circumspect. The book was composed about 1289 and Horn died in 1328. Perhaps this long interval supplied the answer to the problem. "We may have before us the work of a young man who grew wiser as he grew older. In the *Mirror* he sowed his wild oats. He began, as clever youths often will, with the romance of law, with a very 'general jurisprudence', with history written *a priori,* with a full persuasion that he is wiser than the judges and that those who differ from him live in 'mortal sin.' He lived, as perhaps even a clever youth sometimes will, to love the document and collect materials for the Selden Society . . . Were we sitting as a jury to try Horn for the publication of this book, we should have to give him the benefit of the doubt, though we could hardly say that he left the court without a stain upon his character."

If to read the riddle of the *Mirror* was an agreeable pastime, the preparation of *Bracton and Azo* was a sterner task. That Maitland should return to Bracton is natural. But it is tempting to suspect that his appetite for *Bracton and Azo* was whetted by some words of Maine. As scholars the two men were opposed in aim and in method. Maitland told Pollock that he always talked of Maine with reluctance, "for on the few occasions on which I sought to verify his statements of fact I came to the conclusion that he trusted much to a memory that played him tricks and rarely looked back at a book that he had once read." Maitland undervalued Maine and his gift of imparting a ferment which is one of the marks of genius; but he recoiled from soaring generalizations detached from detailed evidence. It seems clear at least that the theme of *Bracton and Azo* was given by a passage in Maine's *Ancient Law*. "That an English writer of the time of Henry III should have been able to put off on his countrymen as a compendium of pure English law a treatise of which the entire form and a third of the contents were directly borrowed from the Corpus Juris, and that he should have ventured on this experiment in a country where the systematic study of the Roman law was formally proscribed, will always be among the most hopeless enigmas in the history of jurisprudence."[51]

Maitland quickly disposed of Maine. The study of Roman law was not proscribed in Bracton's England. There was no putting off if Maine thereby meant that Bracton offered other men's thoughts as though they were his own: the thirteenth century knew no property in ideas or in sayings. Nor did Bracton seek to pass off Roman as English law. He only assumed, as "plenty of other people have done, are doing and will do in many parts of Europe," that Roman law might fill the gap in national or provincial custom. In form Bracton diverged decisively from the Corpus Juris. In matter he borrowed directly from Roman law not a thirtieth, and from Azo not more than a fifteenth, of his whole book.

Maitland then sought to assess for himself Bracton's debt to Roman or Romanesque law. He concentrated on two sections of the treatise: folios 1–10 and folios 98b–107. In the first of these sections Bracton used Azo's *Summa* in an attempt to state the principles or "general part" of English law. He had only to copy intelligently whatever in Azo seemed appropriate for his purpose. "Is this task well performed? What would Azo have said if one of his scholars had brought him this abstract?" Maitland could not give Bracton many marks. "The distance between him and Azo in their treatment of Roman materials is, when stated in academic terms, the difference between a low third class and a high first." In the second section Bracton's task was harder. "He could not simply copy from Azo: he had to go to the Institutes themselves. He desired to find there the general principles of a law of contract; he desired also to fit our

English actions into the Roman niches." Here his work was not bad—but it was not good. This was not surprising. He used Roman where English law failed him, and he could not draw on his own experience as a judge. But he at least learned how to think and how to write about law. "When he uses an Italian book as a model he does well; when he uses it as a 'crib' he does ill."

This severe verdict Maitland tempered with two reflections. What judgment would have to be passed had the position been reversed and Azo had sought to make an abstract of Bracton? "He would have been guilty of many a wonderful mistake. If *praescriptio verbis agere* was Greek to Bracton, a *placitum de vetito namii* would have been Hebrew to Azo." Maitland suspected, moreover, that he might not be reading what Bracton had really written. The manuscript was not unique. "In the margin is a large mass of matter which has passed into the body of other manuscripts . . . and there is a strong presumption that the manuscript which makes Bracton say what Azo said is better than the manuscript which makes Bracton flatly contradict his teacher."

Maitland's judgment has been reversed on appeal. Vinogradoff wrote: "I do not go further than to claim for Bracton an acquaintance with Roman law at second hand by means of *Summae* and collections of extracts. Even with this qualification Bracton's use of civilian jurisprudence remains a remarkable monument of the scholarly interest and of the ingenuity of an English lawyer bent on rationalising the laws and customs of his time and country."[52] Professor Thorne's devoted and masterly study of the text has now settled many points and enabled important conclusions to be drawn. Vinogradoff need not have made his qualification: Bracton knew at first hand the Institutes, the Digest, and the Code. There are certainly in the Roman parts of the book defects which need to be explained. Hermann Kantorowicz suggested that these were the errors of a redactor who knew some English but little Roman law and who was at work after Bracton's death. Was this creature a man or a myth? George G. Woodbine denied his existence. Plucknett accepted him but thought that he had worked under the eyes of Bracton.[53] Professor Thorne has shown that the redactor indeed existed; that between 1272 and 1277 he copied and assembled the material left by Bracton at his death in 1268; that the archetype thus made was the ancestor of all the surviving manuscripts; that it contained defects in the English as well as in the Roman law; and that the redactor was responsible for both. Maitland had assumed—as did his contemporaries—that the text provided by the manuscripts, within a greater or smaller margin of error, was in essence the text which Bracton had written. This assumption was mistaken. Bracton never saw the text as it has come down to us, and there is no extant original.

Maitland ended his introduction to *Bracton and Azo* with the unusual plea of *ignorantia juris*. He himself, "whatever may have been Bracton's case, was no instructed Romanist, but had acquired the very little, the almost nothing, that he knew of Roman law painfully, late in life, and in order that he might understand some sides of English history.[54] He may not have visited upon legal texts the distaste he felt for the classics as school exercises, but he thought that, even in the Tripos, it was soon possible to have enough of Roman law. He put his mind to it only when he must. For his present purpose he had sought the help of colleagues and especially of William Warwick Buckland, upon whose reminiscences all who write of Maitland must draw. Buckland had become a Fellow of Caius College in 1889, and he fell under Maitland's spell. Friendship was cultivated both in Cambridge and in the Canaries. Maitland encouraged Buckland to write his book on *The Roman Law of Slavery*,[55] and he would have rejoiced at its publication in 1908 and at Buckland's election in 1914 as Regius Professor of Civil Law.

Chapter VII

Downing Professor

The Years from 1888 to 1898 (II)

Maitland felt ever more insistently the fascination and the urgency of historical research. He had much to remind him that "life is short and history the longest of all the arts."[1] In 1887 Vinogradoff had published in St. Petersburg *Investigations into the Social History of Medieval England.* He sent a copy to Maitland, and Maitland struggled with the Russian. "*Cuius linguam ignorabant*—I feel now the full force of these words—I am *in tenebris exterioribus* and there is *stridor dencium;* but I heartily congratulate you upon having finished your book and thank you warmly for the copy of it that you sent me and for the kind words that you wrote upon the outside. Also I can just make out my name in the Preface and am very proud to see it there. Also I have read the footnotes, and they are enough to show me that this is a great book, destined in course of time to turn the current of English and German learning."[2]

In 1888 Vinogradoff came again to England. He had been preparing an English translation of his book and wished to discuss it with Maitland. H. A. L. Fisher's parents had taken for the summer a house in the hinterland of Sussex. The Maitlands were staying there and Vinogradoff was asked to join them. The Fishers long remembered his visit. He arrived without luggage and remained immaculate; at a dinner party he spoke at length of the Sussex county families, some of whose members were his fellow guests, traced their evolution and named the holders of their estates in the Middle Ages. In the following winter he sent Maitland the first half of the translation. Maitland relished its quality and was eager that it should make its proper mark upon English opinion. Vinogradoff's command of language was as powerful as his mind. It was, indeed, too exuberant, and he had to be restrained from such forays into the vernacular as his description of King John's death: "John had taken his hook." Maitland had also to suggest the danger of inferring political sympathies from historical views, of identifying Stubbs with progressive thought and Seebohm with conservative reaction. This would be received as paradox. "All that you say about Stubbs and Seebohm and Maine is, I dare say, very true if you regard them as European, not merely English, phenomena and attribute to them a widespread significance—and doubtless it is very well that Englishmen should see this. Still, looking at England only and our insular ways of thinking, I see Stubbs and Maine as two pillars of conservatism, while as to Seebohm I think that his book is as utterly devoid of political importance as, shall I say, Madox's *History of the Exchequer*. But you are cosmopolitan and I doubt not that you are right. You are putting things in a new light—that is all. If 'the darkness comprehendeth it not', that is the darkness's fault."[3] In the autumn of 1891 Maitland reported that every page had been passed for the press, and the book was published early in 1892 under the title of *Villainage in England*.

In the ensuing years Vinogradoff wrote at intervals to English friends and sent occasional articles to the *English Historical Review*. But he was increasingly disturbed by the political state of Russia, by the intrusions of the government into academic life, and by the disruption of the universities. In January 1895 he wrote a despairing letter to Maitland. "I may be dismissed or constrained to tender my resignation any day. Common prudence obliges me to look about for other work and means of livelihood. And so I am brought to ask you a question of which I have been in dread for some time. Is there any possible opening for me in England?" Maitland had to reply that the outlook at Cambridge for a historian was bleak: there was no money for any new post. He asked Fisher if Oxford offered better prospects. "I feel sure that in course of time a man of P.V.'s power would come to the front at O. or at C.; but I fear that at C. he would have a long struggle for his first bread and butter. I wish to heaven that I were prime minister at this moment! I would risk a war to put P.V. in the vacant chair."[4] For the rest of the century Vinogradoff remained in Moscow, struggling amid turmoil to advance education and foster research.

From their first meeting in England Maitland's relations with Vinogradoff were unusually intimate. Of the other European scholars whom he admired Felix Liebermann of Berlin was almost the only one whom he came to know as a man.[5] Liebermann was a dedicated scholar with wide interests, especially in Anglo-Saxon and early medieval English law. He was an authority both on Glanvill and on Vacarius; but his great work, the fruit of patient research over many years, was *Die Gesetze der Angelsachsen,* ultimately published in three volumes between 1903 and 1916. He had the eye of a lynx for original documents wherever they might be lurking, and for his "Anglo-Saxon Laws" he found and examined one hundred and eighty manuscripts in forty libraries. Maitland had known his work since 1888, and they met three years later. Liebermann called attention to a vital source for the *Mirror of Justices,* and he asked Maitland's help in obtaining admission to English libraries. In 1892 he was trying to settle the text of the *Leges Edwardi Confessoris.* He possessed variations of ten manuscripts, but knew that twenty more existed. Three of these were to be found at the College of Arms and in the libraries of the Marquis of Bath and of the Duke of Northumberland. He might venture to visit the College of Arms, "but to those two noblemen I don't yet see how to find my way." Did Maitland know anything of their characters? He hoped also to visit Cambridge, but did not know the Librarian. Could Maitland assure the latter that "I neither rob nor spoil manuscripts and that the use I should make of all the treasures under his care would serve our knowledge of the English past and tend to no other aim?" In June 1896 Maitland persuaded the University to grant Liebermann an honorary Doctorate, and gave a dinner for him to which he invited young scholars who would otherwise have had no chance to meet him.[6]

With four English historians Maitland was brought, for differing reasons, into special contact. Reginald Lane Poole was the son, the brother, and the father of scholars. He spent his life in Oxford: a lecturer at Jesus from 1886 to 1910, a research Fellow of Magdalen from 1898 to 1933, the university lecturer in Diplomatics from 1896 to 1927. Not a prolific and certainly not a popular writer, he was a man of profound and precise learning and of pervasive influence. When in 1886 the *English Historical Review* was founded, Mandell Creighton was its editor with Poole as his assistant; and when in 1891 Creighton was made a bishop and was succeeded by S. R. Gardiner, Poole continued in virtual control of the *Review*. From 1901 to 1920 he was its editor, "the trusted guide of all his contributors, from his friend and admirer Maitland to the humblest beginner."[7] Maitland, indeed, rich in ideas, vivid in expression, owed much to his cool but sympathetic judgment.

John Horace Round was four years younger than Maitland and survived him for twenty-two years. As an undergraduate at Balliol College, Oxford, he was one of the few whom Stubbs took as a pupil. Poole, another of the few, described Stubbs's method of tuition. He sought "to introduce one to the mass of learning which he possessed and to train one in judgment of affairs and criticism of authorities. He never attempted to supply gaps which we ought to have supplied for ourselves."[8] No method could have been more congenial to Round. Inheriting ample means, he wished, intellectually as well as financially, to be sufficient unto himself. He accepted no academic post but followed his interests wherever they took him. He was ferocious in the pursuit of detail, disdained secondary sources, and strove, at his own pace and in his own way, to re-create the structure of medieval society. Three of his books were pioneer works which left their mark upon English history. In *Geoffrey de Mandeville* (1892) he portrayed the anarchy of Stephen's reign; *Feudal England* (1895) was a landmark in Domesday studies; in the *Commune of London* (1899) he cast new light on the origin of the Exchequer.

Round was a great historical scholar. But he had flaws of temperament and character which prevented him from being a great man. He was an example, perhaps a cautionary example, of the virtues and the temptations that might adorn or assail the leisured class of the late nineteenth century. He avoided the dissipation of drudgery, but he missed the discipline of routine and the daily intercourse with intellectual equals which might have tempered his egotism. Of all his books *Geoffrey de Mandeville* alone was sustained history. The others were miscellanies in which brilliant aperçus and solid learning were interspersed with triviality. He pounced upon the mistakes of rivals and, like many who dissect eagerly the work of others, was acutely sensitive to the possibility, and resented violently the fact, of retaliation.

In 1888 he sent to Maitland the proof sheets of *Ancient Charters* which he was preparing for the Pipe Roll Society. But it was not until 1892 that the two men regularly exchanged letters. In that year both became interested in Domesday Book, and Round was anxious to warn competitors off his own chosen ground. "It would be an awful pity," he wrote to Maitland, "if, as fellow workers, we tumble over one another in our researches. You see I don't know in the least what you are working for, what form your work will appear in, or what line you are specially going on . . . The hide system is my *pièce de résistance,* but all through I approached the subject on new lines, trying, as it were, to get behind Domesday and puzzle out the method of its compilation . . . Now what are your lines? I hope we are not running on the same rails."[9] Maitland reassured him; and when, three years later, the *History of English Law* was published, Round was generous in his praise. "You are a most wonderful man. Here have I been marvelling for years at your output, with which no one else's can compare. And now you top it all with this monumental work as if you had had nothing else to do all these years but write it. My own efforts seem very puny in comparison, and 'scraggy'." He was glad to see that Maitland, and presumably Pollock, had used his own books.

> Their case they ground
> At times on Round
> Who shoulders rubs
> (In notes) with Stubbs.[10]

So long as Round wished to conciliate Maitland their correspondence was friendly and fruitful. But Maitland understood the delicacy needed to sustain it; and two incidents first impaired and then destroyed their relations. The first was trivial but tedious. In Round's words, "the fiercest historical controversy of this generation began with an article of mine entitled *Professor Freeman* published in the Quarterly Review for July 1892." Round attacked Freeman's account of the Battle of Hastings and especially his insistence that Harold had fortified his position with a palisade. The campaign of 1066, short and sharp, was a mere affair of soldiers and paled before the bitter and protracted war of scholars which raged from 1892 to 1899. Freeman was as truculent as Round, and physical immunity allowed and encouraged charges and countercharges. In the early years of the struggle Maitland was ready to be entertained. "Is *the* battle over yet?" he asked in the summer of 1894. "It has amused me much, and I hope that you are not quite worn out by this terrific conflict." Six months later he was becoming weary of it. "As to the battle, I think that it is only *per finem duelli* that a *concordia* can be made." As the years passed he wished only to dismiss it from his thoughts. "That infernal palisade," he wrote to Poole, "I hope that no more will be heard of it."[11]

The second incident was serious. An edition of *The Red Book of the Exchequer* was contemplated for the Rolls Series, and Round was appointed joint editor with Hubert Hall of the Record Office. But they differed in their views of Swereford, the thirteenth-century compiler of the book, and Round resigned. In 1896 Hall reviewed Round's *Feudal England* in the *Quarterly Review*. He was generous in its praise, but he indiscreetly repeated his opinion of Swereford. Round told Maitland of his resolve to crush Hall, and Maitland sought to dissuade him. "I quite agree that [Hall] has a weak spot in his love for Swereford—but I think that this is evident enough and will do no harm, certainly not to you nor I think to any one else; and as there are but few people in the world who are of such a right good sort as he is, I am hoping that you will be content with the status quo. I am thoroughly convinced that you can 'afford' to let the matter be. Pray do not think that I am 'tendering advice'—nothing of the kind. I am pleading for a friend." Round was undeterred; and, when the *Red Book* was published in 1897, he was delighted to detect errors which he could, and did, expose both in reviews and in a pamphlet entitled *Studies on the Red Book of the Exchequer*. Maitland read the pamphlet with misgiving and was distressed when Poole asked him to review it. He begged Poole to excuse him. He could not be objective: his head was with Round and his heart with Hall. There had indeed been blunders. But, even if all that Round had said were true, he was still "using language which should be reserved for cases of a very different sort—some of which have occurred in the Rolls Series. Poor Hall has a curious fluffy mind but never scamps work, besides being (but this alas is irrelevant) the most unselfish man I have ever known."[12]

Maitland's magnanimity had been sorely tried and the breaking point was near. In 1899 Round published a collection of studies under the title *The Commune of London,* in which once again he turned upon the unfortunate Hall. But he had found another victim. Kate Norgate, the author of *England under the Angevin Kings,* had dared to support Freeman in the "Battle of Hastings." She in her turn must be taught a lesson. Maitland could endure no more, and he spoke his mind when he reviewed *The Commune of London* for the *Ath-*

enaeum.[13] He gave praise where praise was due. But "Mr. Round gives his readers too much controversy and too little history. Their interest in the twelfth century is always being distracted by the castigation of some unfortunate being who lived in the nineteenth." To expose error is necessary if unpalatable; but the good historian "will execute justice as noiselessly and as painlessly as may be." "It cannot be said that Mr. Round has always done this. To give one example: he has obtained our ear for an interesting episode in the history of London. He tells his readers that Henry II was offered *quingentas marcas,* and then adds, 'Miss Norgate says *five thousand;* but one must not be severe on a lady's Latin.' That takes their thoughts from King Henry and sets them waiting for the moment when this ungracious remark will come home to roost. If Mr. Round or his printer misspells the name of Scheffer-Boichorst, we do not say that his acquaintance with the German tongue is but gentlemanly. Miss Norgate, however, must be dragged in and battle-axed; she took part in the modern battle of Hastings. The reader is also informed that 'a little *clique* of Oxford historians, mortified at my crushing *exposé* of Mr. Freeman's vaunted accuracy, have endeavoured, without scruple and with almost unconcealed anger, to silence me at any cost.' They must be simple folk down there at Oxford if they think that Mr. Round will ever be silent about his own 'crushing' rightness and the crushed wrongness of Freeman and his followers." Maitland realized that the breach was irreparable. "I am sorry," he told Poole, "that Round has taken offence. I tried to do him full justice and thought that by this time he would have lost the taste for unmitigated praise such as is rightly bestowed upon promising young persons." He foresaw that he should have Round as an assailant for the rest of his life.[14]

The third English historian with whom Maitland made close contact was William Henry Stevenson. He was the son of a Hull timber merchant and as a youth went into his father's business. There he learned Norwegian from the sailors he met, but nothing else. After tasting life as a clerk in a solicitor's office he determined to pursue learning at whatever cost. His success was acclaimed by Sir Frank Stenton. He was "the first scholar to use modern methods of diplomatic for the criticism of Old English charters; he set a new standard of accuracy in the identification of English place-names; he was one of the first historians to appreciate the strength of the Scandinavian element in pre-Conquest England."[15] Maitland relied upon him for philology in general and for place names in particular, and in his preface to *Domesday Book and Beyond* spoke of the "unrivalled knowledge of English diplomatics generously placed at my service."

All that Stevenson knew he had taught himself, and to make a living he had to take whatever work was available. Between 1882 and 1889 he edited four volumes of Nottingham Borough Records. In 1888 he was employed by Merton College, Oxford, to calendar their muniments. In 1892 he began to edit the Calendars of Close Rolls and by 1908 had produced eleven volumes. More congenial was his collaboration with A. S. Napier as joint editor of *The Crawford Collection of Early Charters and Documents now in the Bodleian Library,* published in 1895. At the end of that year his qualities were at last recognized by election to a Research Fellowship at Exeter College, Oxford. Maitland congratulated him, and he replied from his lodgings in Tooting Bec. "I hope to join the array of resident dons at Oxford (a) for agreeable society; I am a hermit here, (b) to attend Napier's lectures, (c) in order to get my task-work done as I could never do it if distracted and exhausted by Close Roll calendaring. In vacation I shall continue calendaring, which will be supportable for short periods. I am wasting weeks over an introduction to the four volumes of Edward II, a task that is little preferable to suicide. I wish I had your capacity for composition which to me is a dreaded and much-shirked task. I don't think any ordinary lifetime would be long enough for me to write two volumes the length of your History."[16] In 1898, on Maitland's recommendation, he was appointed Sandars Reader in Bibliography at Cambridge and gave a course of lectures on the Anglo-Saxon Chancery. Maitland repeatedly urged him to publish them and wrote from the Canaries to say that if, on his return, he did not find them in print he would swear in

Spanish.[17] Even this desperate expedient failed, and the lectures remained in manuscript.

Poole, Round, and Stevenson may all be regarded as Maitland's contemporaries. Herbert Albert Laurens Fisher was a year younger than his sister Florence and fifteen years younger than Maitland. After obtaining a first class in Literae Humaniores he was elected in 1888 to a Prize Fellowship at New College, Oxford, and spent the next two years, as the terms of his election allowed, studying history in France and Germany. In Paris he shared rooms with William Rothenstein and regaled him with stories of Taine and Renan and the other great men by whom he had been received. Rothenstein enjoyed his company and observed him with a painter's eye. "Despite a somewhat grand manner he had a very human and affectionate character."[18] These attributes Fisher retained throughout his life. On his return to Oxford Fisher taught and lectured on Modern History. Maitland welcomed him with warmth as a brother-in-law and with sympathy as a young historian. In 1890 he congratulated him on his first publication: a paper on Fustel de Coulanges, the leader of the Romanist school of medievalists. "Your stay in Paris has enabled you to write about Fustel in a way that very few Englishmen could have done, for the reader is made to feel that you are 'in the swim' and can judge the work from the proper point of view."[19] Fisher in turn helped Maitland in a variety of ways: procuring French and German books, looking at Bodleian manuscripts, and reading proofs. In 1894 Maitland encouraged him in his design to write a volume on *The Medieval Empire,* and four years later the book was completed. Maitland read it on his first visit to the Canaries. "I have read few books so greedily and am now re-reading it. I feel that I am your debtor for some hours of unalloyed enjoyment and for much information that was entirely new to me. My one and only doubt is whether you have not a little underrated English ignorance of German affairs—but there! you were not writing a schoolbook, and it is a good thing to bring home to people like me their lamentable lack of elementary knowledge." He wrote also to Poole: "I have been enjoying Herbert Fisher's *Empire*. I hope that it is well spoken of by those who know."[20] He was ready to be pleased with it himself and anxious that it should please others, but it was not a success. It was marred by errors and omissions; it was "amateurish, and much worse it was dull."[21] Fisher was not a medievalist, and it was only when he turned to Napoleonic studies that he found his métier. While he was a scholar he was also an administrator; and his later career suggested that he was better fitted to be the latter than the former. But he never swerved in his devotion to Maitland and he never lost his hold on Maitland's heart.

Between 1888 and 1899 Maitland wrote for the *English Historical Review* fourteen articles and twenty-two reviews. He knew well the tricks of the reviewer. When he was reading the manuscript of Vinogradoff's *Villainage in England* he urged the need to prepare the opening chapter with special care. "Introductions are of crucial importance, by which I mean that they are of importance to critics, being often the only parts of a book which casual reviewers care to read. As a matter of prudence, therefore, I put into an Introduction a passage about the book which I mean critics to copy, and they catch the bait—it saves them trouble and mistakes."[22] Unlike the random reviewer for whom he set his trap, Maitland came to the reading of a book with his whole mind and without prejudice—eager to learn, happy to praise, resolute at the call of scholarship to challenge. If the book was the work of a seasoned writer, he judged it on its merits;[23] if it was a first flowering, he nursed the sensitive plant. A Mr. Herbert had contributed to the *English Historical Review* a hitherto unpublished "revocatio" by Henry II of his antiecclesiastical claims. Maitland had doubts of the text and wished to state them. "It may be expedient," he wrote to Poole, "that a word should be said of that Canterbury document . . . but who is Herbert? (I fear that I argue myself unknown). If he is a young man he might like the opportunity of having a second word about his document, and I should be unwilling to hurt his feelings."[24]

These years, though fretted by illness, were big with achievement. In addition to his Selden volumes, Maitland published *Memoranda de Parliamento, 1305*,[25] *The History of English*

Law before the Time of Edward I, Domesday Book and Beyond, Township and Borough, and *Roman Canon Law in the Church of England.*

In 1886 Henry Maxwell Lyte had been appointed Deputy Keeper at the Public Record Office and rescued it from perennial crisis. Among the commitments which he inherited was the Rolls Series, started thirty years earlier in order to print the sources, predominantly the literary sources, of English medieval history. It had proceeded on no clear plan and with editors of varying capacity. Francis Hingeston had prepared two volumes of Henry IV's correspondence, the second of which had to be destroyed as soon as it was printed. Sir Travers Twiss published an edition of Bracton. Of the edition printed in 1569 by Tottell, Selden had said: "Menda sunt perplurima eaque crassissima, partim e librariorum inscitia, partim ex operarum incuria." Of the Rolls edition Vinogradoff wrote that Sir Travers Twiss had contrived to add to both classes of errors. When Twiss later prepared an edition of Glanvill, Maxwell Lyte sought Maitland's advice and as a result suppressed the book. Six copies fortuitously escaped destruction, giving them "a value to the book collector which they never had for the reader —a remarkable consolation for literary damnation."[26] Such bêtises must be set against work of outstanding merit: the Year Books edited by A. J. Horwood and by L. O. Pike, and, above all, the seventeen volumes produced over a quarter of a century by Stubbs. These monuments of learning marked the golden age of the series and indeed of its editors. Stubbs was paid £500 for *Benedict of Peterborough* and £1,200 for *Roger of Hoveden.*[27]

At the end of 1888 Maxwell Lyte asked Maitland to edit a volume of Petitions to Parliament. Maitland was attracted by the proposal and, though doubtful of time and health, decided to accept it. In the summer of 1889 he realized the implications of the task. There were at least ten thousand petitions to be examined, strips of parchment some five inches long and from one to three inches broad. He must first date them by the character of the handwriting and the names of the persons mentioned. To date 1,000 petitions he thought would be a good year's work. In October 1889 he proposed a new plan. Instead of a mere collection of petitions conjecturally dated, he would edit the roll of the Lenten Parliament of 1305 which had never been printed. The opportunity would thus be given "for the publication of one of the very oldest Rolls of Parliament in an instructive form; for I should propose to illustrate the enrolments of the petitions and responses (1) by the petitions themselves which in many cases are extant, (2) by the writs whereby effect was given to the responses. The petition, as enrolled, is but a Latin abstract of the petition itself, which is usually in French. By comparing the two we can get a curious insight into the manner in which the business was conducted . . . The relation between the response and the consequent writ throws a great deal of light on the meaning of the response and the connection between the different parts of the governmental machinery."[28]

The new plan was approved in November. But for two years Maitland made little or no progress with it. Apart from his Cambridge duties, he was busy with the Selden Society, he was struggling with the initial stages of the *History of English Law,* and he was only too often ill. He was also awaiting a list of the Parliamentary Petitions which was being prepared. In November 1891 he wrote to ask Maxwell Lyte how this work was proceeding. "A time is coming when, if I have good luck, I may be able to take up again the Parliament Roll of Edward I . . . I am beginning to feel that I am somewhat of an impostor, and I have to work under so many restrictions imposed by doctors that I am unable to make definite promises about what I will do in the future."[29] In March 1892 he received the list and made a serious start upon the Roll. As always, when health allowed, he worked at high pressure, and in May he could tell Maxwell Lyte that enough text was ready "to keep a printer at work until the whole is printed." By September the printer had received the rest of the text, and in January 1893 the first part of the introduction was finished. The second part was completed in the summer, and the book was published in November.

It made little impression. Maitland, when he thanked Round

for a kind review in the *Athenaeum,* said that his praise was the more welcome "because no one else out of Scotland has said one word of the book."[30] Not until 1910, when C. N. McIlwain published his *High Court of Parliament,* was it realized that, while Stubbs's *Constitutional History* remained the point of departure for serious study on the evolution of Parliament, it must be read in the light cast upon it by the *Memoranda de Parliamento.* Maitland himself was not so ungrateful as to disparage the work of his mentor. In his obituary of Stubbs he stressed the immense scope of the *Constitutional History* and the ease with which the enormous mass of material was moved and controlled. It was "extremely well documented, as the French say, and those who have had occasion to criticise any part of it would willingly confess that its footnotes were the starting-points of their own investigations." Stubbs had used his vast knowledge of the written sources to compose a picture which was "marvellously concrete." Maitland summoned the legal records to balance the literary evidence.

Cross-examination of the roll, the petitions, and the writs enabled him to summarize the business which Edward I had in mind when he ordered a parliament to be held: (1) the discussion of affairs of state, more especially foreign affairs; (2) legislation; (3) taxation or supply; (4) the audience of petitions; (5) judicial business. In 1305 it was the problem of Scotland which engrossed attention under the first of these heads. There was little legislation and no tax was imposed. The bulk of the roll was occupied by entries concerning the audience of petitions presented by individuals, by religious houses, by the two universities, by boroughs, and by counties. They did not normally ask for anything that could be called legislation, and they did not necessarily involve a legal hearing, "though the line between the hearing of petitions and judicial business is not very sharp." Maitland's conclusion was that Parliament was a court of justice before it was a law-making instrument, and an expanding council—aristocratic and bureaucratic—before it became a representative body.

Subsequent research has qualified some of Maitland's conclusions. The roll which he examined was not so complete as he had supposed, and he underestimated the political importance of the work done by king and council in parliament. But he had sought, from primary evidence, to determine the character and purpose of the session with which he was concerned and to remove the accretions and assumptions of later years. Under his scrutiny the "model assembly" which Stubbs had found already framed in 1295, ready to serve as a pattern for the future, was seen to be a myth. Maitland's analysis of the word parliament and its implications pierced to the heart of the problem. "The petitions of which our roll speaks are neither petitions by parliament nor yet are they petitions addressed to parliament. We see at once that they are very different from those petitions of the commons (*petitions de la commune, petitions des communes*) which will occupy the greater part of almost any parliament roll of Edward III's day. But again they are not addressed to 'parliament' or to 'the lords of parliament' or to either house of parliament. They are addressed either 'to the king' or 'to the king and his council.' In a certain sense they are parliamentary petitions, they are presented in or at a parliament. But at present 'parliament' or 'a parliament' is not conceived as a body that can be petitioned. A parliament is rather an act than a body of persons. One cannot present a petition to a colloquy, to a debate. It is but slowly that this word is appropriated to colloquies of a particular kind, namely, those which the king has with the estates of his realm, and still more slowly that it is transferred from the colloquy to the body of men whom the king has summoned. As yet any meeting of the king's council that has been solemnly summoned for general business seems to be a parliament."[31]

The History of English Law before the Time of Edward I is the central point of Maitland's work. Its evolution may be traced through his letters. He had first thought to write a history of the manor, a subject to which he had been drawn when engaged on the second volume of the Selden Series. But he decided that too little research had yet been done upon the sources to warrant generalizations which would be safe or sound.[32] In the summer of 1889 the Maitlands took a house at Haslemere in Surrey. Three miles away, in Hindhead, Pollock had bought and enlarged a cottage, surrounded by eight acres of woodland. There the Pollock family spent their holidays, with cricket and tennis in the summer and skating and ice hockey during the hard weather which, at least in recollection, seemed to return each Christmas and New Year.[33] Pollock now suggested collaboration in a book on English legal history. Throughout August, as Florence Maitland recorded in her diary, the project was discussed: interesting enough for her husband, but less entertaining for herself. "The Pollocks came after breakfast and stayed to luncheon . . . Dined *again* with the Pollocks . . . Walked to Hind Head Copse: lots of Lady Pollocks in black having tea on the verandah."

By the end of the vacation the decision had been made to write the book, and in November Maitland told Bigelow that he and Pollock had "mapped out a big work, too big I fear for the residue of our joint lives and the life of the survivor." Pollock, for his part, reported the project to Holmes, who gave it his blessing; but, though he started work upon it, his enthusiasm soon seems to have evaporated. In March 1890 Maitland wrote to Ames: "Pollock and I had a hope of turning out a historical book, but I am not sure now that he will be able to give his time, and if that be so I shall hardly get very much done in my lifetime."[34] Maitland came to realize that he and Pollock were not thinking of the same book. He designed an intensive cultivation of the soil; Pollock a broader survey of a wider field. In October 1890 he offered Pollock release from a burden which he might not wish to bear.[35]

> I want to speak about the size of our book. I go on writing and writing, for I have so arranged my lectures that I have little else to do. Thus matter accumulates at a great rate. I know that some of it deals with rather minute points; but the more I see of cents. XII and XIII the more convinced am I that their legal history must be written afresh with full proof of every point . . . This means a great pile of stuff. For example, for six weeks past I have had "juristic persons" on my mind, have been grubbing for the English evidence and reading the Germans, in par-

ticular Gierke's great book (it is a splendid thing though G. is too metaphysical). Now I don't think that any good would come of speaking of such a matter in a few brief paragraphs—if I am to write about it I can not but write at length. So you see the person that you have to deal with, and if you decide to dissolve partnership I shall not be in a position to complain of the decision. I quite see that a brief history of English law is much wanted and might be written, but I also see that I cannot write it[36] . . . I hardly hope to bring the history beyond Edward I because there seems to be matter for two good volumes in the earlier time.[37] But I feel that I may be hampering you and preventing you from writing a famous book. No one living could deal with the YBB as you could—do you like the notion of having to lay down pen just when they are coming into sight? There—I have delivered my soul of its burden. In time—there is no hurry—you will tell me what you think.

Pollock did not accept the offer of release, and for the next twelve months he continued to do little and Maitland to do much. In November 1891 Maitland reported progress. "I have now written in rough five big chapters—Tenure—Status—Jurisdiction—Domesday—Origins of Feudalism. My next task will be the general history from 1066 to 1272. Then the way will be clear for 'private law'." Six months later he unburdened himself to Vinogradoff. "F.P., who is now in the West Indies and may go to India in the winter, has written an Anglo-Saxon chapter. *Between ourselves* I do not like it very much, partly because it will make it very difficult for me to say anything about A-S law in any later part of the book. My effort now is to shove on with the general sketch of the Norman and Angevin periods so that my collaborator may have little to do before we reach the Year Book period—if we ever reach it."[38]

On January 20, 1893, the Syndics of the Cambridge University Press accepted the *History* for publication. Maitland had made the proposal and retained the copyright. By this time Pollock had ceased to take any substantial part—or indeed any urgent interest—in it. He would have preferred a commercial to an academic publisher. Had he not written a life of Spinoza and had it not sold? But he gave Maitland a free hand to make what terms he pleased, provided that he acted in his own name and in his own right. In the unlikely result of profit, he would accept such sum as Maitland thought proper.[39] He continued, none the less, to think of himself as the joint author; and Leslie Stephen, with abundant literary experience, was anxious that the true position should be made clear. He wrote to Maitland:[40]

> If the question were simply between you and Pollock I should say no more. Be as generous as you please would be my only remark. But you have in my opinion to consider two other points. The first is that the public has some right to say that they shall not be asked to buy a book by a statement as to the authorship which certainly gives an inaccurate impression of the facts. My other point is one of more importance . . . When the book comes out the intelligent and the experts will see clearly what are the real shares of the work . . . The impression which will be made upon them will be that Pollock has been claiming a great deal more than he has any right to claim . . . I am sure that such things will be said in private. There are a good many people who don't like Pollock: he is rather a dab at giving offence, and a chance of making unpleasant remarks about him will not be missed . . . The whole difficulty may be got over by the simplest possible expedient. Write a preface, just showing the facts as they are in the most businesslike way. "F.P. wrote chaps. so and so: F.M. wrote chaps. so and so" . . . After that no complaint can be made. You will have given fair notice.

Maitland replied at once.[41]

> I am grateful beyond words for your long and kind letter . . . You certainly have put before me one aspect of the

> case that I had overlooked. My difficulty has been that in this matter I have really been having my own way. The original scheme would have divided the work into approximately equal shares—but I soon discovered (as I suppose a "collaborator" often will) that I wanted one thing while my yoke-fellow wanted another . . . Perhaps it would have been well if difference had led to discord; but the discrepancy was but slowly borne in upon me and, when it was becoming apparent, I pushed on my work in order that as much as possible might be done in the way which—rightly or wrongly—I like . . . You see therefore that I cannot accuse [F.P.] of not doing his fair share, for I did not want him to do it. What I have always been fearing was not that he would get any credit that would belong to me but that he would take chapters out of my hand. I must add that only a little time ago he said of his own accord that the preface must notice the unequal division of labour, and of any wish to get praise (if such is to be had) for what is not his own I hold him absolutely innocent. But as you very truly say—and I had not thought of this before—there is some chance, especially in America where we hope for a little sale, that his name may be attractive—it certainly ought to be so among lawyers—and therefore I will be the more careful that the preface warns readers to expect a lot of me.

Maitland finished the book on All Souls' Day, 1894; save for the index it was through the press at the beginning of March 1895;[42] and it was published later in that month. Pollock had written a note to the preface. "It is proper for me to add for myself that, although the book was planned in common and has been revised by both of us, by far the greater share of the execution belongs to Mr. Maitland, both as to the actual writing and as to the detailed research which was constantly required." Five months later he named his contributions in a letter to Holmes. "I want to tell you how little of the History is my writing: *viz.* the Introduction (not quite all), the chapter on Anglo-Saxon Law, and the bulk, not the whole, of the chapter on Early History of Contract, which is expanded and rearranged from an article in *Harv. Law Rev.*"[43]

Unlike the *Memoranda de Parliamento,* the *History of English Law* won instant recognition. English and American opinion was unanimous. Vinogradoff in Russia, Brunner and Gierke in Germany, Tardif and Saleilles in France, all acclaimed it. Henceforth, throughout England, young historians were to be "excited by the latest work from the hand of Maitland."[44] Four months after publication it was selling so well that Maitland could anticipate the opportunity of revision. "If that opportunity comes," he wrote to Thayer, "I hope that I shall have courage and industry enough to make both retreats and advances." In the next year he was able to tell Thayer that a new edition was required and to ask for his suggestions: "the correction of my blunders is to me a pleasure." The second edition was published toward the end of 1898.[45] There were three major changes. The first reflected the movement of Maitland's mind upon the problems of personality: the chapter on "Fictitious Persons" was reframed and rechristened as "Corporations and Churches." The second involved a revision of "The Borough," which Maitland had found both attractive and perplexing and in which he now confined himself to stating the legal questions. "Answers will come in due course, I hope." The third change was the most ambitious. He wrote a new introductory chapter "about continental affairs in the dark time. I want to tell people a little about the Salica and so forth and help them to get their centuries straight."[46] In the opening words of this chapter he proclaimed the cardinal article of his faith. "Such is the unity of all history that any one who endeavours to tell a piece of it must feel that his first sentence tears a seamless web."

To attempt a critical analysis of the work as an interlude in a biography would be impertinent. Such a task demands a Firth on Macaulay or a Bury on Gibbon. A few observations may be offered and forgiven.

In the *Memoranda de Parliamento,* though he brought new light to bear upon English constitutional development, Maitland had Stubbs behind him. The *History of English Law* was new in conception, in design, and in execution. It is true that John Reeves, at the end of the eighteenth century, had seen what ought to be done. In his own history he had declared his resolution "to forget every alteration that had been made since" and to teach "the law of the time in the language of the time." Maitland spoke generously of him. "It is greatly to his credit that, writing in a very dark age (when the study of records in manuscript had ceased and the publication of records had not yet begun), he had the courage to combat some venerable or at least inveterate fables." But his zeal outran his performance. "His work is very technical and, it must be confessed, very dull; no attempt is made to show the real, practical meaning of ancient rules, which are left to look like so many arbitrary canons of a game of chance."[47] If Maitland had forerunners, they are to be sought in the scholars who between 1660 and 1730 were engaged upon English medieval history, and especially Thomas Madox. In the preface to *The History and Antiquities of the Exchequer of England,* published in 1711, Madox had announced his purpose "to give such an account of things as might be elicited and drawn out of the memorials cited from time to time, and not to cite memorials and vouchers for establishing of any private opinions preconceived in my own mind." Of all the sources "the Publick Records of the Crown and Kingdom are the most important and most authentick; and these are the Foundation which sustain the whole Fabrick of this History." By the side of the *History of the Exchequer* Maitland set a second book by Madox, the *Firma Burgi.* "No one is likely to make much of a contribution to British municipal history who does not know and admire his Madox; and yet, in a very popular history of England, a list of authorities for the tale of our boroughs . . . said nothing of the *Firma Burgi.* Our boroughs have not been very happy in their historians; few have been able to approach the story of their early adventures without some lamentable bias towards edificatory doctrine or some desire to prove a new and inadequate thesis. Madox was one of the few. 'In truth, writing of history is in some sort a religious act.' Coming from some people we should resent such words as cant: we do not resent them when they come from Madox."[48]

The field which these remarkable scholars made their own in the seventy years after the Restoration was abandoned when they died; and it was only in the last third of the nineteenth century that English historians, through German precept and practice, were recalled to the records. Madox and his contemporaries were read anew, and by none more eagerly than by Maitland. He admired their aims, he improved their technique and he exploited it on a scale and with a catholic interest beyond their aspirations or their powers. In the result he did for legal history what he felt his grandfather had done for ecclesiastical history. *The History of English Law* is "a book which 'renders impossible' a whole class of existing books. I don't mean physically impossible—men will go on writing books of that class—but henceforth they will not be mistaken for great historians."[49] This could not have been said of it had not Maitland been left, or been able, to make the book his own. The attempt to collaborate with Pollock had revealed an incompatibility of temperament, of method, and of ultimate ideals. Each man liked the other, and Maitland never forgot the encouragement he had received when he was first drawn to a scholar's life. Of Pollock's ability there was no doubt. His learning was firmly based on the traditions of Eton and of Cambridge. He was familiar with the literature of France, of Germany, and of Italy, and acquainted with Spanish and Persian. At home he was a master of the common law. But he lacked Maitland's questing mind, his passionate desire to lift the veil of the past, his humility in the pursuit and in the face of truth. To Pollock the promise that the meek should inherit the intellectual world was a paradox: a confident approach offered more likely and more tangible results. Maitland sought to ask the right questions and to suggest solutions; Pollock knew the answers. Pollock was a man of all the talents; Maitland had the power to see, and to make others see, beneath its skin, the anatomy and the character of a subject, which is one of the marks of genius.

The history of law is a history of institutions and of ideas.

Institutions indeed, "those spiritual things,"[50] are only ideas imperfectly realized. But ideas are the creation of men by whom the realms of thought are won or lost. To understand them it is necessary to understand their makers. In a changing environment the nature of man remains a constant factor. Medieval people, said Jowett, "were much like ourselves, only dirtier in their habits."[51] But in each generation individuals react to circumstances in their several ways. According to taste or temperament, strength or weakness of mind and will, they seek to propitiate their world or to transform it. Knowing and feeling this, Maitland set himself to find the facts and to draw such a picture as they seemed to him to warrant. Because he brought to this task both the scholar's love of detail and the imagination to stand in other men's shoes, he cut deep into the quick of medieval life. Nor did he forget that a historian is not to be judged by his relevance to his own age. The past is not to be exhumed so that it may serve the whims of the present—though the living may learn from the achievements of the dead that they themselves, if they have the will, have also the power to remake their own institutions in their own image. For his part Maitland had no dogma to impose. In 1896 he wrote to Dicey:[52] "I have not for many years past believed in what calls itself historical jurisprudence. The only direct utility of legal history (I say nothing of its thrilling interest) lies in the lesson that each generation has an enormous power of shaping its own law. I don't think that the study of legal history would make men fatalists; I doubt it would make them conservatives. I am sure that it would free them from superstitions and teach them that they have free hands. I get more and more wrapped up in the middle ages, but the only utilitarian justification that I ever urge *in foro conscientiae* is that, if history is to do its liberating work, it must be as true to fact as it can possibly make itself; and true to fact it will not be if it begins to think what lessons it can teach."

In his inaugural lecture Maitland had raised the question why the history of English law had not been written. It may perhaps be asked why, after he had set his hand to the task, he stopped at the year 1272. In the last pages of his book he explained his choice. The period between the accession of Henry II and the death of Henry III demanded and repaid special study. "It is an age of good books, the time of Glanvill and Richard Fitzneal, of Bracton and Matthew Paris, an age whose wealth of cartularies, manorial surveys and plea rolls has of recent years been in part, though only in part, laid open before us in print. Its law is more easily studied than the law of a later time when no lawyer wrote a treatise and when the judicial records had grown to so unwieldy a bulk that we can hardly hope that much will ever be known about them." The period was significant not only in itself but for the light, fitful though it might be, which it cast upon the dark years before it. "Our one hope of interpreting the *Leges Henrici,* that almost unique memorial of the really feudal stage of legal history, our one hope of coercing Domesday Book to deliver up its hoarded secrets, our one hope of making an Anglo-Saxon landbook mean something definite, seem to lie in an effort to understand the law of the Angevin time, to understand it thoroughly as though we ourselves lived under it." The years which opened with the accession of Edward I presented new problems, to be attacked through new sources. In 1890, when Maitland had offered Pollock a dissolution of partnership, he feared that he might be stifling a great book. "No one living could deal with the Year Books as you could." But he had since come to feel that, in their existing state, they were not fit for learned comment: they must first be purged of corruption. A start had been made by the devotion of Horwood and Pike, and he was thinking seriously of following their example. He had not yet realized the immensity of the task; but he was sure that "a new, a complete, a tolerable edition of the Year Books was the first and indispensable preliminary" to any study of the later medieval law.[53]

While at work on the *History,* Maitland had begun to examine Domesday Book. In April 1891 he told Bigelow that he was "up to his eyes" in it and that it involved a great deal of drudgery. With Maitland to approach a problem was to become immersed. A year later he wrote to Round: "Domesday Book 'intrigues' me the more one reads it. I lectured on it for a whole term and wrote all that I said; but I have no intention of publishing anything, at any rate for a long time to come. You will probably save me from the necessity of printing anything about it. I shall not be sorry." He hoped also that Vinogradoff might soon write a sequel to *Villainage in England,* and he was reluctant to anticipate him. For the next two years, however, he reserved judgment and concentrated on the rest of the *History.* Only at the end of 1894 did he finally decide to withhold from it the Domesday pages. He was in part influenced by the wish not to "collide" with Round whom he knew to be completing *Feudal England,* and still more by the sheer bulk of his material. This would have overbalanced the *History* even if, as he had at one time thought, it had been extended to a third volume.[54] But he did not wish to waste the many hours of research; and, after contemplating a number of articles for the *English Historical Review,* he resolved to write a complete and substantial book. Early in 1897 this was published under the title of *Domesday Book and Beyond.*

Maitland saw in Domesday predominantly an instrument of taxation. "One great purpose seems to mould both its form and its substance; it is a geld-book . . . Materials were to be collected which would enable the royal officers to decide what changes were necessary in order that all England might be taxed in accordance with a just and uniform plan." Subsequent research has suggested that this was an oversimplification, and that the object of the survey if primarily was not exclusively fiscal. But Maitland's view was shared both by Round and by Vinogradoff, and only fifty years later was it seriously challenged.[55]

There were other problems on which he had to pronounce; and two of them, the meaning of the manor and the origin of the borough, he approached with careful diffidence. "The word *manerium* appears on page after page of Domesday Book, but to define its meaning will task our patience. Perhaps we may have to say that sometimes the term is loosely used, that it has now a wider, now a narrower compass, but we cannot say that it is not a technical term. Indeed the one statement that we can safely say about it is that, at all events in certain passages and certain contexts, it is a technical term." Upon this assumption he ventured to offer a definition. A manor "is a house against which geld is charged." The origin of the borough was an even darker problem, and Maitland introduced it with a special warning. "The few paragraphs that follow will be devoted mainly to the development of one suggestion which has come to us from foreign books, but which may throw a little light where every feeble ray is useful. At completeness we must not aim, and in our first words we ought to protest that no general theory will tell the story of every or any particular town."[56] How did the line come to be drawn between the borough and the vill or rural township? The word *burh* meant at first merely a fortress; it was extended to include a fortified group of houses; and at latest during the struggle between the Danish invaders and the West Saxon kings the establishment and maintenance of fortified towns became a matter of urgent policy. Another factor contributed to the development of the towns. "Long before the Conquest a force had begun to play which was to give to the boroughs their most permanent characteristic. They were to be centres of trade. We must not exclude the hypothesis that some places were fortified and converted into burgs because they were already the focuses of such commerce as there was. But the general logic of the process we take to have been this:—The king's *burh* enjoys a special peace: even the men who are going to or coming from it are under royal protection: therefore within its walls men can meet together to buy and sell in safety . . . Thus a market is established."

Domesday Book and Beyond was sent on publication to the *English Historical Review,* and Poole in turn sent it to James Tait, then a young lecturer at Manchester. Tait, in a survey as courteous as it was searching, questioned Maitland's conclusions. He gave cogent reasons for supposing that the vill rather than the manor was the unit of taxation and he even shook the one foundation which Maitland had felt to be secure. Was "manerium" a technical term and did it in truth have any precise meaning? Nor was Tait reassuring on the origin of the borough. Maitland had exaggerated its military at the expense of its commercial function, and the fortress theory was drawn too trustingly from German scholars and German analogies.[57] Few reviews have had greater effect. Tait was at once recognized as a scholar of rare quality, and Poole wrote to him: "I admire the review very much and am sure Maitland will be all the more pleased because you are critical. He has suffered from too much adulation." The best commentary is to be found in Maitland's own letter, written to Tait on October 20, 1897. "Will you allow me to take an unusual step and to offer you my warm thanks for the review of a book of mine which you have contributed to the *English Historical Review*? If the step is unusual (and I have never done anything of the kind before) the occasion also is unusual and in my experience unprecedented, for I have never seen a review of anything that I have written which has taught me so much or gone so straight to the points that are worth discussing. If ever I have to make a second edition of that book I shall have to alter many things in it in the light of your criticisms. Certainly this would be the case in the matter of the boroughs, and I must confess that you have somewhat shaken one [of] my few beliefs in the matter of the *manerium*, namely that this term had *some* technical meaning. I can't give up that belief all at once, but may have to do so by and by."[58]

Despite just and extensive criticism *Domesday Book and Beyond* holds its own as a work of living scholarship. It bears the inimitable marks of Maitland's mind and method—not least in his insistence upon the changes wrought by time in the meaning and value of ideas and of words. Verbal anachronism is especially insidious. It is pleasant to fancy that in a dissolving society language can remain constant. To most persons thinking is a rare and uncomfortable necessity, and the stock of technical words is small. It is easy, and gives a comforting sense of stability, to meet the demands of a new age by repeating old formulas and investing them, half consciously, with fresh meaning. The historian who shuts his eyes to this process lives in a world of his own creation. Maitland was alive to the risk and took out his insurance. "The most efficient method of protecting ourselves against such errors is that of reading our history backwards as well as forwards, of making sure of our middle ages before we talk about the 'archaic', of accustoming our eyes to the twilight before we go out into the dark."[59]

The book is not without the characteristic flashes that lighten and point the argument. But, perhaps inevitably, it is packed close with detail, and the reader is unusually aware of the burden of research. The weight lay heavily upon Maitland himself. "I have sweated over it," he wrote to Vinogradoff, "and what I have written reeks with sweat." In the third essay he apologized for having to face the "dreary old question" of the hide, and again for the "dreary and inconclusive discussions" of Domesday statistics. After the book had been published he "felt sorry for any one who has to read [it] unless he is of the small number of the Elect who were predestined to fall under the Conqueror's spell." In 1900 he wrote to Poole: "It grieves me that you should brood over my Domesday. Of all that I have written that makes me most uncomfortable. I try to cheer myself by saying that I have given others a lot to contradict." He might have agreed with Stubbs who, when a protégé said that he "intended to go into Domesday Book," replied that it was "much more important to get out of it."[60]

In 1896 S. R. Gardiner had inaugurated the Ford Lectureship at Oxford with a course on "Cromwell's Place in History." In February 1897 Maitland was invited to give the second series of lectures. The invitation was embarrassing. "What on earth to talk about," he wrote to Fisher, "I don't know . . . At present my mind is turning towards a favourite theme of which we have talked before now—the haziness of medieval ideas about 'property', 'communities' and so forth, and the consequent disputes." He also asked Poole to help him in the choice of a theme. "Since I received the astounding letter from your V.C. I have been perfectly miserable. To tell truth, I have completely emptied myself into books which contain all that I know, and a good deal more. Several projects have been flitting before me, and I want to ask your advice about one of them. You owe me some aid since you put me into this pickle. I have been thinking of 'English boroughs and German theories' as a possible theme for my discourses. Now does this strike you as a suitable subject? I don't know that I have much to say that I have not implicitly said already, but nothing better occurs to me and I think that in the course of a vacation I might put together some fairly new stuff." There was another possibility. He had been examining unpublished documents dealing with the town and fields of Cambridge. "I am enjoying myself," he told Sidgwick, "over a terrier of the Cambridge common field. I think of making it the basis of my lectures at Oxford."[61]

Maitland had long been fascinated by local history. He regretted that so few boroughs had published their records—the indispensable preliminary to any comprehensive study;[62] and he was provoked by the cult of folklore fostered without discretion by enthusiastic antiquarians. In 1890 George Laurence Gomme had published *The Village Community, with Special Reference to the Origin and Form of Its Survivals in Britain.* Gomme had explored the foundations of village and borough alike and had spoken in particular of the "archaic" tribal constitution of Malmesbury. "All the talk about chiefs and tribesmen," Maitland said to Pollock, "is I feel sure pure bosh"; and he dissected the unfortunate Gomme in an article in the *Law Quarterly Review* in 1893.[63] He opened and developed his attack with ominous urbanity.

> That land was owned by communities before it was owned by individuals is nowadays a fashionable doctrine. I am not going to dispute it, nor even to discuss it, for in my judgment no discussion of it that does not deal very thoroughly with the history of legal ideas is likely to do much good . . . My present purpose is merely that of raising a gentle protest against what I think the abuse of a certain kind of argument concerning "village communities"—the argument from survivals. Some quaint group of facts having been discovered in times that are yet recent, some group of facts which seems to be out of harmony with its modern surroundings, we are—so I venture to think—too often asked to infer without sufficient investigation that these

> phenomena are and must be enormously ancient, primitive, archaic, pre-historic, "pre-Aryan" . . . . I need not expand this warning into a lengthy sermon; it has been given once and for all in words that shall never be forgotten—"Praetorian here! Praetorian there! I mind the bigging o't."[64] If these words should be always in the ears of every one who is hunting for "survivals", they should, so it seems to me, be more especially remembered by those who, not content with the phenomena which they can find in the open country, are looking for exceedingly ancient and even pre-historic remains within the walls of our English boroughs.

It was only too easy to happen upon "a funny old custom" and to discover a survival from the primitive past. But "the archaic times of which it tells" are likely to be "the archaic times of Queen Anne or some king of that primeval dynasty, the illustrious house of Hanover." Mr. Gomme had offered as a candidate for survivorship an elaborate "custom" determining the allotment of land between burgesses in the borough of Malmesbury. Maitland examined in detail the evidence assembled for its antiquity, and doubted if it could be traced beyond the end of the middle ages or the beginning of the Tudors. "When asked to call it or any part or trait of it pre-historic, I feel as if I were being told that Henry VII's chapel at Westminster was the work of 'neo-lithic man'."

Of the three themes which Maitland mentioned to Fisher, to Poole, and to Sidgwick, "English boroughs and German theories" might have seemed the most promising; he admired Gierke and felt the lure of corporate personality. But a discourse on metaphysical jurisprudence was scarcely within the province of the Ford Lecturer in English History. Maitland decided to take as his text the Cambridge terrier, to use it as the base for tentative advances into local history and to say no more of legal persons than was needed to keep the way open for later exploration. At least he could suggest to the future historian of the English boroughs, whoever he might be, the main subjects of inquiry: "the transition from rural to urban habits and the evolution among the townsmen of that kind and that degree of unity which are corporateness and personality." These were two phases of one process and must be traced along the borderland of law and economics.[65]

In the autumn of 1897 Maitland gave six lectures under the title of "Township and Borough." For the solecism of preaching to his Oxford hosts on a Cambridge theme he offered an apology which, to the uninitiated, may seem a little arch. "Will you think me ill bred if I talk of the town in which I live? What else have you left me to talk of? What fields has not Oxford made her own?" But Cambridge had fields, fields in the medieval sense: "vast, hedgeless, fenceless tracts of arable land, in which the strips of divers owners lay interspersed . . . fields which were open and commonable." The bucolic character of Cambridge long persisted. "Erasmus accused the Cambridge townsmen of a pre-eminence in boorishness. *Vulgus Cantabrigiense inhospitales Britannos antecedit, qui cum summa rusticitate summam malitiam coniunxere.*" As late as 1624 the Vice Chancellor of the University and the Mayor of the Borough made a joint order to regulate the number of cattle which the townsmen might pasture on the common land. "Thus through the crust of academic learning, through the crust of trade and craft, of municipality and urbanity, the rustic basis of Cambridge is displayed." But was Cambridge thus unique? Maitland could not think so. All was *rusticitas;* Cambridge was *summa rusticitas.*[66]

Agrarian Cambridge might thus be taken to exemplify the English medieval borough. How did it move from rural to urban habits? Maitland paid tribute to Tait's criticism of *Domesday Book and Beyond* by reducing the fortress theory from a dominant to a single element in the process. Three other elements were to be observed. The borough was a political entity. "Throughout a wide tract of England there were in 1086 no boroughs which were not or had not been in some distinct and legal sense the centres of districts, the chief towns of shires . . . Shire and burh are knit together. The shire maintains the burh; the burh defends the shire." The borough was a judicial unit. Its court stood on a level with the hundred courts. Maitland cited the Cambridge terrier. "I can not find that Cambridge has ever been deemed a part of any of the adjacent hundreds, and by Cambridge I mean some five square miles of land. Five hundreds touch that tract; they converge upon it; but it lies outside them all." The borough was also a mercantile center. "The market is another link, and it is a legal link. Men are not to buy or sell elsewhere; that is to say, if they buy elsewhere they imperil their necks. Cattle-lifting must be suppressed. Men must buy cattle before a court of law or before official witnesses in a borough, or else they must take the risk of being treated as thieves." But none of these elements is to be thrust too blatantly into the foreground, nor is the borough to be deemed the mere creature of the law. "The history of our towns must not be merely the history of legal arrangements. The trade winds blow where they list and defy the legislator. It were needless to say that half-fledged boroughs such as Manchester, and mere villages such as Birmingham, will outstrip the old shire-cities. But even in the middle ages there were ups and downs in the fortunes of the boroughs. I think that both Oxford and Cambridge had good luck."[67]

It was harder to trace the evolution of anything that might be described as communal personality. "The borough community is corporate; the village community is not. That is a real and important difference. In the fifteenth century it stands out in the clear light." How did it emerge from the darkness? The various parts which the borough had to play—political, judicial, and commercial—all demanded the recognition of an entity which the law could recognize and which could be set against the individuals with which it had to deal. "The Town which has rights and duties, the Town which owes and is owed money, the Town which can make a contract even with one of the townsmen, the Town which can be landlord or tenant, the Town with which the treasurer can keep an account, slowly struggles into life. If we are to understand the process we must study at close quarters the methods in which the affairs of the borough are conducted, the growth and expenditure of a revenue, the incidence of profit and loss . . . What I may call the business side of municipal life must come by its rights. Political and constitutional history will thereby gain a new reality. If we fail to see this need, it is because we carry our methods of business into an age which knew them not and our thoughts into an age which did not and could not think them."[68]

In these lectures Maitland repeated the warning he had given in *Domesday Book and Beyond* against the besetting sins of the historian. The attempt to give universal significance to ideas was a delusion. "I am not very hopeful of a portable village community which we might take about with us from one quarter of the globe to another. A Natural History of Institutions is a fascinating ideal, but we must have a care or our Natural History will bear to real history the relation that Natural Law bore to real law. Explorations in foreign climes may often tell us what to look for, but never what to find."[69] The snare of anachronism was equally dangerous and more common. More than one great man had fallen a victim to it. "Sir Henry Maine has said that 'the Family, in fact, was a Corporation.' But then he has also told us that 'the Patriarch, for we must not yet call him the Paterfamilias,' was a 'trustee for his children and kindred,' and 'in the eye of the law' represented the collective body. This patriarchal trustee, who represents a corporation, looks to me, I must confess, suspiciously modern. He may be a savage, but he is in full evening dress. At any rate he is an individual man; and, if he is treated as trustee and representative, there is law enough for individuals and to spare. If we speak, we must speak with words; if we think, we must think with thoughts. We are moderns and our words and thoughts can not but be modern. Perhaps, as Mr. Gilbert once suggested, it is too late for us to be early English. Every thought will be too sharp, every word will imply too many contrasts. We must, it is to be feared, use many words and qualify our every statement until we have almost contradicted it. The outcome will not be so graceful, so lucid, as Maine's Ancient Law."[70]

Thomas Seccombe, who heard the lectures, said that they held "a large audience, strange to the subject, spell-bound by the sheer force of personality and style."[71] The first two lectures, even in cold print, are scintillating—so brilliant, indeed, that they cast a shade over the remainder. The reader of the later lectures is left with some sense of disappointment, or at least of anticlimax. The subject was too large for its setting, and Maitland had not allowed himself space to develop his arguments. He was himself uneasy. In December 1897 he wrote to Fisher.[72] "I want you to do for me a really brotherly act and to tell me from the bottom of your heart whether those lectures to which you were kind enough to listen are worth print. I have got stuff for a book about the Cambridge Field and this I am minded to publish in any case. My thought had been to make the stuff an appendix to my lectures; but now I am hesitating. Every one at Oxford was enormously kind, but just for this reason I feel sadly in need of a little objective criticism. I do not want to emphasize a failure. There is no one I can appeal to or should think of appealing to but you. So do tell me how it strikes you. I shall be grateful beyond words. I don't want you to say much or to put you in an awkward place. 'No' will be quite enough. And 'Rewrite in a more serious vein' will be quite enough. And my gratitude for these or any other brief remarks of the kind will be very true." Fisher's reply has not survived. But Maitland decided to publish the lectures as they had been delivered, with the "Cambridge stuff" as an appendix to supply the evidence for the views that he had advanced. The appendix, filling more than half the book, is a formidable contribution to topographical scholarship which later research has not displaced. But its very substance tends to deepen the impression of inequality. As the first two lectures overshadow the other four, so the appendix is out of proportion to the text.

Maitland had amassed the material for *Domesday Book and Beyond* while he was writing the *History of English Law;* his interest in *Township and Borough,* awakened before the *History,* was strengthened by it; and it was through the *History* that he was forced to consider the place of the canon law in England. The first result of his inquiry was a paper on Henry II and Becket, published in the *English Historical Review,* in which he sought to prove "that Henry had a very respectable amount of canon law in favour of his way of treating the criminous clerk." He knew that he had set sail on stormy seas, and he expected "to be accursed by both parties."[73] As he continued with the *History* he found that he must persist in this perilous exploration. The medieval law of marriage had been reviewed by the House of Lords in *The Queen v. Millis*.[74] In that case, heard on appeal from the Irish courts, the House had to determine the validity of a marriage performed in Ireland by a Presbyterian minister. The six lords were equally divided; the judges whose opinion they sought were against the validity; and in the result the marriage was held to be void. Three of the law lords maintained that "by the ecclesiastical and by the civil law of England the presence of an ordained clergyman was from the remotest period onwards essential to the formation of a valid marriage." If this thesis were right, the results were strange. "We have been asked to suppose that for several centuries our church was infected with heretical pravity about the essence of one of the Christian sacraments, and that no one thought this worthy of notice. And an odd form of pravity it was. She did not require a sacerdotal benediction; she did not require (as the Council of Trent very wisely did) the testimony of the parish priest; she did not require a ceremony in church; she required the 'presence of an ordained clergyman.' "[75]

After the *History* was published, Maitland felt free to examine in greater detail the place and authority of the canon law in medieval England. He had at once to digest the report of a Royal Commission appointed by Gladstone in 1881 "to inquire into the constitution and working of the Ecclesiastical Courts as created or modified under the Reformation Statutes of the 24th and 25th years of King Henry VIII, and any subsequent Acts." On the Commission law was represented, inadequately, by Lord Coleridge, Sir Robert Phillimore, and Sir Francis Jeune; history, by Stubbs and Freeman. Lawyers and historians eyed each other with suspicion, but the dominant figure was Stubbs. He attended each of the seventy-five sittings from May 1881 to July 1883, and he supplied to the report five historical appendices. His, and the Commission's, conclusion was that the church in medieval England could accept or reject Papal legislation as it thought fit and that, unless accepted, Roman canon law was not binding on the English ecclesiastical courts.[76]

The conclusion was comforting to all who felt the danger of Erastianism and who sought to stress the continuity of the Anglican Church. The sixteenth century was to be seen as an age not of revolution but of evolution: all churches had been out of step save the English. Maitland doubted the legal and historical foundations on which this conclusion was based.[77] He turned to William Lyndwood's *Provinciale,* the authoritative work on the canon law in medieval England.[78] The more he read the more he doubted. He was left with the impression that there was "next to nothing that can be called *English* canon law," and that "the English canonists were very strong papalists, or rather I should say very helpless papalists." He hoped that Poole would let him "trail his coat" through the pages of the *English Historical Review,* though he warned him that what he was writing might "irritate some good folk." He was now deep in *Domesday Book,* but he found the canon law a refreshment from those stern labors. Two papers appeared in the *English Historical Review* in 1896 and a third in 1897.[79]

In 1898 he resolved to publish as a book all that he had written on the canon law. He had already sent the material to the press when he heard from Poole that Stubbs resented, or at least regretted, their reappearance. "I hope and trust," he replied, "that you were not very serious when you said that the bishop was 'sore'. I feel for him a respect so deep that if you told me that the republication of my essays would make him more unhappy than a sane man is whenever people dissent from him, I should be in great doubt what to do. It is not too late to destroy all or some of the sheets. I hate to bark at the heels of a great man whom I admire, but tried hard to seem, as well as to be, respectful."[80] Poole's reply is missing; but Maitland, reassured or satisfied that only a thin skin could be chafed by his presentation of a reasonable case, published *Roman Canon Law in the Church of England.* To the essays printed in the *English Historical Review* in 1896 and 1897 were added three other papers: "Henry II and the Criminous Clerks"; " 'Execrabilis' in the Common Pleas," a note on the conflict of jurisdiction which had appeared in the *Law Quarterly Review* in 1896; and "The Deacon and the Jewess; or Apostasy at Common Law," an early contribution to the *Law Quarterly Review,* slight but charming.[81] But the substance of the book is to be found in the first three essays: "William Lyndwood"; "Church, State and Decretals"; and "William of Drogheda and the Universal Ordinary." The others, though they are concerned with the respective spheres of church and state, and are written, and may be read, *con amore,* are in essence supplements. In the preface, amid the tumult of theological warfare, Maitland proclaimed his disinterested neutrality. "At a time when the perennial stream of Anglo-Roman controversy has burst its accustomed channels and invaded the daily papers, the assumption will be readily made that anyone who writes about those matters of which I have here written is an advocate of one of two churches, the English or the Roman. Therefore it may be expedient for me to say that I am a dissenter from both and from other churches."

Maitland began the first essay by stating the issue. "The doctrine that is in possession of the field I take to be that of the Ecclesiastical Courts Commission. The Commissioners (among whom were historians whose every word deserves attention) gave us the following sentence: 'But the canon law of Rome, although always regarded as of great authority in England, was not held to be binding on the courts.' Now, if by 'the courts' the commissioners meant (and no doubt they did mean) the ecclesiastical courts, and if they were speaking of the three centuries which immediately preceded the Reformation (and no doubt they did intend to include that age), then I can not but think that their *dictum,* carefully worded though it be, is questionable and should be questioned." The crucial evidence was that of William Lyndwood, canonist, dean of the arches, bishop, in whom could be heard the authentic voice of the fifteenth century. Maitland examined what may be called the English sources of ecclesiastical law, and in particular the provincial constitutions of the archbishops of Canterbury upon which Lyndwood had concentrated. To these Lyndwood's reaction was that of a lawyer faced with rules made by a nonsovereign legislator. In modern terminology they were bylaws and were open to the challenge of *ultra vires.* In the rare cases in which they seemed at variance with papal decretals Lyndwood, as judge and as scholar, sought to reconcile them. This was to be accomplished by preferring the superior to the inferior law. Provincial legislation could not derogate from the *ius papale,* the common law of the universal church, to which the constitutions of the archbishops were only an appendix. Maitland cited the problems of marriage. "There is no English law of marriage. If you want to know whether you are old enough to marry, whether you may marry your late wife's second cousin or your godmother's daughter, whether a religious ceremony is essential to a marriage, whether you have good cause for a divorce, you will find your answer in the *ius commune* of the church."

A second source of ecclesiastical law was to be found in local custom. In England this was not extensive, and, if it were pleaded, it must be proved not only to be of long standing but to be reasonable. It would be reasonable if it gave the canonist more, but not less, than he found in the *ius commune.* An English custom to make the parishioners liable to maintain the nave of the church would be good; a custom to pay no tithes would be bad. It is significant that the English ecclesiastical courts knew no case law; and this at a time when England was "producing the Year Books and the most thoroughly national system of temporal law that the medieval world could show. But, whereas the English state was an independent whole, the English church was in the eyes of its own judges a dependent fragment whose laws had been imposed upon it from without." Maitland cited a passage from the report of the commission. "The constitutions of the archbishops, from Stephen Langton downwards, and the canons passed in legative councils, ratified by the national church under Archbishop Peckham, were finally received as the texts of English church law under the hands of the commentators John of Ayton and William Lyndwood. These commentators introduced into their notes large extracts from and references to both the canon and the civil law of Rome, but these were not part of the authoritative jurisprudence." "That this may be true of what happened 'finally'," said Maitland, "is very possible, for the world did not come to an end at the Reformation." But the contrast between Lyndwood and the Commissioners was startling. "The last is put first and the first last; the inferior prelate takes the place of the pope." Had Lyndwood imagined that his book would have been cited for such an inversion, he would have burnt it; and Stubbs, together with all his colleagues, unless they recanted and adjured so heretical a doctrine, would likewise have been committed to the flames.

At the outset of the second essay, "Church, State and Decretals," Maitland stated two propositions which were to be found in the works of ecclesiastical historians and in the dicta of judges: "(1) That in England the state did not suffer the church to appropriate certain considerable portions of that wide field of jurisdiction which the canonists claimed as the heritage of ecclesiastical law. (2) That the English courts Christian held themselves free to accept or reject 'the canon law of Rome.'" The propositions were distinct; but it was easy, and disastrous, to slide from the one to the other. The first was doubted by nobody and was irrelevant. The second, upon which the argument of the Commissioners depended, was avowed by many and proved by none. Stubbs, in an appendix to the report of the Commission, had stated that "the papal law-books were regarded as manuals but not as codes . . . A knowledge [of them] was the scientific equipment of the ecclesiastical jurist, but the texts were not authoritative." To support his statement he cited the Council of Merton in 1236, when "the English barons and the king refused to allow the national law of marriage to be modified by [the papal texts], and it was held that they were of no force at all when and where they were opposed to the laws of England." Stubbs here asserted the second proposition but offered evidence of the first. Maitland pursued the implications of the Council of Merton. "What is the good old story? In the twelfth century the church in England and elsewhere had become definitely committed to the doctrine that a marriage between two persons might legitimate their already born children. This doctrine was unacceptable to the king's court . . . At Merton the bishops asked the barons to change the English law of inheritance and received the well-known reply: *Nolumus leges Angliae mutare*." If the barons would not, the bishops could not alter their position; they were bound by the *ius commune* of the church. By the canon law the children were legitimate. By the law of England they were bastards; and bastards the barons were resolved they should remain. Each party maintained its own ground. But the state found a way to circumvent the obstinacy of the church. Instead of sending questions of legitimacy to the ecclesiastical courts, it sent them to a jury. Maitland drew the conclusion. "The honours were divided, but the state took the odd trick. Here, then, we may see a collision between the claims of the church and the claims of the state. But there was no collision between the law of the church of England and the law of the church of Rome: quite the contrary. The principle for which the English bishops struggled was part and parcel of the canon law of Rome."

A second instance of conflict between church and state, and therefore of Maitland's first proposition, was offered by the problem of patronage. Was an advowson spiritual or temporal property? This struggle had been lost and won in the twelfth century. Pope Alexander III, in a decretal addressed to Henry II, had insisted that disputes over the right of patronage belonged exclusively to the courts of the church. "But, in spite of Alexander and Becket, Henry established as English law the very opposite of this proposition . . . A vast volume of litigation was thus diverted from the ecclesiastical forum, to the impoverishment of the canonist and the enrichment of the serjeants . . . The advowson is temporal property; the laws of the church and the courts of the church cannot touch it."

In these and other disputes the vital question was to determine the theory of the Papal decretals which prevailed in the English ecclesiastical courts during the later Middle Ages. Were they regarded as statutes or did the English church feel free to pick and choose among them? The church's right of selection had been asserted in books and judgments of the eighteenth and nineteenth centuries, but Maitland could find little or no evidence to support it. "The proof of which we are in search must be found, if anywhere, before the breach with Rome . . . Are we entitled to suppose that the treatment which 'the foreign canon law' received in our courts Christian before [that breach] was substantially the same as the treatment [after it]

. . . ? I cannot believe that this, or anything like this, is true." The history of the church in England from the middle to the modern age is not a record of continuity. The reign of Henry VIII saw "a sudden catastrophe in the history of the spiritual courts": they must now enforce acts of the English Parliament.

In the third essay, "William of Drogheda and the Universal Ordinary," Maitland turned to discuss the pope not as legislator but as judge. That he should be supreme arbiter was evident; it was equally true, and not so obvious, that he should be a judge of first instance. "The apostolic see is an omnicompetent court of first instance for the whole of Christendom . . . The jurist could state the matter thus: Normally the competent judge is the judge ordinary of the defendant's domicile; but Rome is the common fatherland of all men, as we learn from the Digest, and the pope is the judge ordinary of all men, as we learn from the Decretum." This doctrine was expounded during the reign of Henry III not only by Bracton but more abundantly by William of Drogheda in his book on the canon law known as *Summa Aurea*. William of Drogheda, an Irishman, taught at Oxford for twenty years before he was killed by his servant in a house in the High Street, still called Drawda Hall. His book, though meant primarily for the Oxford law school, was eminently practical. "He is going to teach his readers to win causes and begs that a few of the fees that they earn may purchase masses for his soul. His object is to trace an action through all its stages, to solve the questions about procedure which will beset the practitioner, to supply him with useful formulae or models for the various documents which he may have to indite and to offer him sound advice in the shape of *cautelae*. This last word we can hardly translate without condescending to the slang of 'tips' and 'wrinkles' and 'dodges'; and in truth some of William's *cautelae* do not deserve pretty names, for they are none too honest." The England of Henry III was full of judges ordinary: the bishop in his diocese, the archbishop in his province. But William assumed that as a matter of course all big and remunerative litigation would be heard at first instance not by them but by delegates appointed for the occasion by a papal writ. For this practice there was more than one reason. Appeals had been so much encouraged that it was economical to go at once to the highest authority. The plaintiff who went to the pope for a writ enjoyed considerable liberty in the choice of judges. The cause might involve a delicate question of jurisdiction. "You might wish to sue as co-defendants a man who lives at Lincoln and another who lives at York. No English prelate has power over both these men. In the judicial system Canterbury is a unit and York is a unit; but England is no unit."

Such was the doctrine that was taught "in an Oxford, in an England, which did not love the pope, but growled and grumbled at him and at his exactions." But to rebel against the pope, to deny his authority, was not only impossible but inconceivable. "Every principle that the pope could demand was being conceded to him . . . Nor must we throw all the blame upon the canonists, upon such men as William of Drogheda. In our own day and country the medieval canonist is defenceless. Some of us do not like lawyers; some of us do not like priests. Upon the man who was half priest, half lawyer, many dislikes are concentrated . . . But William was only drawing practical inferences from premisses that he shared with the theologian. He merely registers the fact that the pope is the universal 'ordinary' in order that he may teach his pupils how fame and fees are won. It is Grosseteste, the theologian, the bishop, the immortal Lincolniensis, who will preach with fervour the doctrine that the whole of a bishop's power is derived from, or at all events through, the pope."[82]

Maitland had expected to be attacked for inconvenient arguments and unpalatable conclusions—to be dispassionate in theological controversy was in itself an affront. The essays were indeed resented by individual members of the High Anglican party.[83] But Stubbs himself did not reply to them. In the preface to the third edition of his *Seventeen Lectures on Medieval and Modern History,* published in 1900, he simply, and a little pathetically, affirmed that his appendices to the Report of the Royal Commission contained "true history and the result of hard work." Maitland, like the tactician at the Bar who knows when to press a point and when to leave it alone, let the essays speak for themselves. A similar silence, he thought, would be recommended by the more astute of his opponents. "I see," he wrote to Sidgwick in February 1899,[84] "that the Right Reverend Father in God whom we used to know as G.F.B. has passed the word that the Canon Law is a pathless wilderness. My lord of London said to me something of the same kind. I think that these highly prudent prelates will discourage their young men from excursions over ground which, whether I am right or wrong, is certainly full of ugly holes for Anglicans. To express a tolerant contempt for lawyers will be the popular and the safe course. Lawyers have written a great deal of nonsense in all ages: the middle not excepted." Subsequent research has suggested two valid criticisms of the essays. On the one hand Maitland underestimated the influence of provincial constitutions in glossing the Roman canons; and on the other hand he exaggerated the area of conflict between the jurisdiction of the royal and of the ecclesiastical courts.[85] But after seventy years his central position remains intact.

A reader today need have no special interest in its subject to find the book fascinating. Maitland displays in his most attractive manner the dual qualities of historian and lawyer. He isolates the vital issues, marshals the evidence, makes all concessions consistent with his case, and presents conclusions which seem to emerge irresistibly from the premises. His cause was the discovery of historical truth; but it is not fanciful to see in the technique the experience of his years in chambers. Six years after the book was published he told Fisher that he had "got more fun out of it than out of any job I ever did."[86] In *Township and Borough* there is an underlying sense of strain. Maitland was not sure that he had found the right theme for the occasion; and the wit, though not forced, is not always an integral element of the thesis. In the *Canon Law* gaiety pervades the whole adventure. The "fun" is not ornamental but structural. Wit is the medium of argument. The shafts are keen but not barbed; if their victims wince, it is because the aim has been shrewd and the target pertinent.

Chapter VIII

Family Life

The Maitlands, on their marriage, lived first in a house which they leased at 15 Brookside, Cambridge.[1] Here their elder daughter, Ermengard, was born on December 20, 1887. The Downing Professorship carried with it an official house in the College court known as West Lodge; to this the Maitlands moved in the autumn of 1888. Here, on February 21, 1889, their younger daughter, Fredegond, was born. The front of the house was covered with virginia creeper and the back with ivy and with wistaria. A large garden ran behind most of the west side of the court and as far as the lane beyond Addenbrooke's Hospital. Hiding the lane were large trees with wild parsley beneath them. The lawn was cut up by a fountain and by a flower bed in which Maitland grew the dark velvet roses and the parrot tulips that he loved. On the ground floor was the study, a plain square room looking on to the court, and the dining room. The drawing room was upstairs—a set piece with Morris paper, black and gold cabinet with matching chairs, and chintz curtains inherited from Maitland's predecessor. The family preferred the lecture room which opened out of the dining room and had steps into the garden. Here Florence Maitland made a sitting space with comfortable chairs and a piano, and here she indulged her music, had small tea parties, and sat after dinner. She spoke of it in a letter written to Bigelow on February 28, 1897.[2] "We sit a great deal in our favourite room, the lecture room, when lectures are not going on. In fact I am writing this at one of the long tables by the fire, for we are spending the evening there. In the lecture room we get every bit of sunshine that is to be had in the day, and that is a great advantage at this time of year—also the bareness and the amount of table room is conducive to writing and painting and every sort of untidy occupation."

To both parents the children were not creatures who belonged to them but independent personalities to be met with imaginative insight. Florence peopled their world with characters: Mrs. Tattlecow, Mrs. Gravelrat, and their friends. She drew Mrs. Gravelrat in her purple and yellow dresses and supplied her with conversation. Crabs, prawns, and lobsters were the fare that she and Mrs. Tattlecow grew fat on, and both had triple chins. Ermengard recalled the tact with which her mother came to her rescue when nurses pressed unwanted food upon her.

> Like most good children I was a slow eater. They put too much on my plate, they gave me porridge which would not float, they expected me to eat fat, they offended my eye by vermicelli mould. I picked and chose and was told "Many a poor child would be glad of what you leave." The poor child was quite welcome—why didn't they give him my plate straight away? Why bother me at all with stuff that would give him such pleasure? If my mother was near she would take pity on me, would tell me stories while I ate, or invent verses. Many an unwanted meal was eaten to the magic words:—
>
> A Farmer's dinner is mostly suet;
> He sits down and does justice to it;

> Then he rises up quite fat
> And puts on his Great Straw Hat.
>
> I wanted to be a farmer, I wanted suet, I wanted to wear a Great Straw Hat; so, bit by bit, down went the dinner, even if it were mutton.

Her father was as comforting as her mother.

> After the fashion of those days whisky and water was prescribed for me when I was ill, and only my father's patient care got it down me. He sat on my bed and spooned it out to me with long pauses during which he told me the story of The Drunkard's Journey from Gloucester to Stroud. We visited the New Inn at Tuffley, the Four Mile at Brookthorpe, the Gloucester House at Edge, and at each inn we talked and drank and then we rolled on. I knew that rolling well, for a slow procession of brewers' drays, drawn by magnificent glossy shires encrusted with brass ornaments, passed us twice daily. I can still smell the mixture of beer and horse. At the water trough they drank and slobbered and champed their bits. The draymen, red faced and leather aproned, puffed and blew, for they had walked up the long hill and some of their walking was far from steady.

Despite Maitland's endemic illness, the children thought of him as essentially gay. "He gave us no impression of being an invalid—he was far too active and alive. My sister and I always thought of him as young; and now I see him as belonging to no age, not a great Victorian, certainly not a heavy Victorian father, for while his own conversation was fastidious and modest he never rebuked our wilder tongues."[3] He moved with "light quick steps like those of a mountain creature," whistling, as the fancy took him, the Preislied from the Meistersinger, airs of Schubert or Mozart, or tunes from Gilbert and Sullivan. In the last summer of his life, when both girls were ready for the King's College ball, he danced round and round the room first with one and then with the other until Florence cried, "Oh Fred, you will crumple them and make their hair come down."

Portraits could not do him justice: the life was in the brilliant eyes and the mobile features, and when asked to pose he became rigid. Fredegond, with a poet's insight, saw him as a "vivid flame-like presence." To him "with his young sparkling face we spoke of what we felt most interest in."

"Are you rich?"
"Very rich?"
"The richest man in Cambridge?"
"Who is the *greatest* man here, next to *you*?"
"Is Charlotte Brontë greater than George Eliot?"
"Is Leslie Stephen the greatest philosophy?"
"What is philosophy?"[4]

Gwen Raverat, who was two years older than Ermengard, wrote of Florence Maitland as "strange and beautiful."[5] That she was beautiful nobody doubted: tall, slender, brown eyes, hair brighter than brown but not so bright as red-gold. That she was strange depends upon definition. She came to Cambridge from a country life where she had not been encumbered with convention—certainly not the convention of a university town, with its mélange of intellectual pressure, or pretension, and the gossip of a closed society. She was amazed to hear the dons' wives talking of servants and "marrying off their daughters"; and she never forgot the lament of the professor's wife that her maid had put out gloves with a hole in one of the fingers and that, wearing them, she had the embarrassment of meeting Lord Acton. For ignorance, or even innocence, the Cambridge ladies were prepared. But Florence was hard to tame and she had interests which she pursued to unseemly lengths. Photography might perhaps be condoned, especially in one whose great aunt had been the celebrated Mrs. Cameron and who could be chaperoned by Mrs. Frederic Myers.[6] Music was an elegant accomplishment, but it had a time and a place whose limits Florence did not or would not understand. She was a good pianist, a very good violinist, and experimented with the guitar even upon Bach. She was not content to play for her husband's delectation or to set the tone of an informal party: she gave violin lessons and invited young men to join her in trios and quartets. In 1892 Ralph Vaughan Williams went up to Trinity as an undergraduate. "There was a great deal of music-making in [the Maitlands'] house at Downing. Ralph admired both Maitland, a vivid and attractive man whose lectures and writings illuminated the dusty archives of legal history with humanity and wit, and his wife, who was a beautiful and original young woman and a fine amateur violinist. Among the most constant visitors to their house were Ralph's friends Nicholas and Ivor Gatty. Nicholas was a violinist, Ivor played the horn, Ralph the viola, and other undergraduate musicians joined the group for 'scratch' chamber music. Sometimes Florence's younger sister Adeline stayed at the Lodge, and, as she was able to play the 'cello if no one else was available, though her real talent was for the piano, she was a welcome addition to the party."[7] In June 1893 Adeline was with Florence at Downing when Tchaikovsky, who had come to Cambridge to receive an honorary degree, was a fellow guest. Florence and Adeline played for him and pinned roses in his buttonhole before he left for the ceremony.

Above all there were the animals. A rare catalog of fauna may be compiled from letters and diaries. Dogs and cats were obvious members of the household in Cambridge and in Gloucestershire. But they had a succession of more curious companions. Ermengard had first one piebald mouse and then a second "to be a possible mother of a charming little family." Fredegond had a white rat which, to her delight, crept round her neck under her hair. In 1894 Florence bought a "wonderful little Peruvian cavie." In July 1895 Maitland told Bigelow that "Madame's menagerie has been enriched by a meerkat from South Africa—an amusing little beast—and a stolid English badger." The meerkat sat on its hind legs, walked about like a miniature kangaroo, and followed the family all over the house. In October 1895 Florence wrote to Bigelow: "I have by me now a charming little Harvest mouse—you would adore it. I caught it in the wood one evening and it is now quite tame and sits on my hand and eats there and washes its face in the most attractive manner. I hope I shall be able to keep it in spite of our two dogs and three cats, to say nothing of my sister's mongoose who is here on a visit." In January 1896 she made a more ambitious experiment. "I have a new inmate of my menagerie—a small monkey, neither affectionate nor intelligent but very strange to look at. He has twice jumped into the fire—each time without disastrous results." But he tore the paper from the walls, pulled up the rugs, picked the embroidered stool to pieces, and spilled ink over the carpet; and Florence had to harden her heart and part with him. Undaunted, she acquired a second monkey, "a South American capuchin, very nervous and irritable and bad tempered—but all the same rather attractive." Its fate is not recorded.[8]

It is easy to understand Florence's impact upon contemporary Cambridge—or indeed upon Oxford had marriage set her there. But Maitland cared little for conventional society and nothing for its strictures. He had his own passion for music and, as ill-health increasingly curtailed visits to opera and concert, he welcomed all that Florence could give him. Upon the "menagerie" he looked with affectionate amusement. Others, indeed, thought the atmosphere of West Lodge unbecoming to a scholar. R. L. Poole once entered Maitland's study to find it shared by a monkey which had to be put in a box on a chair with Madox's *Exchequer* as a lid. Precise in mind and habit, the focus of his own domestic life, reverently solicitous for old books in general and the *Exchequer* in particular, he found the combination of circumstances horrifying. But Florence did not see Maitland, and he did not see himself, as the Head of the Family. He grudged the time and care that she bestowed on her animals no more than she weighed his devotion to learning against his love. Neither was self-conscious and neither sentimental. Each had complementary qualities which the other respected and never sought to reduce to a common pattern. "In those days," Ermengard wrote, "a child took its parents' happiness together for granted, but I had a good nose for trouble and I never smelt even a whiff of fire save over miracles and the Boer War and he for Dickens, she for Thackeray. I do not believe that her menagerie of animals, her hours of violin playing, her feeding of tramps and gypsies, her photography and pony-driving, her story-telling and play-writing were ever anything but a pleasure to him."[9]

Save for one term at a day school near Downing and attendance at "Miss Mary Greene's Wednesday Drawing Class" and "Miss Ratcliffe's Dancing Class" of which Gwen Raverat has given so lively an account,[10] neither Ermengard nor Fredegond had any formal education. Florence's father had seven sons to send to school and she herself had to grow up without it. Maitland remembered all that he had learned at home in the holidays and the blessings that he had called down upon the treasures who had guided the steps of Sela and Kate.[11] While the children were at Downing two worthy ladies successively came in the mornings and taught them round the dining room table: history, geography, elementary arithmetic and algebra, French, and a tentative approach to Latin. Florence taught them music and encouraged Ermengard, when not yet seven, to play her violin on the platform at London Bridge Station to entertain the porters. She also helped to lead the children further into French. Fredegond looked back upon "the rainy summer afternoons when we essayed to learn our French irregular verbs in the dining-room window and, instead, were lulled to sleep by the grey and rose coloured parrot which grated her beak gently against the cage bars, chiming with the raindrops sweetly and incessantly as they fell."[12]

French grammar, Latin grammar—these were useful aids to learning. But English grammar was not to be taught; it was to be absorbed by reading and again reading and by trying to write. There was plenty to read and to absorb. The house was full of books and the children were free to browse where they would. Maitland had been initiated by his grandfather into the England not only of Chaucer but of the eighteenth-century poets, and well-worn volumes from Dryden to Crabbe were on his shelves at Downing. He had been nourished upon Scott and Jane Austen and the Victorian novelists; William Blake as poet and as artist he discovered for himself. When Ermengard was twelve or thirteen he took her into the University Library. "I had never been in it before and I walked beside him filled with pride: I can feel it still. A book illustrated by Blake was laid on a table before us and he turned the pages, admiring and explaining. It is clear to me that he had been to see it before and that he needed to communicate his great pleasure to someone else. Just how great the impression made on him was I should have realised in 1906 when, during his last illness, the mosquito nets round his bed were translated into Blake's angels. He spoke of them several times to me, not as one speaks of a vague likeness but of a living reality."[13] Of contemporary writers both he and Florence knew and revered Meredith as poet, novelist, and man, and Meredith gave Florence as a wedding present a set of his books. Maitland shared the current taste for Browning; but he had a deeper and more sympathetic appreciation of literary quality than some of his friends. He enjoyed Henry James when Sidgwick found him "unmitigatedly serious and naively wearisome," and he sensed the poetic mind of Thomas Hardy when he was generally regarded as a novelist who had strayed clumsily into verse. When Hardy sent him a sonnet upon Leslie Stephen, Henry Jackson, to whom he showed it, was contemptuous. "If Hardy is not a poet, I think that the sonnet is a very fair piece of verses but without inspiration. If Hardy sets up to be a poet, I don't think the sonnet justifies his claim." Maitland was unconvinced: he liked the poem and put it into his book.[14]

The manor of Brookthorpe and Harescombe which Maitland had inherited, while it imposed responsibilities, offered a respite from Cambridge. He took its duties seriously, improving the existing property, building a new farmhouse and three new cottages, and, as was required of the lord of the manor, maintaining the chancel roof of the church. The income did little more than balance the expenditure; but it was a place of delight to the whole family, and until 1899 almost every vacation was spent in Gloucestershire. As his own houses were occupied, he had to find substitutes. In 1890 he took Brookthorpe Vicarage for a month's holiday, but in succeeding years he found a happier solution. Brookthorpe lies on the road from Gloucester to Stroud and is nearly equidistant from each. A mile or more of steady climb from the valley, and outside Maitland's property, is the village of Edge. Here his sister Sela owned two houses. To one of these—Horsepools House—she came in 1887 when her husband left Cambridge, and there they lived until 1896 when Dr. Reynell became Rector of Tidenham, near Chepstow. Next to it was Little Horsepools House which Maitland leased from his sister and which he came to look upon as a second home.

The family set out for Gloucestershire with a sense of high adventure. Maitland shared the feeling of gaiety—not because he would be idle but because, free from the trammels of lectures and University business, he could work at what he liked in the countryside which he loved and in which he had his own special interest. They rose early, breakfasting in winter by candlelight, caught the train to Liverpool Street, and then drove across London to Paddington. The expedition was formidable. Ermengard, looking back, could see the "mountain of luggage, the bird cages, the cat baskets, the dog on leash, all waiting for the train to back slowly into its appointed place. In we got, crowding the third class seats with our treasures and talking loudly of chicken pox to keep out strangers. Luncheon baskets were handed in, containing large helpings of cold chicken and salad and buns and apples."

In *A Child's-Eye View* she described the house and its immediate surroundings.

> Little Horsepools House was a small three-storied Cotswold house said to have been an inn. Certainly there was near the kitchen a stone-flagged room with a bow window, and this we looked on as the bar. There we kept our parakeets, or "screechers" as we rightly called them, and there on the window panes my mother inscribed with a diamond the birthdays of our dogs and cats. For all I know the birth of Wogs Augustus, Earl of Gloucester, may still be thus commemorated. There was also a tiny drawing-room where we were given piano lessons by my mother, and a dining-room whose walls had been rendered permanently damp by the breath of old Miss Aubrey who had sat there all day, long before we knew. In memory the room is enlivened by having been the scene of one of our greatest thrills. Lunch

was laid in state, for visitors were due. Monkey was in cage at safe distance. Safe distance was but an incentive to monkey. Cage was rocked until it was possible to stretch out paw and pull tablecloth. As was natural, china, glass, silver, flowers and water came too. The result was two little girls and one monkey thoroughly pleased with life.

Upstairs was my father's large study with windows on two sides: I remember the sense of urgent work. Nearby were our day and night nurseries connected by a sort of cupboard passage. One night we were awakened by sounds of jollity. We crept into the cupboard, listened and squinted. My sister's barrel organ was being turned. The maids were dancing and there were young men to partner them. My mother and father were away and there was a cask of beer in the cellar. Above this floor was a delectable region that included a spare room, space at the top of steps where we acted, and space where the marmot—Wishton Wish—lived. There was also the cook's room from which she once issued in the middle of the night and in wild grey disorder, calling aloud the one word "Earthquake!" She then banged the door and went back to bed. And the house rocked. In the stone stables at the back of the house were, at various times, a badger, rabbits, a cock that flew in our faces, a donkey and a pony.

In front of the house and across the road was the fall to the Severn Valley; a wide map of fields outlined by elms. The eye jumps over them to rest on the silver swoops of the river and canal and then goes on to the Forest of Dean and the Welsh mountains—that is as far as eye can go.

At Horsepools Maitland welcomed the American friends with whom he had exchanged letters on legal history. Charles Gross came twice, and the first visit was preceded by two characteristic notes. On July 5, 1893, Maitland invited him. "I can promise you pretty country and we can have a long talk about coroners." When Gross accepted the invitation, Maitland wrote: "I rejoice. If on arriving at Stroud station you do not find a fly from Horsepools at one side, try the other."[15] With

Bigelow and his family the Maitlands were on closer terms, and Florence's letters to them are full and frank. They had stayed in Downing in 1889, but they were at Horsepools in 1894 and again in 1897. Among Maitland's own colleagues a frequent visitor was Henry Bond. The son of a prosperous Cambridge grocer, he had been elected in 1887 a Fellow of Trinity Hall of which he was to be Master from 1912 to 1929. He was at Horsepools on a memorable afternoon when a "County" lady paid her call and felt that she should explain why this was belated. She had known that Maitland was a professor but had thought him to be nothing more. Looking round the small drawing room, she said: "You see, University men so often marry back into the class from which they sprang. I did not realise that you were landowners." But of Cambridge guests perhaps the most welcome was W. J. Whittaker. He could help Maitland with work, he was a comfortable man about the house, he was ready to join in any adventure. Ermengard has recorded an excursion by pony and train to Sharpness on the Severn: mother, father, children, and stout, round, jovial "Wicks."[16]

> We had lunch on the shore, and my sister excited, but not beyond words, by so much water and such a picnic, rose to great conversational heights. "Why don't you bathe, Wicks?" And then aware that some change in clothing might be well, "Make yourself some drawers of brown paper and stick them on with jam." Finding that this had gone down quite well, she thought it a good moment to resolve a doubt that had come to her. "Where do you sleep, Wicks? Oh, I know . . ." And then followed the most naive, the most satisfactory solution that could occur to her loving heart. I remember the gasp, the feeling that the grown-ups were suffering from some strange convulsion, but by the time they had recovered my sister was deep in excitement of another sort; she had begun to sink in the soft river mud. We went to her rescue, holding on to each other as in a tug-of-war. The more we pulled, the more mud and glory we acquired. On Sharpness station we weighed ourselves and boasted of our added substance. It was one of those lumi-

nous and timeless days that remain when greater occasions have faded away.

Descents upon Horsepools by Pollock were recurrent, and not to be averted. To Maitland they were pleasant, but Florence awaited them with misgiving. "I *fear,*" she wrote to Bigelow on September 16, 1897, "that Sir F. Pollock meditates a visit to us very soon. I know you will sympathise with me for this." She felt, perhaps unjustly, that he patronized Maitland and accepted her as his protégé's wife. The children were nervous of him, though he paid them attention, drawing pictures and giving them trinkets and books. The books, indeed, were sometimes strange choices and accompanied by notes not easy to decipher or to interpret. When Ermengard was eight years old, he gave her for her birthday an illustrated edition of *The Marvellous Adventures of Sir John Maundevile, Kt.,* with a Latin inscription comparing the relative credibility of Maundevile and of St. John the Evangelist. Ermengard took the book to her father that he might translate the words. He was amused; her mother was not.

At Harescombe Grange lived Crompton Hutton, a county court judge. "Crump" was an engaging figure, even if Ermengard and Fredegond accused him of tarring his gates to prevent them from being used as swings. He admired Florence—who, when she was busy, would station the children to give warning of his approach. He disapproved, indeed, of her taste for gypsies and "vagabonds" and regretted that he could not turn them off Maitland's land. But her music and her looks were ample compensation. He wanted her to play Beethoven (pronounced like the vegetable) but not Wagner (like the dog's tail). The son of a coachbuilder, he had made his own way in the world and gave himself no airs.

Farmers and cottagers were not only tenants to be visited but friends to be made and personalities to be treasured. Mrs. Hawkins of Chambers Farm dressed in black silk, and the children found her alarming. "She entertained us to lunch—a very stately meal—and showed us the cheese room with its shelves of 'double Gloucester'." Mrs. Carter of Brook Farm wore a black cotton sunbonnet both in and out of doors. It was tilted over her face and its ribbons were untied. "She gave us very good teas, she smelled of milk and she took us to see the dairy. The younger daughter took us to see calves and cut roses for us. The elder daughter leant her head on the tips of her long fingers and took no active part in the proceedings." Mrs. Moss, shrewd in wisdom, broad in speech, as kind as she was brave, brought up in her cottage ten sons and two daughters and then took charge of three "charity children." They came from the workhouse and their underclothes were stamped Gloucestershire County Council. It was Mrs. Moss who, after Maitland's death, welcomed back to Brookthorpe Florence and the children and who asked if the Venus de Milo had been born without arms. Other local characters enriched the village life: the reputed witch who prepared love potions and, according to taste, produced or removed warts on people and murrain on cattle; the fern man who gathered moss and ferns as he stalked silently before his wife; the sand carrier with his sacks of silver sand and the donkey which he grazed in Maitland's wood, near the gypsies whom Florence protected.

The calendar was marked by the weekly excitement of the market and by the annual haymaking. On market day the village was transformed. Herds of cattle and strings of horses passed along the road under the charge of drovers in ragged clothes. Farmers, in their best breeches and with their bowler hats, set out for Gloucester in gigs or traps or spring carts—horses and vehicles as trim as their masters. Lesser folk traveled in the carrier's van. Late in the day a less orderly procession returned. Horses might take their owners home without guidance and the carrier's shouts awaken early sleepers. Haymaking was always welcome. "One woke early to the leisurely sound of mowing machine or swish of scythe, the rick-i-tick of tedders or the yanking release of horse-rake. Horses rumbled their great red and blue wagons over the fields, and they looked like galleons on wheels. Large stone jars or little wooden barrels of cider stood in the shade of the elms, and women and children brought out bottles of cold tea and 'doorsteps' of bread and cheese. The women remained to rake or turn, and the children begged rides on the wagons. The men wore strings round the legs of their stiff pale corduroy trousers, and on their heads were great straw hats. The women wore tightly fitting dark woollen bodices buttoned down in front, flowing skirts of the same material and white aprons." The Maitlands had their own small part in the festival. They made hay in the wood for the upkeep of their pony, "Little M" by name, "for we had bought him from the baker and the baker's name was Mortimer. In cotton sunbonnets we tossed and raked. Little M. brought out tea and my father joined the party. We sat in the hay and then carried it in the cart."[17]

Maitland took Ermengard and Fredegond for walks through the woods or along the common to Haresfield Beacon, where he found for them fossils and Roman snails and orchids, and they imagined the valley turned back into sea. Longer days were spent in Gloucester. Florence drove the children to the fair, to ride on merry-go-rounds and sample all manner of allurements magically evoked by steam. Maitland infused city and cathedral with the sense of the past—"the stout Norman pillars stained to a short man's height with what he believed to be the warmth of the medieval crowds." The belief might be unjustified, but the picture remained to tempt the imagination. He took them to Llanthony Bridge to see the docks, the tall warehouses, and the canal barges; and he led Ermengard "into a very potent wine and spirit vault to see a bit of Roman wall" and brought her up quickly "while the going was good."[18]

December and January days brought their own duties and their own content. At Christmas it had long been a practice to give a parcel to each cottage tenant. When Florence married Maitland, she added toys for the children and chose them with careful pleasure. "The parcel contained a length of navy blue serge (black for widows), a cardigan for the man and calico and flannel for the children's petticoats. These parcels came from an ancient firm in the City of London, presumably instructed by the family solicitor." The parcels, while appreciated, came to be expected as if they were an official or statutory grant. Ermengard remembered a Christmas when a tenant returned a length of serge and demanded another: there was a burn on it and it had arrived in that condition. "We replaced the length but had our doubts."[19]

In the evenings and in bad weather Ermengard and Fredegond read or had books read to them, drew and made music, invented games and acted. If invention flagged, Florence suggested new themes, which in later days were developed into *Plays for Village Children* and published. She devised for adult amusement parodies of Ibsen into which she introduced travesties of family and friends and neighbors. "Rector Reynell," "Judge Crump," Henry Bond, and Maitland himself as a "Professor" hawking white mice to the strains of *The Magic Flute* were all dramatis personae and jostled such local eccentrics as the old woman at Painswick who compounded and sold pills and whom the dramatist's license could use for more dangerous ends. The parodies were read aloud and received with acclamation; and, though for obvious reasons they were not to be published, the manuscripts of two full-length plays survive. The setting and opening dialogue of one of them, entitled *Drugs,* may be offered as a sample.

> Act I, Scene I. A room in Pastor Melland's house. To the right is a door leading to a passage, and to the left a cupboard, the open door of which shows bottles of a blue colour, boxes, scales, weights, mortars, etc. By the window is a plain deal table at which Mrs. Melland sits, rolling pills. From time to time she looks out on the rain that is falling heavily. She is dressed in a simple gown of black stuff with plain white collar and cuffs. A black bag and an antimacassar lie on the soft to the left. The walls are hung with family portraits of clergymen and officials.
>
> A knock at the door.
>
> *Mrs. M:* Who's there? I am busy.
>
> Voice from outside: It is Mrs. Richard. May I come in?
>
> *Mrs. M.:* (without rising) Come in, dear, we can have a long comfortable chat together; for if I am not mistaken, we two take the same view of life. Yes, Araminta, we two can clasp hands as friends. We have the same firm and joyous grip on the world around us.

Mrs. R.: (entering) You, dear, have this. I am still one of those who grope. I have never gripped.

The impression of family life thus gained is of prevalent happiness, and especially at Horsepools where parents and children felt the more intimately their interdependence. But the picture will not be complete without some inquiry into the religious or ethical background against which this happiness may be measured. Maitland had grown up in a Christian household, and so long as Aunt Louisa lived, whatever his reservations, he would not hurt her by avowing them. When she died he ceased to attend the services of the church. The current of intellectual opinion was setting against orthodoxy, and it would have been strange if Maitland had been unmoved by it. The year of Aunt Louisa's death was the year in which he met Leslie Stephen. Stephen, though he had been ordained in the Church of England, had renounced his orders. In 1873 he had stated his position in "Essays on Free-thinking and Plain-speaking"; and in an essay in 1876[20] he had put into wide circulation the word agnosticism, first coined six years previously by Huxley. Where all is conjecture, it is not improper to suppose that Maitland's admiration for Stephen helped to confirm his separation from the Anglican Church.

Henry Sidgwick had long felt similar doubts; but, unlike Stephen, he could not be positive. In 1870 he had written to Frederic Myers: "I can neither adequately rationalise faith nor reconcile faith and reason nor suppress reason . . . But in an irreligious age one must not let oneself drift, or else the rational element is disproportionately expressed and developed by the influence of environment, and one loses the fidelity to one's true self. This last is the point . . . My true self is a Theist, but I believe that many persons are really faithful to themselves in being irreligious, and I do not feel able to prophesy to them." Through the next ten years he sought painfully to find a *via media* between the materialist and the mystic. He clung to the idea of duty, "to me as real a thing as the physical world." In duty he must believe; if this faith failed him he should feel that the "last barrier against complete philosophical scepticism, or disbelief in truth altogether, was broken down."[21] But a perplexed spirit was unlikely to be appeased by an abstraction. A pertinent question was put to a friend by Benjamin Jowett, whom the most obdurate free-thinker could not accuse of bigotry. "Having shut yourself out from any relation to God as an incentive to duty, does this moral atheism satisfy human nature?"[22] Sidgwick still craved an ultimate sanction; and in 1882 he became the first President of the Society for Psychical Research.

In things of the spirit as in those of the mind Sidgwick was the last man to seek proselytes. But Maitland could not have been his devoted pupil and have remained impervious to his views. Nor was Florence's influence to be cast decisively into the balance against them. She came from a home where church attendance was at least irregular. Her brother Herbert disliked professional religion. She herself, indeed, remained outside the church rather from loyalty to her husband than from choice; and, while unorthodox, she did not feel it necessary to subordinate faith to reason. To her "miracles were no bother at all—the only miracle would have been that there were no such things."[23]

Ermengard said of her father that his position "was that of a very Protestant agnostic, I might almost say a Low Church agnostic." Such he was in general repute, even to the next generation. In the one term in which Ermengard and Fredegond attended school in Cambridge they were met by mocking comments from other children: "Oh, you don't go to church. I suppose you hold a service in your own little dining-room." It is hard to catch and harder to convey the fine shades of doubt. Even the phrase "Protestant agnostic" may give too sharp an outline to Maitland's position. He would never have surrendered the right of private judgment and he recoiled from anything that, to his mind, suggested superstition; but he could wonder "whether, after all, Comte was not right about Protestantism:—not a stage on the main line, but a siding out of which you must back." He was a "dissenter from all churches";[24] but though he was anticlerical, he was not anti-Christian. He sought no substitute for orthodoxy and, unlike

Clough, he did not mar with vain questionings the sparrow flight of life. Agnostic or not, he could not, and would not if he could, renounce the inheritance of the Bible. Its words and images permeate his writing. He was no literary apostate, and language shapes thought in many secret ways. He wished his children to know something of Christ's teaching so that they might have the material upon which, as they grew up, they could make their own decisions and perhaps find their own faith. He read to them the Gospel of St. Mark which he thought the most helpful to young minds.

Above all, it was not in Maitland to be intolerant, save of shifty conduct or lazy thought. Ermengard remembered "how we came as quite small children to my father and told him that we had been talking to our cook—dear Mrs. Bowers with her tight black bodice, her rosy face and high, wheezy laugh—told him that Mrs. Bowers had said something outrageous but highly entertaining about Catholics or the Pope. I cannot remember his exact words but I well remember a stir in the atmosphere and a feeling that my mother was distressed. Roughly his judgment was that Mrs. Bowers and her like were the salt of the earth and the strength of England. My sister recounted his indignation when she admired one of the images carried round the streets of Telde on a feast day; yet when she asked him if she could become a Catholic there was no protest, only the statement that when she was twenty-one she could do as she thought best. His friends were, of course, within and without all folds, his daughters were free to make their own way, the fruits of his learning dropped on either side of the Anglo-Roman fence."[25]

The happy life in Downing or in Gloucestershire was checkered, not by religious doubt or difference, but by the shadow of ill-health which, ever since his election as Professor, had lain across Maitland's path. Throughout 1898 it was darkening. "The cold of an English June" culminated in an attack of pleurisy, and in August, when Gross paid a second visit to Horsepools, Maitland had still to spend his time "unprofitably and in bed." In September he had finally to dismiss from his thoughts the invitation to America with which Gross had tempted him. "I fear that the time has come when I must write to you and 'make the grand refusal'. I hate doing it: the prospect has been so honourable and so pleasant. You know how I regard the Harvard Law School: I feel as if I lived in the 12th century and was rejecting a 'call' to Bologna. But really I am hopeless and must not allow you to hope that you have found a substitute for your 'sabbatical'. This vacation has been to me a sore disappointment. Not only have I left undone many things that I meant to do, but I am none the better for my idleness. If I do a couple of hours work I become useless, and already I am dreading next term."[26] At the beginning of October his doctors insisted that he must escape to the sun, and he had hastily to beg leave of absence from the University and make suggestions for a deputy Professor.[27] At first he thought, or tried to think, that one season would cure him. But he had soon to admit that winter exile was henceforth to be the condition of survival.

This sentence broke the pattern of family life. The months abroad had each year to be paid for not only in money but in unremitting work at Cambridge when the summer brought Maitland back to his lectures, his books and his libraries. Visits might still be made to Gloucestershire, but they were fugitive echoes of the past. Sela, now in the rectory near Chepstow, sold the Horsepool houses, and the loss was poignant. Florence went to Brookthorpe for a fortnight in the June of 1900. "It was sad," she wrote to Bigelow, "to see the little house in the possession of others, and it looked uncared for and desolate."[28] To the last year of his life Maitland thought unavailingly of his "beloved Horsepools."

Chapter IX

Winter Exile

The merits of many resorts were discussed by Maitland and Florence: Palermo, Málaga, Algiers, Morocco; but they decided upon Grand Canary. Save for the winter of 1904–05, when they went to Madeira, they remained faithful to their choice. They stayed at first at the Hotel Santa Catalina on the outskirts of Las Palmas. From there Maitland wrote to Sidgwick on October 31, 1898. "I am idle in such idleness as is impossible in Europe. For the first time in my life I am feeling that mere existence is pleasant. In spite of all that I had heard, I did not believe in the demoralising effect of the sun." To Leslie Stephen on November 5 he said something of his environment.

> At first sight I was repelled by the arid desolation of the island. I suppose that I ought to have been prepared for grasslessness, but somehow or another I was not. But then the wilderness is broken by patches of wonderful green—the

> green of banana fields. Wherever a little water can be induced to flow in artificial channels there are all manner of beautiful things to be seen. I have picked a date and mustered enough Spanish to buy me a pair of shoes in the "city" of Las Palmas—a dirty city it is with strange smells; but we are well outside it. Between Las Palmas and its port there is a little English colony. This hotel is so English that they give me my bill in £. s. d. and my change in British hapence which have seen better days. Indeed now I know where our coppers go to when they have become too bad for use at home. Also the "library" of this hotel seems a sort of Hades to which the bad three-voller is sent after its decease. But the proposition that all the worst books collect there is (as you must be aware) not convertible into the proposition that only bad books come there, and I see a certain *Life of Henry Fawcett* which you may have read.[1]

A month later they moved to the Hotel Santa Brigida in the district of Monte, southwest of Las Palmas and fourteen hundred feet up in the hills, where, after Christmas, they were joined by Maitland's sister Kate. Hotel life had its drawbacks. There was little privacy and the only refuge was a deserted billiard room. Here the children did their lessons, learned Spanish, and acted little Spanish plays; and here Florence read to them *Mansfield Park* and *Persuasion,* and Maitland *Old Mortality* and *Woodstock.* But for days on end they were able to live out of doors. The children rode on donkeys and they all had picnics on the hillside among almond trees, geraniums, and roses. When it was not too hot, Maitland enjoyed long walks whose only drawback was the troop of boys who took "a fiendish pleasure in dogging the steps of an Englishman who obviously is deaf, dumb and mad. Attempts to reason with them only lead to shouts of Penny! or Tilling!—I cannot even persuade them that Tilling is not an English word." He occasionally secured a companion. "I took to myself," he wrote to Leslie Stephen, "the soundest looking man in a hotel full of invalids and got me up into the hills . . . and we succeeded in mastering not indeed the highest but the most prominent mountain of the island, if a mountain may be no more than 6000 feet high. This raised me in my own conceit, and certainly I had a very enjoyable time. I doubt whether in any of your good ascents you can have seen so gorgeously coloured a view as that which I beheld. A great part of the island lay below me; many of the rocks are bright orange and crimson, and these are diversified by patches of brilliant green. The whole was framed in the blue of sky and sea. It was like a raised map that had been over-coloured." On February 25, 1899, he could tell Sidgwick that "for three months I have enjoyed such a relief from all fleshly woes as I have not known for a good many years, and I shall be everlastingly thankful to the University which has allowed me this bath of blessed sunshine." When the time came to return to England it was with many regrets that he left his island refuge. "But if I am not strong enough for England now I never shall be, and I am anxious to see books once more."[2]

Through the summer of 1899, as the combined effect of his winter abroad and of good weather at home, Maitland was abnormally well. But in September he was once more ill, and in the middle of October he was ordered "to scuttle out of the country as fast as possible." The sudden demands of health made it awkward, in this as in later years, to arrange passages from England; and, as Las Palmas was an intermediate port of call, the return voyage might also present problems. Maitland had to study the chances of freighters as well as liners and of foreign as well as English vessels. One winter he heard good reports of a Hamburg line and asked a German living in Grand Canary if their boats were comfortable. "Oh, yes," he was told. "There is a band and it plays at every meal." "Yes," said Maitland, "I dare say it is very splendid, but that is not quite what I mean. Is it really comfortable?" "Comfortable!" the German exclaimed, "I should think it was! Why, they open a fresh cask of beer every day." In the autumn of 1899 Maitland had to leave by himself for Tenerife and thence by a little Spanish steamer, butting its way through bad seas, to the port of Las Palmas. Florence and the children followed a week later by a Union Castle liner.[3]

They decided to be independent of hotels and found a finca near the village to Santa Brigida. The house belonging to the property lay below the highway from Las Palmas to Santa Brigida and was built on one of the narrow cultivated terraces characteristic of the country. The highway was reached either by a steep stony lane or, less violently, by a path which, though it narrowed as it neared the road, was broad around the house; and there, in the shade of chestnut trees, Maitland set the chaise longue in which he worked or idled. "It is downright wickedly pleasant here," he wrote to Jackson. "By here I do not mean Las Palmas[4]—which stinketh—but some seven miles out of it and some 1300 feet above it, in a 'finca' that we were lucky enough to hire: that is something between a farm house and a villa. The Spaniard of the middle class is a town-loving animal. He likes to have up country a house to which he can go for six weeks or so in the year and where he keeps a major domo (= bailiff) who supplies the town house with country produce. Such a finca we hired for £1 a week, and there we live very comfortably and very cheaply among vines and oranges and so forth. Life here would have been impossible if my wife had not acquired the Spanish, or rather the Canario, tongue with wonderful rapidity. I fancy that some of her language is strong; but if you want anything here you must shout."[5]

The finca had two stories, with outside stairs leading from the one to the other. The majordomo lived on the ground floor with his wife and a baby who thrived on wine and chicken bones. The Maitlands had the upper story, with windows on all sides commanding long views. Florence liked it none the less because it was remote. On her return to England she wrote to Bigelow: "We saw no one but Spaniards all through the week, but every Sunday we dined at the English hotel and met 'Europeans'. The Spaniards are very nice and we got so fond of the cottage people around us. The little girls acted some tableaux for them before we left and they enjoyed this very much."[6] They were happy in the finca and they rented it again in the following winter. They did not regret their decision, though Maitland described to Henry Jackson the condition in which they found it. "I fancy that the comparison that you instituted between the life of the Roman and the life of the Spaniard as seen by me in these islands might be extended in a good many particulars. When, as happens for about eleven months in the year, you are not living at your finca, you occasionally pay it visits with a party of friends—male friends only—whom you entertain there. You eat a great deal and you drink until you are merry: then late in the evening you drive back to town twanging a guitar and, if you can, you sing inane verses made impromptu. Our landlord had one of these carouses the day before he handed the house to us, and my wife's account of the state in which the house was when she entered and got some servants to scrub it is not for publication. Apparently, as host and guests fill up with meat and drink, they become cheerfully careless of the manner in which they make room for more. Isn't this rather classical?"[7]

In the winter of 1901 to 1902 they found a house with a good garden in Telde, a large village eight miles south of Las Palmas. "This year," Maitland wrote, "our finca is in the midst of a 'pueblo'. The front of our house faces a high street which is none too clean; but then you keep the front of your house so shut up that you see nothing of the street, and at the back all is orange and coffee and banana and so forth. Telde is the centre of an important trade in tomatoes—the whole village is employed in the work of packing them for the English market and sending them off to the ships in Las Palmas." The house was owned by an English firm whose local representative was a Mr. Leacock, whom the Maitlands were to meet again in Madeira where he had his own interests as a wine merchant. The rooms opened out of a gallery and were almost bare of furniture. Florence improvised tables and other necessaries from packing cases covered with bright material. To this house they returned on each subsequent visit to Grand Canary save from December 1902 to April 1903, when they rented a house in Tafira, a small village between Las Palmas and Santa Brigida with a church, a sugar mill, and an inn kept by a hostess who prided herself on her emancipation from the local dialect and who gave Maitland lessons in Spanish.[8]

During his first winter abroad Maitland had to pay for ten

years of crowded achievement by complete rest. But indolence is an acquired taste; and in later visits he preferred to dilute it with work. In the winter of 1899–1900 he completed two tasks. The first was an article on the History of English Law for the *Encyclopaedia Britannica*—"the work of a bookless imagination, though dates were brought from England."[9] The second was more ambitious. Sidgwick had long been interested in Gierke's interpretations of law and politics and especially in his discussion of medieval political theories developed in the third volume of *Das deutsche Genossenschaftsrecht.* He thought that these passages at least might command an English market and suggested that Maitland should use his leisure to translate them. Maitland welcomed the suggestion and obtained Gierke's consent. The appropriate rendering of German words and phrases presented peculiar problems. The title of the relevant section—"Die publicistischen Lehren des Mittelalters"—was itself refractory. Dare he venture on "Publicistic Doctrines of the Middle Ages"? He wrote to Sidgwick: "The choice between Jargon and Verbosity is ever present. To which extreme would you lean? I suppose that I must not say (e.g.) Organic Idea when I mean that society is organic: but, fleeing Slang, I wander in a maze of *whiches* and *thats.*" Sidgwick replied: "When I got your postcard I tried to make a rational choice between Jargon and Verbosity in the abstract, but I did not find it possible. They have to be presented in the concrete before the faculty of choice can make any pronouncement. There are writers who prefer the two in combination, and they are by no means irreconcilable. Have you still any remembrance of Sir William Hamilton who, I think, was still living an *examinational* life—if no other—in your day? I seem to remember that, in a polemic against Brown, he accuses that philosopher of 'evacuating the phenomenon of everything in it that desiderates explanation.' Don't you call this J. and V.?" Maitland decided to opt for Jargon. "I want 'nature-rightly' very badly, and perhaps 'private-rightly' too. F. Pollock is shocked by "publicistic', which however implies more than 'political'. What is one to do? I can't make Otto G. into an Englishman. He resents the attempt."[10]

On January 22, 1900, Maitland reported that "after a sort" the translation was finished; and he now "shivered on the brink of an Introduction." In its first pages he apologized for an unhappy necessity. Were the whole of Gierke's book to be published in England it would have required neither introduction nor, indeed, the "distorting medium" of translation.

> But what is here translated is only a small, a twentieth, part of a large and as yet unfinished book bearing a title which can hardly attract many readers in this country and for which an English equivalent cannot easily be found . . . Now though this section can be detached and still bear a high value, and though the author's permission for its detachment has been graciously given, still it would be untrue to say that this amputating process does no harm. The organism which is a whole with a life of its own but is also a member of a larger and higher organism whose life it shares, this, so Dr. Gierke will teach us, is an idea which we must keep before our minds when we are studying the political thought of the Middle Ages, and it is an idea which we may apply to his and to every good book. The section has a life of its own, but it also shares the life of the whole treatise . . . [It] is a member of a highly organised system, and in that section are sentences and paragraphs which will not yield their full meaning except to those who know something of the residue of the book and something also of the controversial atmosphere in which a certain *Genossenschaftstheorie* has been unfolding itself. This being so, the intervention of a translator who has read the whole book, who has read many parts of it many times, who deeply admires it, may be of service.

Maitland finished the introduction before he left the Canaries. The proofs came to him in the summer of 1900, and the book was published as *Political Theories of the Middle Age* before the end of the year. But on August 29 Sidgwick had died. When Maitland heard the news, his mind went back to the lecture which he had attended at the end of his first year as an undergraduate and which had taught him the meaning of scholarship.[11] With love and veneration he added two last sentences to the introduction. "Last year, being sent from England, I was encouraged to undertake this translation by Professor Henry Sidgwick. What encouragement was like when it came from him his pupils are now sorrowfully remembering."

In addition to the *Gierke* and to the article for the *Encyclopaedia Britannica* Maitland had hoped, on this second visit to the Canaries, to copy two Year Books for the Selden Society. But the complete freedom from illness of his first visit was never repeated. Perhaps the recipe for health was not sunshine alone, but sunshine and rest. "The crumpled rose-leaf is that if and so long as I am very lazy I am very well." Maitland desired the sun, but rest was not to be torpor; and he was distressed when days in bed made work impossible. Still, he told Jackson, he had "managed to do some things that he should not have done at home," and he thought of his return to England "with the mixedest feelings. I am going to give Cambridge a last chance. If it cannot keep me at about 9 stone I shall 'realise' such patrimony as I have and buy a finca. Then for the great treatise De Damnabilite Universitatis."[12] If he had not copied his manuscripts, at least he had read them and his appetite had been whetted. Henceforth the study of the Year Books was to be his chosen "holiday task."

In one winter he had to pay a debt of friendship. In the autumn of 1901 Leslie Stephen had undertaken to write on Hobbes for the Men of Letters series. In April 1902 Stephen learned that he was suffering from cancer; and, though an operation in December brought relief, he knew that he was doomed. He met his fate with courage. Confined successively to his house, to his room, and to his bed, he strove to write for two or three hours a day on "that delightful old cuss, Thomas Hobbes of Malmesbury." The book was finished, "the work of a man who was dying by inches." Maitland, when he left England at the end of November 1903, "carried off the manuscript and proof-sheets after receiving some lucid instructions, and saying or trying to say farewell."[13] During the next three months he prepared the book for the press; and on March 5,

1904, he heard of Stephen's death. "I suppose that we ought to be glad," he wrote to Fisher, "that Leslie has gone to his rest—and certainly be glad that he suffered so little. Still when the event happens, though one has been expecting it, there is a bad time for those who remain behind . . . I cannot tell you how much I admired him." He asked Fisher to check his revision of the proofs. "A second eye will be useful in this case, for when I take them up I hear his voice, and that may make me inattentive to commas and the like. I think that people ought to say that the book is quite as good as its predecessors—there could be no question as to authorship, if it were an anonymous work: only one man could have done it." In the summer of 1904 he added a note to explain the abrupt ending of the book, and later in the year it was published.[14]

When he was well, Maitland took his exercise by walking or cycling. He walked alone or with Florence or with his daughters, and he sometimes prolonged the excursions by driving to the foot of the mountains in a *tartana,* a light two-wheeled wagonette drawn by either mules or horses. Fredegond recorded her memories of these days: "the early breakfast and start before the heat began, the drive in the dewy freshness when we could see the sea all around and hear the workers singing in the maize. Best of all was the mountain hamlet, with its forge and smithy, its jingling of harness and of goat bells, its tinkling waters, the ferns and violets growing in the crevices of its high walls." At the hamlet they dismounted and began the ascent. "The rocks grew pinker and the heat danced on the stones. We would eat our fruit and sandwiches in the last of the shade." Upon another expedition beyond Atalaya, the cave dwellers' mountain, after looking out upon the circle of cinder-covered hills, the blue basin of sky, and the sparkling ring of sea, Maitland said to Fredegond, "It seems pretty good to me, but you can never tell what an artist would say because there is that in the artistic temperament which makes them like to contradict."[15]

Cycling had its anxieties and its endurances. Roads and tracks were more or less navigable according to the weather.

In one winter, after a prolonged drought, "El Senor Cura clapped on the prayer for rain so very effectually that he had to protest before all the saints that he had not meant quite so much as all that." But the Canaries kept "a really working sun that is up to a sun's business and converts the most appalling mud into dust in the space of a few hours." Maitland had his experiences on the road. "The Spaniards," he wrote to Jackson, "are fond of using mere initials: after a dead person's name you can put q.d.h.e.g. = que Dios haya en gloria. The case that amuses me most is that you can speak of the Host as S.D.M. (his divine majesty—just like H.R.H.) One day in Las Palmas I had to spring from my bicycle and kneel in the road because S.D.M. was coming along. But I have just had my revenge. I have been mistaken for S.D.M. They ring a little bell in front of him. I rarely ring my bicycle bell because I don't think it a civil thing to do in a land where cycles are very rare. However the other day I was almost on the backs of two men so I rang. They started round and at the same time instinctively raised their hats—and instead of S.D.M. there was only an *hereje*."[16]

In the evenings there was music or Maitland played chess with Ermengard, who became so skilled that she won as many games as she lost. He remembered the bookless desert of his first visit and was careful thereafter to import what literature he could. On the second visit he brought with him the six volumes of Creighton's *History of the Papacy* and the ten volumes of S. R. Gardiner's *History of England, 1603–1640*. When he returned, he declared, he would be a well-informed person. He confessed that he had "misjudged Creighton's Papacy. It cannot be tasted in sips. Reading it straight through, I became deeply interested. I would that I could say as much of Gardiner." Despite his precautions, intermittent bouts of illness consumed his store of books. He had to fall back upon Spanish translations of Zola or on Perez Galdos, by birth a Canariot, who aspired to be a Spanish Balzac. "He is not bad, though he writes too much. I have lived in the society of fighting priests and so forth, very queer beings but well-drawn I should suppose."[17]

The children had somehow to be taught. Twice a governess accompanied them from England. Professionally neither was a success; but one remained vividly in Ermengard's memory.[18]

> *Tiens! Il est decoré.* The words were spoken on the quay of Las Palmas. We had but that moment landed and our big black Arks were round us. Small boys were singing "Ta-ra-ra-boom-de-ay" under the natural impression that it was our national anthem, and my mother was busy dealing with boat men and hotel porters in her best kitchen Spanish. The speaker was a French governess brought out to care for us during our winter's sojourn, and the object of her exclamation was a tall dark man wearing a red ribbon in his button-hole. My sister and I were standing with the feeling of the sea still in our legs—standing and staring; and we sensed after our fashion that the words were the subject of some sort of comic song. *Tiens! Il est decoré.* She did not leave it at that; before we left the quay she had found out that he was the French Vice-Consul and had gladly given him the information that we were going to Quiney's Hotel.
>
> The next day my mother left Las Palmas and went out to the country to arrange our rented house, engage servants, unpack the Arks and get things ship-shape before the arrival of my father in a few weeks' time. We were left at Quiney's in the charge of Mademoiselle—and then the fun began. The Vice-Consul came morning, noon and dewy night. They sat together among the flowers, they drank glasses of wine in the patio. We were foresaken. There was no one to take us in to meals at the proper times, and strange ladies had pity on our awkwardness. The Spanish servants talked to us with vehemence; *La sin verguenza,* they said—"the shameless one". We played it up to the top of our bent. *Las pobrecitas,* they said. We drank it in, feeling not poor but rich.
>
> When we joined my mother, there was much to tell. The kind ladies followed and added their versions. Mademoiselle was talked to and pleaded love at first sight, and was cer-

tain her love was returned, and of course he was decoré, and all would be well if only my mother would help. My mother was used to the rôle of confidante; the love tales she was told on our voyages would have filled a book. She told Mademoiselle to invite the Vice-Consul to tea. Day after day Mademoiselle sat all tidied up in the long galeria, listening for the sound of horses' hooves; for, like all tall, dark, decorated men, he rode. "He cometh not," she said.

The next thing I remember clearly was that we were to go to town for the day. HE wished to see HER, to see her alone. She dressed with added prettiness—I think she had a natural grace, though we did not see it then. Off we went in the *tartana,* along the dusty road, by peppertrees, banana groves, maize fields and glimpses of the sea, until we reached the city. Lunch at Quiney's, and then my mother took us on a long round of shopping: into dark, cool drapers' shops, to dealers in African parrots, to the market with its blaze of fruits and its strange fishes, into the bank where we were served by a man said to be a descendant of the aboriginal Guanches. It was his large head and high cheek-bones that showed it, they said. At last my mother felt that we had given the pair time to propose, accept and rejoice and, in a state of intense excitement, we returned to Quiney's.

The Vice-Consul had departed, and we saw before us a woe-begone figure.

"He talked to me of his dead fiancée," she said. My mother did not let grass grow: she got in touch with the French Consul. He was a kindly old man and was distressed that Mademoiselle should have fallen for his Vice. There were interviews, tears, letters, and finally he got her a passage back to France. We were left with an unforgettable phrase for our Book of Tunes:—*Tiens! Il est decoré.* It took its place with Come into the Garden, Maud: Say that you love me, do: Onaway, awake beloved: 'Ave you bought the street, Bill: Daddy wouldn't buy me a bow-wow:—and, of course, our national anthem.

This experience was enough. Florence resumed the teaching

of French and Maitland, as he told Pollock, "played the schoolmaster. How they have turned the Latin grammar inside out!—and I miss my Rule of Three."[19] He gave lessons in mathematics and Latin and even in Spanish grammar. Fredegond was stupid at sums and dreaded going to her father with them.[20]

> "You are *not* trying."
> "Oh I *am.*"
> "No, it's no good—you *can't* learn them".
> I used to creep away in guilty misery to the kitchen, where I would soon be shouting and boasting in Spanish to the cook.
> He tracked me down.
> "Come back, I think you have a gift for language—you must learn Spanish—there are two verbs for *to be* and two for *to have*—the one is . . . the other . . ." I grew interested because he made the richness of two kinds of "being" and "having" so real to me.

Occasional visitors came from England. In November 1901 W. H. Stevenson traveled out with Maitland and remained until Christmas, but lack of time and money forbade him to come again. In the winter of 1902–03 G. T. Bennett of Emmanuel College, though he did not stay with Maitland, walked and rode with him. Maitland's gratitude for his company was tempered with trepidation. "Heaven send," he wrote to Jackson, "that in his demoniacal cycling he kills no child—for homicide, when committed by an 'inglese', is sometimes seriously treated."[21] Buckland paid two visits to Grand Canary, the first and longer, with his wife and daughter, from January to March 1902. The Maitlands were then living in Telde, and the Bucklands stayed not with them but in a house outside the village. As the postal service was incalculable, all their letters were addressed in the first instance to Maitland. "Every mail day we used to watch for Maitland, who, as soon as the letters came, used to mount his bicycle and bring down ours. As he approached the bridge he sounded his bell and shouted 'Post! Post! Post!' till he had attracted our attention, at first to the amazement and afterwards to the amusement, of the local people."[22]

Buckland recorded his tours with Maitland on cycle and on foot.[23] The central road of the island was twenty-three kilometers long and rose three thousand feet in one unbroken ascent. It was Maitland's ambition to ride to the summit, but he persisted in trying to take it by storm: he started off at high speed and could not last the course. There were mule tracks as well as roads on which to ride. "We took our bicycles, sometimes shouldering them over these tracks into places where no cycle, or indeed any form of wheeled traffic, had ever been."

> But there were places to which no bicycle could go—in particular the Cumbres, the tops of the mountains, about 6,000 to 7,000 feet. On one occasion we made an expedition to these heights, stopping the night before at the highest hotel on the island, about 4,000 feet below. We had a good day on the summit and then started for our homes, not much above sea level; but we had not realised what was involved in a descent of 6,000 feet down a mountain side with which we were not familiar. We had one or two thrills, and we lost our way. We got very tired; and every now and then Maitland gave a loud groan or bellow, which at first alarmed me, for I supposed the labour was too much for him. But seeing this he explained—I think not merely to ease my mind but with truth—that it was only letting off steam and he found it refreshing. Dark had fallen before we reached a little mountain village, Valsequillo, and after that it was plain sailing. We were very hot. There was an inn in the village. The conclusion from these premisses is obvious. I had the pleasure of seeing Maitland enjoy a drink, and a very long drink. There was but one beverage, for the beer was undrinkable. This was vino-vermouth, a mixture of the local red wine (*vino tinto*), which is sold, even to foreigners, at about sixpence a gallon and is not worth so much, and cheap Spanish vermouth. The mixture is sold in litre bottles, and Maitland disposed of a bottleful immediately. To avoid misconception I had better say that

> I did the same. He finally reached home dog-tired, and early in the morning I went up to his house in some trepidation as to the effect of the fatigue on him. I found him in his garden, smoking and transcribing a page from a photographed Year Book and looking perfectly fit. He told me he felt better than he had felt for months, and, as a matter of fact, he had no more illness that winter. Whether it was the vino-vermouth or the unusual fatigue, I do not know.

While Buckland was still on the island Maitland had another visitor, George James Turner.[24] Born in 1867, he was an undergraduate of St. John's College, Cambridge, and in his last year at the University was placed among the senior optimes in the Mathematical Tripos. In 1893 he was called to the Bar and for a few years practiced as a conveyancer. But his abiding interest was in medieval law and its background. As early as 1892 he began to take part in the work of the Selden Society. In 1896 Maitland, when he meditated a prolonged attack upon the Year Books and wanted help, told Lock that he was thinking of Turner. "I know no one who looks more hopeful . . . He and I could work together and supply each other's defects."

During the next ten years Maitland thought ever more highly of Turner as a scholar and became ever fonder of him as a man. He also discovered his defects. Turner was at once endearing and exasperating. He had enough private means to choose his own tasks and to pursue them with provocative deliberation. As a thief of time he was without rival. "When I tell him of it," Maitland wrote to Poole, "he only laughs. That is the worst of it—but I need not say more to you, for I saw that you love the little man. I love him very much."[25] He was not indolent; he was beset by intellectual scruple. His delight was to find a problem, and if none was apparent he would devise it for himself. A proof sheet was an invitation to change his mind and start afresh upon a new scent. The result of his travail was admirable, but the gestation was prodigious. He was once induced to write some articles for the *Encyclopaedia Britannica.* A friend asked him how they progressed. His answer was to produce from his pocket a sheaf of reply-paid telegram forms, all unused. In 1894 he undertook to edit a volume for the Cambridge Antiquarian Society. The Society's annual report for 1899 stated that the book would be "issued shortly." In 1902 publication was expected "before Christmas." In 1904 it was "nearly ready." It appeared in 1913 through the desperate intervention of the Society's honorary secretary who verified points upon which Turner was still in doubt and sent the proofs to the press. In the preface Turner thanked him for his help—"kindness which I value the more because the assistance was rendered on his own initiative and without my knowledge." Plucknett's comment is just. "If Maitland's work leaves the impression of light coming in a sudden flash of intuition, Turner's seems to show the almost imperceptible dawn breaking after a long night of contemplation."[26]

Turner was a lifelong bachelor; once challenged to avow his political faith, he declared himself a "Liberal Misogynist." But, like many bachelors, though he was shy of women he enjoyed the taste of domesticity. When he came to Telde in December 1901, he was made welcome by the family and responded with nervous pleasure and diffident generosity. "Little T" or "Twidlums," as Maitland and the children called him, had his difficulties. Ermengard recalled him looking like a newly fledged bird and bringing presents for her and for Fredegond. "They were wrapped and placed in the hall: we took no notice. He moved them into the gallery: we passed them with averted eyes. They were moved again, but what could we do about them? My mother had to rescue us all, bringing giver, receivers and presents together." When Maitland had to return to Cambridge for the Easter term, Florence and the children stayed behind for some weeks, and Turner remained to escort them home. He had "fallen in love with the land of *mañana*."[27] With all its embarrassments the visit had been a success, and it was repeated in later years.

But English visitors were rare, and Maitland had usually to rely upon letters. Fisher sent news of the family and of Oxford; Poole discussed the prospects of the *English Historical Review;* Lock reported on the Selden Society. Pollock offered tantalizing peeps of the great world: his experiences on the hustings in the General Election of 1900, "stumping the country from Spalding unto Barnstaple," his purchase of an "ingenious steam motor car," his links with the Comédie Française, his cultural tours of Italy and of France. Verrall wrote gaily of Christmas holidays and literary adventures. "We spent the greater part of the vacation in London, and put in a theatre, concert or something of the kind on more than half our days. The thing I enjoyed most was the *Messiah* at the Albert Hall; but the Drury Lane pantomime also pleased my catholic taste. The ballets were splendid. There was not much satire; the best was a supposed view of London from an air-ship. 'Now we are over the Surrey side. The roads are all up, and it looks *lovely*' . . . Do you know anything of a musician called Smetana? A quintette was performed here last Wednesday and I liked it much. He is quite new to me . . . I am in the middle of William James' *Psychology,* two enormous volumes, *awfully* difficult to poor me! But such is my passion for self-improvement! I was cheered up at finding that Miss Bates in Jane Austen's *Emma* is a signal example of 'Impartial Redintegration'. Then I felt that I was at any rate within the sphere of my observation, however the terms might tax my comprehension. What *would* dear Jane herself have said 'if she had been thought worthy to know'—as Peter Featherstone's relations remark about the ultimate fate of his property."[28]

Alex Hill and Kenny kept Maitland in touch with college business and Buckland with university politics. "You will have heard," Buckland wrote in December 1903, "that a syndicate has been appointed to see what we must do, academically speaking, to be saved. It is expected to report that we must sell all we have and give it to the Professors of Science. They are a greedy race . . . I will endeavour to keep you informed of University happenings as seen from the lower levels. Your other local correspondents are dignitaries." The most august of the dignitaries was Henry Jackson. An undergraduate of Trinity, he was elected a Fellow in 1865 and remained in Cambridge until he died in 1921. He was a man of robust personality and, though he published comparatively little, of ripe scholarship. In his own words, he wrote "mainly for experts and mainly in technical periodicals." His papers in the *Journal of Philology* on Plato's later theory of Ideas were a decisive contribution to learning. He was a teacher of unusual power and influence, and early in 1906 was elected Regius Professor of Greek. Maitland sent his congratulations from Telde. "I feel," he said, "that I am in a position to write to you an interesting letter full of good advice from an old to a young professor. I could tell you that you have illusions and beg you to retain them as long as possible for your own sake. Lord! what a lot I meant to do when I was elected!" Jackson replied that he had received "a strange diversity of advice: (1) address yourself, about Greek culture, to people who know *no* Greek, (2) give *no* lectures to men who are reading for a Tripos, (3) do just what you are doing, (4) no one expects anything from a professor."[29]

Jackson was not only a scholar. He was an observer of life, so far at least as life may be observed from an ivory tower. He relished all aspects of university business and, though a "reformer," he was the repository of Cambridge tradition. He delighted, by letter and if possible by reunion, to keep in repair both personal and college ties. At feasts and festivals old members thronged to his rooms. Desmond MacCarthy, who was an undergraduate at Trinity at the end of the century, wrote to Leonard Woolf after he had come up for a night in March 1905.[30] "Then we went to Jackson's at home. You know the scene: clouds of tobacco smoke—a roar of conversation—dozens of whist tables with lighted candles on each—clay pipes—boxes of cigars—a piano and someone singing God knows what . . . Then songs with choruses, school songs—the various representatives of different schools, gathering round the piano and shouting with defiant patriotism." From 1900 to 1906 Jackson was the most prolific of Maitland's correspondents, and the echoes of Cambridge life came gratefully to the exile. The two men were on comfortable terms; and, save on the rare occasions when they differed on university policy and tact was expedient,[31] Maitland could talk and write to him without taking tedious thought to spare susceptibility. But it is difficult to sense in the letters the warmth of intimacy. In all but scholarship Jackson was the antithesis of Sidgwick, and he could not replace Sidgwick in Maitland's heart.

Despite relapses and disappointments the winters abroad achieved their end. This success owed much to Florence's courage and common sense. "It was on the crest of her essential practicality, her belief that all things were possible, that we were able to winter in the Canary Islands when it seemed necessary for his health. Looking back, I realise how little can have been spent on clothes, luxuries and education, so balancing the comfort of service and warm winters. Those winters were themselves (if not rough-and-ready) at least plain, with half-furnished houses, half-trained servants and my mother making bread, jointing meat and bargaining at the door."[32] Despite these preoccupations Florence enjoyed her winters—above all, as she wrote to her mother, when there were no visitors: "no regular meals to think of, and getting to bed early and just letting things go." "Mr. Turner is very nice," she continued, "but I long to be alone. All Fred's time is going, and we never can do anything together." An island home, whatever its drawbacks, was essentially simple: "no stairs, no fires, no shopping and no horrid English servants with their brazen ways." She returned each spring to Cambridge with spirits renewed and, if not reconciled to the conventions of university life, steeled to encounter them.

Chapter X

Downing Professor

The Years from 1899 to 1906

Winter sunshine supplied Maitland each year with a reserve of strength upon which he could draw until the late autumn. But he did not expect, and he did not achieve, complete freedom from ills and pains. Sometimes he had to blame his own imprudence; more often the vagaries of the English climate. The letters tell their tale. In May 1900 he had to postpone a visit which Gross was to have paid to Downing. In July 1901 he was compelled to neglect the Selden Society. "I felt very much ashamed of myself," he told Lock, "for not being at the Council meeting, but your very kind letter turned the scale; and I think that I did well, for I am out of pain now though absurdly sleepy." In 1902 he was especially unlucky. In May he wrote to Jackson: "After the walk from Newnham the other night I had a bad bout with the fiend that persecutes me and I am compelled to argue *post hoc ergo propter hoc.* Just for a bit I must forswear going out of nights—otherwise I may be useless." At the end of August: "the devil has me and I am compelled to be abed." A month later he had to refuse an invitation to attend the commemoration of the Bodleian tercentenary. "I am much better," he told Poole, "but do not feel sure of getting to Oxford. It is of great importance to me to get through a course of lectures without a break-down." In the autumn of 1903 "one unfortunate ride in the rain squelched numerous projects" and "the damp has been sinking into me."[1] But when he was not driven to his bed he could be vigorous and hopeful. He made up lost time by lecturing, if need be, every day in term and by giving courses in the Long Vacation. He still took his share of University business; and in two controversies he played a characteristic part.

The first was a "battle of the books." Mrs. Rebecca Flower Squire, who died on November 26, 1898, left part of her estate in trust to build and endow a law library. In June 1900 the Senate formally accepted the bequest. But the library had not only to be built but to be equipped; and the solution of this problem was long sought and hotly debated. Jackson and Maitland held conflicting views. Maitland wished, in Jackson's words, "to stock the Squire from the University library"; and Jackson opposed him on the ground that such a course would jeopardize the privilege granted by the Copyright Act to the University of claiming a copy of each book published in the United Kingdom. "If we give out our books to departmental libraries, our defence against the publishers—that we hold the books as a great collection for the use of the nation—is gone." Maitland was not deterred and throughout the summer and autumn of 1904 urged the needs of the Squire library. Before the crucial vote was taken in the Senate he had to leave England. Buckland took his place and was able to report a victory by eighty votes to sixty-three. But he warned Maitland that Jackson was resolved to renew the fight and asked him to intercede. Maitland had misgivings. "I will feel my way once more. I say 'once more', for I made an attempt and found that [Jackson's] manner underwent a sudden change as I approached the subject. Something or another—or perhaps I should say someone or another—has riled him." But he wrote to Jackson from Funchal in March 1905.[2]

> A while ago I hesitated [to put my proposal to the Senate] partly because I feared that the Squire Library would be made a dumping ground for rubbish, partly because I would rather not remove books from the old building if there were any chance of their being useful while they are there. What brought me to ground was the economic argument. I guess you hardly know how exceedingly bad the Univ. Libr. is as a law library—in the matter of foreign law books and periodicals it is shamefully poor. I don't like taking an American into it: the land is so naked. Now we shall have a little Squire money and I hope that in course of time we may be able to get together a creditable collection of foreign—remember that this includes American and colonial—books. Any way this will be a long job, but even the first beginning of it will have to be postponed for many years if at the outset we have to acquire the first necessaries of life, namely the English reports; and gifts of them we are not likely to get if there are already copies in the place. Then as to the Copyright Act, I don't say that there is no danger, but I do think that the danger is trifling when compared with that which we are incurring all day and every day by allowing books to be taken out of the Library. That, so it seems to me, is our weak point and a very weak point indeed. I feel that it would not be difficult to write a good slashing leader about it on the side of the publishers. On the other hand books are not to go out of the Squire building . . . "Books preserved in separate buildings" seems to me a less attackable position than "books not (continuously) preserved in any building."

Jackson decided not to carry on a guerrilla war after the vote in the Senate. He may have been impressed by Maitland's arguments or he may have feared defeat by the other faculties, whose members would be eager to press through the gate so obligingly opened for them by the lawyers.

In the second controversy Maitland was Jackson's zealous supporter. Jackson sought to abolish Greek as a compulsory subject in the University entrance examination. He explained his reasons in a letter to A. J. Butler.[3] "I think both Latin and Greek excellent instruments of education for the right men; but I think also that in this busy XXth century the wrong men ought not to be expected to take *two* dead languages. By the wrong men I mean (a) men who have no turn at all for languages, (b) men who, for whatever cause, have got sick of Latin and Greek at School . . . It is reasonable to require a modicum of Mathematics—at any rate Arithmetic; and similarly it is not more unreasonable to require a modicum of one dead language than to ask for a modicum of two and get failure in both." Few crusades were more congenial to Maitland, and he helped Jackson to draft proposals. These were debated in the Senate while he was still in England. He spoke of his own experience at Eton: of the "boy at school not more than forty years ago who was taught Greek for eight years and never learnt it; who reserved the greater part of his gratitude for a certain German governess; who, if he never learnt Greek, did learn one thing—to hate Greek and its alphabet and its accents and its accidence and its syntax and its prosody and all its appurtenances, to long for the day when he would be allowed to learn something else, to vow that if ever he got rid of that accursed thing never, never again would he open a Greek book or write a Greek word." He recognized that most of his opponents were moved by the fear—natural if not necessarily justified—that classical studies would wane both in the University and in the schools. But some, he suggested, were thinking more of their own esoteric interests than the needs of education in a changing world. These he compared to Demetrius of Ephesus who incited the silversmiths against St. Paul when his preaching threatened their trade—"so that not only this our craft is in danger to be set at naught but also that the temple of the great goddess Diana should be despised and her magnificence should be destroyed."[4] The passage was indiscreet, and, though nothing could have saved the proposals, it did not enhance the chances of success.

The crucial vote was taken only after Maitland had left for Madeira. When he read the result in the *Times* he was disagreeably surprised by the size of the majority against the proposals. "I made a last guess as I opened my newspaper and said 'Beaten by 200,' and lo! it was worse." The numbers were swollen by the "non-resident parsons" who flocked to Cambridge to defend the classical faith. "I can well imagine," he wrote to Jackson, "that *a Greekless clergy!* was a good cry, but wonder how Greekful our clergy really is." A contributory cause of defeat was to be found in class consciousness. A line of distinction must be drawn between the old and the new Universities. "For a little while past I have been coming to the conclusion that at bottom this is a social question. Having learnt—or what is precisely the same thing—pretended to learn Greek has become a class distinction which is not to be obliterated."[5]

These were the years of wide recognition. In 1899 he was made an honorary D.C.L. at Oxford and an honorary L.L.D. at Glasgow. Doctorates were also conferred upon him by the Universities of Cracow and Moscow. In 1901 he became a corresponding member of the Royal Prussian, and in the next year of the Royal Bavarian, Academy. In 1902, when the British Academy was founded, he became one of the original Fellows. He was in familiar company: Frederick Pollock, Leslie Stephen, William Cunningham, and James Ward, who had defeated him in the Fellowship examination in 1875. He was made, to his delight, an honorary Fellow of Trinity and, to his amazement, an honorary Bencher of Lincoln's Inn. This last election made his "hair stand on end. One of the vacant bishoprics would have been less of a surprise."[6]

While degrees and dignities accrued, Maitland watched with hope or anxiety the fortunes of his friends. In November 1902 he received a letter from W. H. Stevenson, whom he had hoped to take with him for a second visit to Grand Canary. Writing from Exeter College, Oxford, Stevenson explained why he must refuse the invitation. "Alas! I am even more 'unrich' than I was last year, for I have remained here all the Long in the hopes of finishing Asser. My fellowship expires with the year, and I must go back to 'Close Rolling' and London, unless I can summon up strength to 'pisen' myself. I have got considerably blinder this last year or two, so that I have been unable to work on many August and September days. With Close Rolls the disability is like to increase. Another year should finish Edward I, and then I know not what other drudgery, if any, may be open to me. It is a nuisance to be born without the faculty of making a moderate livelihood either by commerce or scholarship, and to get sick of the worthless subjects one has wasted one's leisure over." For the next twelve months Stevenson struggled to support himself, eking out his fees for the Calendar of Close Rolls with such casual work as he could get. In March 1904 Maitland wrote to Jackson almost in despair. "I have very sad news of Stevenson—I think that I introduced you to him, the man who was given a fellowship at Exeter without ever having faced a competitive examination—self taught in an attorney's office. The fellowship has expired and now the poor beggar is almost starving; and yet I am told by a German luminary that something that Stevenson published along with Napier (the Crawford Charters) is out and away the best bit of 'diplomatic' that has ever come from England. It will be a pity and a scandal if he goes to the wall, and he is damnably modest and will not strive nor cry. When I get home I must see whether anything can be done."[7] There was a happy sequel. Two months after Maitland's letter Stevenson was elected to a research fellowship at St. John's College, Oxford, and was at last assured of subsistence.

In Moscow, from 1895 to 1901, Vinogradoff's position became ever more precarious. To him state control of universities was odious, and the noose was constantly tightened. A professor was regarded as the servant of the government, expected to teach "official" history and to report the political views of his students. Vinogradoff, by the very fact of his reputation as a teacher and by the enthusiasm which his lectures aroused, became an object of particular suspicion, and spies were planted in his classes. On the other hand, he detested the revolutionary propaganda which corrupted young minds and he sought to mitigate its effect. He thus stood, as he said, "between two fires": blamed by the government for university disorder and accused by intemperate students of treachery to his own ideals. In 1901 he prepared a scheme for the creation of professorial committees, free from state interference, to keep in touch with the students and, so far as possible, to meet their grievances. It was submitted to the Minister of Public Education and was incontinently rejected. Vinogradoff felt that he could no longer remain in Moscow, and in December, with his wife and children, left Russia for England. For the next two years he lived at Tunbridge Wells. He wrote reviews for English and foreign journals; he prepared material for his book *The Growth of the Manor,* to be published in 1905; and he gave a special lecture at Cambridge on "The Reforming Work of the Tzar Alexander II and the Meaning of the Present Development in Russia."[8]

In 1903 Pollock resigned his chair as Corpus Professor of Jurisprudence, and Vinogradoff was persuaded by members of the Oxford law faculty to offer himself as a candidate. In January 1904, in Grand Canary, Maitland heard the news of Vinogradoff's success. He wrote to congratulate him and recalled the enthusiasm which, twenty years earlier, had kindled his own awakening interest in legal history. "Now I shall look to you to fire some one else. I badly need a coadjutor *cum spe successionis* in my Year Book work. You must find me one, Señor Catedratico." In his reply Vinogradoff said that he was going to Oxford on the first day of March "when my Inaugural will have to be delivered after an 'exciting' theological debate in Congregation. My lecture ought to give a mild relaxation to the impassioned minds of the dons who attend both events. It will treat of Maine, quite a cool subject nowadays. I selected it because it will give me the opportunity of occupying my corner of the chair over which the shadow of a great man still hovers."[9]

Vinogradoff's establishment in Oxford richly atoned for a small but real loss of comfort in Cambridge. In 1901 Whittaker —"Wicks" *en famille* and "The Squire" to his friends in Trinity and in the law faculty—sought his fortune in London. He went into Maitland's old chambers in Lincoln's Inn and taught law at University College and later as Assistant Reader to the

Inns of Court. Maitland missed his loyalty, his even temper, and, when so much had to be done in so short a time, his readiness to shoulder some of the burden of lectures. At the end of 1904 Buckland reported to Maitland in Madeira the rumor of Whittaker's engagement to be married. Maitland was surprised and awaited confirmation before he sent his congratulations. Buckland had soon to report the marriage, and Maitland wrote: "If what you said of the Squire be true, he is a deep 'un—a secretive Squire. The wretch sent me a beery but pretty postcard from the Koenigliches Hofbrauhaus zu Muenchen, and alluded not to the domestic event. Talked of a journey on business to tackle a German lawyer. Honeymoon, I believe—or Meadmoon, if mead be beer and honey." Whittaker soon made his peace with Maitland. "The squire has behaved nobly to me despite his billing and cooing. He has sent me a delightful "baboo" letter and Anatole [France's] last, which I am keeping for the voyage."[10]

A new generation of scholars turned to Maitland as their guide through the marches of law and history. John Neville Figgis was a lecturer of St. Catharine's College from 1896 to 1902 and later became a member of the Community of the Resurrection at Mirfield. His main interest lay in the relations of church and state. In 1896 he wrote his first book *The Divine Right of Kings,* and he gave a series of lectures on "Political Thought from Gerson to Grotius," which he published in 1907. He was deeply impressed by Maitland's papers on the Canon Law and by the introduction to *Gierke,* and he treasured the hours of discussion which they provoked. Religious differences did not inhibit gratitude. For him Maitland was the man who brought the past to life; and he relished the complaint of an undergraduate that he could take no notes at Maitland's lectures because they were so absorbing. A second scholar who thought of Maitland as his master was Gaillard Lapsley. Born in New York in 1871 and educated at Harvard, he became a lecturer at Trinity College in 1904 and University Reader in Constitutional History. Sir Maurice Powicke described him as "for many years the outstanding exponent of medieval history in Cambridge," and recalled a luncheon party given by Professor Hazeltine in Downing at which he and Lapsley were fellow guests. Lapsley explained that they were lunching in the room which had been Maitland's study. He pointed to a place on the wall and said with emotion, "Domesday Book stood *there*."[11]

In 1895 Lord Acton was appointed Regius Professor of Modern History at Cambridge. The Professorship had been founded by George II in 1734, and for the next hundred years its annals were sparse, though, in Maitland's words, "no unfavourable inference should be drawn from the bare fact that the professor's mastery of history was seldom attested by any book that bore his name. Macaulay has said that the author of the Elegy in a Country Churchyard was in many respects better qualified for the professorship than any man living. That may be so: but the habits of the time made lecturing unnecessary, and as a teacher of modern history Thomas Gray must be for us a mute inglorious personality."[12] It was only in the second half of the nineteenth century that modern history was recognized as something more than an ornamental fringe around the solid learning of antiquity. The Professor from 1860 to 1869 was Charles Kingsley, who at least brought to his office a sense of high purpose. Henry Sidgwick liked to tell the story of a pass-man who thanked him for a course of elementary lectures which he had given. "They are the best I ever attended, except perhaps the lectures of Professor Kingsley—but then *his* are intended to improve the mind."[13] If, a hundred years later, some think of Kingsley as a professor, more know him as the luckless antagonist of Cardinal Newman and most as the author of *Westward Ho!*

Kingsley's successor was John Robert Seeley. Already a controversial figure through his *Ecce Homo,* his inaugural lecture was eagerly awaited. Expectation was fulfilled or disappointed according to temperament. It is told of W. H. Thompson, Master of Trinity, that, at the end of the lecture, he remarked to a friend, "I never thought that we should have had occasion so soon to regret poor dear Kingsley." The sentence, nicely compounded of judgment, wit, and malice, has earned its place in academic anthologies. Seeley was a man of decided ideas and forceful personality. The function of the University was to be a seminary of politicians. But "politics were vulgar when they were not liberalised by history, and history faded into mere literature when it lost sight of its relation to practical politics." Upon this text he wrote his most famous book, *The Expansion of England,* and he lectured for the last ten years of his life on English diplomacy. He enjoyed panoramic views and disliked the minutiae of research: the function of detail was to provide the basis of generalization. Despite his apparent simplicity, he was a man of innate contradictions. His taste was for applied history and his talent for narrative; but G. M. Trevelyan, as an undergraduate, was enraged to be told by him that history was a science and that Macaulay was a charlatan. It was largely through Seeley's efforts that the Historical Tripos had been established in 1873; but, when accused of converting it into a Political Tripos, he repudiated the suggestion that the course of historical studies in any University should be influenced by the demands of an examination. "I have always regarded the Tripos," he declared, "as a thing which does not concern me and which might conceivably, though it has not done so, mar the effectiveness of my teaching."[14]

Kingsley and Seeley had been popular choices. Acton, when he came to Cambridge, was almost unknown save by historians. To them he was a scholar unsurpassed in Europe and unequaled in England. The library which he formed at Aldenham in Shropshire speaks of the man and of his methods. After his death it was bought by Andrew Carnegie, given by him to Lord Morley, and by Morley to the University of Cambridge. It comprised nearly sixty thousand volumes and, though it ranged over a wide field, it reflected Acton's predominant interest in ecclesiastical and political history. It was especially rich in French local history and in the history of the Italian and Spanish churches and of the Society of Jesus. Sir Charles Oman went to see it at Aldenham after Acton's death and before its removal to Cambridge.

There were shelves on shelves of books on every conceivable subject—Renaissance Sorcery, the Fueros of Aragon, Scholastic Philosophy, the Growth of the French Navy, American Exploration, Church Councils. The owner had read them all, and many of them were full in their margins with cross-references in pencil. There were pigeonholed desks and cabinets with thousands of compartments, into each of which were sorted little white slips with references to some particular topic, so drawn up (so far as I could see) that no one but the compiler could easily make out the drift of the section. I turned over one or two from curiosity—one was on early instances of a sympathetic feeling for animals, from Ulysses' old dog in Homer downward . . . Arranged in the middle of the long two-storied room was a sort of block or altar composed entirely of unopened parcels of new books from continental publishers. All had arrived since Lord Acton's health began to break up. These volumes were apparently coming in at the rate of ten or so per week, and the purchaser had evidently intended to keep pace with the accumulation, to read them all and to work their results into his vast thesis—whatever it was. For years he had been endeavouring to keep up with everything that was being written. Over all there were brown holland sheets, a thin coating of dust, the moths dancing in the pale September sun. There was a faint aroma of mustiness, proceeding from thousands of seventeenth and eighteenth-century books in a room that had been locked up since the owner's death.[15]

Acton's devoted erudition was manifest. But if he was a historian he was also a moralist; and history must serve morality. In his inaugural lecture at Cambridge he rehearsed his creed and summoned his audience to accept it. "I exhort you never to debase the moral currency, but to try others by the final maxim that governs your own lives and to suffer no man and no cause to escape the undying penalty which history has the power to inflict on wrong." Justice was scarcely to be tempered by mercy. "There is a popular saying of Madame de Staël that we forgive whatever we really understand. The paradox has been judiciously pruned by her descendant, the Duc de Broglie, in the words: 'Beware of too much explaining lest we end by too much excusing.'" By this severe standard he judged even the work of those whom he admired. Mandell Creighton, while engaged on the third and fourth volumes of the *History of the Papacy,* wrote to a friend that he was "busy with the Borgias; and it is like spending one's day in a low police court. But I don't want to show how the Popes lived in Rome, but how they affected Europe . . . The good are not so good as they think themselves: the bad are not so bad as the good think them." When the volumes were published, Acton reproved Creighton for palliating the degradation of the Papacy in the thirteenth and fourteenth centuries. "I cannot accept your canon that we are to judge Pope and King unlike other men, with a favoured presumption that they did no wrong. If there is any presumption, it is the other way—against holders of power, increasing as the power increases. Historic responsibility has to make up for the want of legal responsibility . . . The inflexible integrity of the moral code is to me the secret of the authority, the dignity, the utility of history." Creighton was not convinced that it was the province of the historian to scourge the bad and to applaud the good, if indeed the good could be found. "When you begin to draw definite lessons from history, you cease to be a searcher after truth, because you have a bias which tends to take you to one side or another." Sidgwick may be allowed the last word. "I am inclined to say that it is not the historian's business to be either judge or advocate, but to give the reader such means of judging as his superior knowledge enables him to give."[16]

At first Maitland hardly knew what to make of Acton. Both were members of the History Board, immersed in a chaos of conflicting proposals. "At present," he wrote to Fisher, "Acton = 0. I wish he would bless or curse or do something." But he soon found the man behind the historian. Acton held his learning in trust for all scholars. He had accepted a Professorial Fellowship at Trinity and had rooms in Nevile's Court. "There he was to be found at all hours, accessible to any Cambridge historian from Maitland or Cunningham to the humblest undergraduate, ready to help anyone from the profound stores of his knowledge. He sat at his desk, hidden away behind a labyrinth of tall shelves which he had put up to hold his books, each volume with slips of paper sticking out from its pages to mark passages of importance."[17]

In 1896 the Syndics of the Cambridge University Press proposed to Acton that he should undertake the general direction of a history of the world. Maitland, himself one of the Syndics, thought the project chimerical and persuaded his colleagues to substitute a history of Europe from the Renaissance. Acton accepted the new proposal: "such an opportunity of promoting his own ideas for the treatment of history has seldom been given to any man."[18] Through the autumn of 1896 Acton and Maitland exchanged views on possible contributors.[19] On Acton's tentative list Maitland had reservations. There were too many professors and too few men of promise, too many "eminent outsiders" and too few "historians of pure water." But he welcomed the inclusion of a chapter on the growth of polite literature and urged the claims of Verrall. "He is not a professed student of history but knows a very great deal of England in cent. xviii, has a marvellous power of learning new things and is to my mind the brightest pen that you will find here. If anything is to be done for 'pretty letters', English or French, I believe that he could do it well." Acton asked Maitland to write for the second volume of the History a chapter on "The Anglican Settlement and the Scottish Reformation." Maitland was astonished. As his work on the canon law had shown, he did not wish a historian to be either judge or advocate. But if his approach to the Anglican Settlement would be without prejudice, it would also be without knowledge. On November 20, 1896, he wrote to Acton.[20] "I can not at once bring myself to refuse your offer, the honour and pleasure of working under you and of having my exercises corrected by you would be so very great. But, though you may guess a good deal, you cannot know the depth of my ignorance. I have hardly so much as heard that there was a Queen Elizabeth. Until I was thirty years old and upwards I rarely looked at a history—except histories of philosophy, which don't count—

and since then I have only 'mugged up', as the undergraduates say, one subject after another which happened to interest me. Perhaps in the course of four years I could learn something about Elizabeth and her church, but I am very sure that it would cost you less time and trouble to write the chapter yourself than to teach me how to write it. However, let me play with this dream for a little. Possibly when the Easter vacation is at hand you will devote an hour or two to telling me what I must read."

The offer was allowed to remain open for twelve months, and in November 1897 Maitland accepted it. Once he had made his decision, he allowed no misgiving to hold him back. Acton lent him books which he read greedily. "That is the worst of it: I can't deny that I am greatly interested." He was on the scent of Vatican manuscripts and of "some Documentos ineditos—for in the vacation I ought to wrestle with Spanish." For the next nine months he worked doggedly at his task, and in October 1898 he left on his first voyage to Grand Canary. On November 4 he wrote to Acton from Las Palmas. "My departure from England was hastened by a difficulty with a steam-ship company; but before I left I deposited the 'Anglican Settlement' at the Press so that you can obtain it if you wish to see it. If all goes well I ought to be fit for work at Easter time and be able to revise and verify the chapter if you will then prevent me from wasting time on stuff that will not be wanted: but I shall not have very much time to spare." In the summer of 1899 he revised the chapter and, before he left England again in November, put the new version into Acton's hands. "I never was more relieved than when I got rid of it," he told Jackson. "His Lordship's lordship was considerate to an invalid and only excepted to a few new words that I had made, but I dare say he swore—if he ever swears—in private." He added some general comments on the whole venture. "It will be a very strange book, that History of ours. I am extremely curious to see whether Acton will be able to maintain a decent amount of harmony among the chapters. Some chapters that I saw did not look much like parts of one and the same book."[21]

In the spring of 1901 Acton had a stroke. On June 19, 1902, he died. During his few years at Cambridge Maitland's initial neutrality had changed to admiration. "My own very strong opinion," he told Poole, "is that [Acton] did more than any one else could have done to elevate the study of history here towards the position that it has at Oxford. If we had had him ten years earlier we might by this time be within a measurable distance of you . . . For myself I learnt to admire A. enormously—and on his merits, for I was not by any means prejudiced in his favour."[22] The obituary which Maitland wrote for *The Cambridge Review* repays ample quotation both for the impression made by one great man upon another and as an example of sustained literary power. Maitland first set himself to meet the obvious criticism that though Acton was a man of prodigious learning, he did little with it. "That daily consumption of a German octavo—did it benefit him and the world, or was it only a stupendous feat of intellectual voracity?"[23]

> No one who heard him talk or read what he wrote or borrowed a book from the most generous of book-lenders would for one moment think of him as reading idly, for amusement, for distraction, to pass the time. It was serious work, the reading of history—calling not only for a chair but for a table, pencil, pen and abundant slips of paper. The day's book was mastered. If it was of any value, certain facts had been ascertained from it, and they had been correlated with countless other facts. And the author had been judged: not vaguely consigned to a class, but judged in a reasoned judgment: often condemned. You had but to ask and you might hear the sentence, plain, decided, not what you had expected, for, though there was reticence, though there was irony, a plain question about book or man brought a plain answer and an unconventional. Once it happened that a solemn filler of many volumes, a German too and an historian, whom I supposed to be highly respected, was dismissed with "mountainous jackass" . . .

> . . . No, if the reading had been idler, less purposeful, more might have been written and published. "Everybody has felt . . . that he knew too much to write." These are words that he applied to Döllinger, his friend and master, and in some sort they were true of himself. But the obstacle did not consist merely in the enormous weight of the mass that was to be moved. Huge it was, but in his hands not unwieldy. There was also an acute, an almost overwhelming sense of the gravity, the sanctity of history . . .
>
> It may seem to some a plain untruth that he was more deeply interested in certain great problems of a philosophical kind than in any concrete presentment of particular facts. They may well have thought of him as the man who with wonderful exactitude knew and enjoyed all the bye-play in the great drama:—at home, no doubt, upon the front-stairs, but supreme upon the back-stairs, and (as he once said) getting his meals in the kitchen; acquainted with the use of cupboards and with the skeletons that lie therein; especially familiar with the laundry where the dirty linen is washed; an analyst of all the various soaps that have been employed for that purpose in all ages and all climes. Disclaiming all esoteric knowledge and reading only what all may read, I cannot think of him thus . . . For him, so it seems to me, nothing was too small because nothing was too large. The whole lay in every part and particle: there and there only to be discovered, there and there only to be judged . . . When all has been collected that can be collected and all has been told that ought to be told, it will be clear to the world that the acquisition of knowledge was for Lord Acton not end but means.

Maitland then turned to the *Cambridge Modern History,* the enterprise so eminently fit for Acton's mind and resources and so ironically belated.

> At last came the great opportunity: at last and too late. We saw with wonder how eagerly it was seized and how a project that might have been pedestrian took horse, took

wings and soared. All modern history—the scheme was large enough. Twelve stout volumes—there would be room for minutely truthful work. Stored knowledge, big thoughts, an acknowledged primacy, polyglot correspondence, ramifying friendships, the tact of a diplomatist, the ardour of a scholar—all were to be subservient in a noble cause, to the greater glory of truth and right: to the greater glory, be it added, of a Cambridge that he had learned to love. It was Napoleonic. I know no other word, and yet it is not adequate. I felt as if I had been permitted to look over the shoulder of a general who was planning a campaign that was to last for five centuries and extend throughout the civilised world. No doubt there was some over-estimate of health and endurance and mere physical force, some forgetfulness of the weight of accumulating years. We feared it then: we know it now. But of such mistakes, if mistakes they be, the brave will be guilty. And about mental power there was no mistake. With whatever doubts I had gone to his rooms, I came away saying to myself that if contributors failed, if the worst came to the worst, or perhaps the best to the best, Lord Acton could write the twelve volumes from beginning to end, and (as the phrase goes) never turn a hair. But it was too late: too late by ten or fifteen years.

On October 25, 1902, Arthur James Balfour, as Prime Minister, wrote to Maitland and offered him the chair of Regius Professor at Cambridge. Maitland was surprised but had no doubt of the answer. He replied on the following day. "I must not trifle with the temptation that you have very kindly placed in my way. There are many reasons, all of them sufficient, which would deter me from endeavouring to fill the vacant chair of history: but I will trouble you with only one. For some time past I have been compelled to do very little work and to absent myself from England for some months every winter. Twice I have offered to resign the professorship that I hold, and I have only been able to retain it because the University has gone to great lengths in the way of exceptional indulgence. I must not even think of burdening our rising school of history with an invalid professor, and the very little that I can do to further its interests can best be done from without. I will ask you to regard this letter as final and at the same time to accept my hearty thanks for the great honour that you have done me and my yet heartier thanks for encouraging words that I shall not forget."[24]

Acton's illness and death delayed until 1903 publication of the volume of the *Cambridge Modern History* to which Maitland's contribution belonged. In the intervening years he had written a number of papers and delivered a lecture which may be described as offshoots of his chapter and considered with it as parts of a whole. The period allotted to him by Acton was only from 1558 to 1563; but if it was short it was critical. After the religious turmoil of a quarter of a century a settlement had to be sought which should be more than an armistice. The Anglican Church must comprehend as many Protestants as possible and its relations with the Queen established. Maitland had to walk delicately between conjecture and conflict, policy and prejudice, to draw inferences from scanty or conflicting evidence, and to tell a story whose conclusion, since it was a compromise, would satisfy no enthusiast.

The tortuous tactics of the Queen, her Parliaments, and her Bishops culminated in the Act of Supremacy, the Act of Uniformity, and the Thirty-nine Articles. When Elizabeth came to the throne the statutory religion was the Roman Catholic and she would have made a false move had she sought, on her own initiative, to annul or ignore it. She knew what she wanted and how she might hope to prevail. Her first Parliament met on January 25, 1559, and she set the stage for its performance. "A mass was said at Westminster early in the morning. At a later hour the Queen approached the Abbey with her choir singing in English. The last of the abbots came to meet her with monks and candles. 'Away with those torches', she exclaimed: 'we can see well enough.'"[25] The question of ecclesiastical supremacy, if not handled with discretion, might rend the English Church asunder. Three attempts were made to solve it. A first Bill was introduced into the House of Commons on February 9 and withdrawn or abandoned within a fortnight.

A second Bill was read for the first time on February 21 and seems to have passed through all its stages by March 22. *La Reine s'avisera.* The third Bill was introduced on April 10 and on April 29 received the royal assent. The heart of the problem was the title of the Queen. Should she be pronounced Supreme Head of the Church of England? Maitland had little doubt that these words appeared in the second Bill. But to insist upon them was to invite dissent; and Elizabeth decided not to covet a title which her father had assumed. She would not be Supreme Head of the Church; she would be "the only Supreme Governor of the realm as well in all spiritual or ecclesiastical things or causes as in temporal." The distinction was nice but sufficient. "Catholics suspected that Elizabeth's husband would be head of the Church if not head of his wife . . . Protestant lawyers said that she could take the title whenever she pleased. Sensible men saw that, having the substance, she could afford to waive the irritating name."[26]

Whereas the Act of Supremacy had involved anxious diplomacy, the Act of Uniformity was passed with surprising ease. Maitland summarized its results as they appeared to the men of 1559. "A radical change in doctrine, worship and discipline has been made by Queen and parliament against the will of prelates and ecclesiastical councils. The legislative power of the convocations is once more subjected to royal control. The derivation of episcopal from royal jurisdiction has been once more asserted in the words of Henry VIII. Appeal from the courts of the Church lies to royal delegates who may be lay men . . . There is no 'liberty of cult'. The Prayer Book prescribes the only lawful form of common worship . . . It is not such as will satisfy all ardent reformers; but their foreign fathers in the faith think it not intolerable, and the glad news goes out that the Mass is abolished. The word 'Protestant', which is rapidly spreading from Germany, comes as a welcome name. In the view of an officially inspired apologist of the Elizabethan settlement those who are not Papists are Protestants."[27]

In 1563 a convocation of the province of Canterbury completed the outline of the Anglican Settlement. "A delicate task lay before the theologians: no other than that of producing a confession of faith." Archbishop Parker persuaded them to accept a revised version of the forty-two Articles of Religion for which Cranmer had been responsible under Edward VI; and by a further adjustment these became the Thirty-nine Articles. "A dangerous point had been passed. Just at the moment when the Roman Church was demonstrating on a grand scale its power of defining dogma, its adversaries were becoming always less hopeful of Protestant unanimity. In particular, as Elizabeth was often hearing from Germany, the dispute about the Lord's Supper was not to be composed, and a quarrel among divines was rapidly becoming a cause of quarrel among princes . . . As causes of political union and discord, all other questions of theology were at this moment of comparatively small importance; the line which would divide the major part of the Protestant world into two camps, to be known as Lutheran and Calvinist, was being drawn by theories of the Holy Supper." Elizabeth would have preferred silence. If words must be used an elastic formula should be devised; and, put upon their mettle, "the English divines framed an Article which, as long experience has shown, can be signed by men who hold different opinions."[28]

The scope of the chapter prescribed by Acton required Maitland to deal not only with England but with Scotland. He showed a happy skill in weaving the threads of English and Scottish history—each with its special problems but both moving to a common end. He began boldly by focusing attention upon the state of Scotland. In 1560 a new Pope, Pius IV, set himself to stem the tide of heresy. "Suddenly all farsighted eyes had turned to a backward country. Eyes at Rome and eyes at Geneva were fixed on Scotland, and, the further they could peer into the future, the more eager must have been their gaze. And still we look intently at that wonderful scene, the Scotland of Mary Stewart and John Knox: not merely because it is such glorious tragedy, but also because it is such modern history. The fate of the Protestant Reformation was being decided, and the creed of unborn millions in undiscovered lands was being determined. This we see—all too plainly perhaps—if we read the books that year by year men still are writing of Queen Mary and her surroundings. The patient analysis of those love letters in the casket may yet be perturbed by thoughts about religion. Nor is the religious the only interest. A new nation, a British nation, was in the making."[29]

Scotland was racked by civil war, and a war that involved both England and France. Mary of Guise, the Regent of Scotland, was supported by French troops; and her opponents, the preachers and the Protestant nobles who called themselves "The Congregation," looked for help to Elizabeth. After anxious irresolution she was persuaded by Cecil to intervene. In January 1560 an English fleet sailed into the Firth of Forth and in March an English army crossed the border. Events played into Elizabeth's hands. The Regent died, and the French in the fortified town of Leith, though they repelled assault, could be reduced by hunger. Cecil wrung from them the Treaty of Edinburgh. They were to evacuate the country and the Scots were to be left to their own ploys. "And so the French troops departed from Scotland and the English army came home. The military display, it is true, had not been creditable; there had been disunion, if no worse, among the captains; there had been peculation, desertion, sheer cowardice. All the martial glory goes to the brave besieged. But for the first time an English army marched out of Scotland leaving gratitude behind. Perhaps the truest victory that England had won was won over herself. Not a word had been publicly said of that old suzerainty; no spoil had been taken, not a town detained. Knox included in his liturgy a prayer that there might never more be war between Scotland and England, and that prayer has been fulfilled. There have been wars between British factions, but never another truly national war between the two nations."[30] Here, as elsewhere in the chapter, Maitland used the presence and power of John Knox to bind the fortunes of the two countries. Elizabeth and Knox understood each other, and Maitland appreciated both. "Elizabeth, the deliverer of Scotland, had built an external buttress for her English Church. If now and then Knox 'gave her cross and candles a wipe', he none the less prayed for her and everlasting friendship. They did not love each other; but she had saved his Scottish Reformation, and he had saved her Anglican Settlement."[31]

Maitland's study of the Scottish Reformation has been generally accepted. Reaction to the Anglican Settlement has been less favorable. Maitland sensed, through all Elizabeth's tactics, the urge of religion. "It is not unlikely that at the critical time her conduct was swayed rather by her religious beliefs or disbeliefs than by any close calculation of loss and gain. She had not her father's taste for theology; she was neither prig like her brother nor zealot like her sister; but she had been taught from the first to contemn the pope, and during Edward's reign she had been highly educated in the newest doctrines."[32] A. L. Smith in his two lectures on Maitland supported this view. But the weight of modern opinion is against it. To unravel the skein of diplomacy and above all at the convergence of church and state, to detect and to weigh motives—these are tasks where men may guess but cannot hope to be sure. "It is common learning," said Chief Justice Brian in 1478, "that the intent of a man cannot be tried, for the Devil himself knows not the intent of a man." The historian is no better equipped. But it seems more consonant with Elizabeth's temperament to doubt rather than to accept Maitland's conclusion.[33]

A second criticism is literary. Acton had wished that, when his contributors delivered judgment, nothing in their manner should reveal their identity. "Nobody must be able to tell, without examining the list of authors, where Bishop Stubbs laid down the pen and whether it was Fairbairn or Gasquet, Liebermann or Frederic Harrison, who took it up. Our account of Waterloo, for example, must be one that satisfies French and English, German and Dutch readers alike." The aim was questionable and unrealistic. Maitland at least could not quench his personality. "No one," said A. L. Smith, "could open the chapter at random and read three consecutive sentences without saying 'aut Maitland aut diabolus'. By accident I did so open it at a part I thought was by another writer and found myself wondering who is this on whom Elijah's mantle has fallen? A delightful sort of light touch which is never levity is always his; a sort of ripple on the surface which is not laughter nor jocosity, but a peculiar brightness and gaiety." But even so ardent a reader had to admit the spots on the sun. In the manuscript submitted to him Acton had regretted Maitland's experiments in word-making; if some were deleted, others survived. Maitland described the first draft of the Act of Supremacy as "a bill which went the full Henrician length in its Caesaro-Papalism." Faced, as in his introduction to Gierke, with the choice of Jargon or Verbosity, he chose Jargon.[34]

More serious is the charge of recondite allusion. Miss Cam, when she included the chapter in her *Selected Historical Essays,* felt bound to add a note of interpretation. "It was of importance to Elizabeth," Maitland wrote, "that she should assure the German princes that her religion was Augustan." "Augustan," Miss Cam explained, "means in accordance with the Confession of Augsburg." "The Leipzig *Interim,* the work of the Elector Maurice, had given rise to a quarrel among the Lutherans, between Flacians on the one side and Philipians on the other." Flacians and Philipians were the followers respectively "of Flaccus Illyricus and Philip Melancthon." The chapter, indeed, is a rich incitement to research. When Maitland was describing Elizabeth's attempt to appease all parties, he recalled her distaste for a married clergy. Misogyny, thus qualified, impressed the Catholics. "It encouraged the hope that she might repent, and for some time Rome was unwilling to quench this plausibly smoking flax. But her part was difficult. The Puritans could complain that they were worse treated than Spanish, French and Dutch refugees, whose presence in England she liberally encouraged. Casiodoro de Reyna, Nicolas des Gallars and Utenhove, though the Bishop of London was their 'superintendent', were allowed a liberty that was denied to Humphry and Sampson; there was one welcome for Mrs. Matthew Parker and another for Madame la Cardinale."[35] What would Macaulay's schoolboy have made of these last two sentences? In the amplitude of his *History of English Law* Maitland could embroider his themes and yet keep a firm grip of perspective. In the *Cambridge Modern History* he was cramped for space and fettered by Acton's prohibition of footnotes. He felt that he must make his effect by signs and tokens, by words to the wise, even perhaps by innuendo.

In 1900 Maitland wrote for the *English Historical Review* four "Elizabethan Gleanings" and in 1903 added a fifth. But for Acton's injunction, most of their material would have appeared as notes or appendices to the chapter. Upon the first "Gleaning" a little may be said. It was published in January 1900 under the title "Defender of the Faith, and So Forth." "For nearly 250 years the solemn style and title of the king or queen of this country ended with the words 'and so forth', or in Latin *et caetera*. On the first day of the nineteenth century a change was made. Queen Victoria's grandfather became king of a 'United Kingdom' of Great Britain and Ireland. He ceased to be king of France. He also ceased to be 'and so forth'. Had this phrase always been meaningless? I venture to suggest that it had its origin in a happy thought, a stroke of genius." Elizabeth, Maitland thought, was the first sovereign of this country "to be solemnly etceterated." He recalled the moment when she was doubting whether to invite or reject the name of Supreme Head of the Church. "A happy thought occurs. Let Her Highness etceterate herself. This will leave her hands free, and afwards she can explain the etceteration as occasion shall require." The device would meet most emergencies. "Suppose that sooner or later she must submit to the Pope. She can still say that she has done no wrong. She can plead that, at least in some of his documents, King Philip, the Catholic King, etceterates himself. There are always, so it might be said, some odds and ends that might conveniently be packed up in 'and so forth'. What of the Channel Islands, for example? They are not parts of England and they are hardly parts of France." If, on the other hand, she follows in her father's footsteps, the *et caetera* will signify that portion of his title which, for the sake of brevity, was not written in full. Suppose, again, that the estates of the realm made too great a virtue of Erastianism. She can assert that her ecclesiastical supremacy is independent of legislation and is not to be controlled by Parliament. "Therefore let her be 'Defender of the Faith, and so forth'. He who knows what faith is 'the' faith will be able to make a good guess at the import of 'and so forth'." The argument was attractive; but the premise upon which it rested was false. Mary Tudor had employed the same *et caetera* in the first two years of her reign. Elizabeth, while she made good use of the words, conformed to precedent.[36]

As in his studies of the canon law, so with his inquiries into Elizabethan policy, Maitland knew that he must anger partisans who ransacked the past to serve a present cause. While he was still at work on the Anglican Settlement, he wrote to Sidgwick: "I shall have to say something about many controversial points, and (as footnotes are not allowable) I may afterwards be compelled to defend what I have said with chapter and verse. This prospect is not pleasant, for I was hoping to pass the evening of my days in the medieval towns which are fairly peaceful places: at least they are undisturbed by the *odium theologicum*." In October 1899 Malcolm MacColl, Canon of Ripon, of whom his biographer said that "few political or ecclesiastical controversies escaped his pen," published an article in the *Fortnightly Review*. He asserted that the Prayer Book authorized by Parliament in 1559 had been sanctioned at the same time by Convocation. This fable Maitland at once exposed.[37]

It was generally known that "just at the critical time a mysterious silence falls upon the official journal of the House of Lords." Canon MacColl set himself to fill the void. "Something evidently took place," he wrote, "which has escaped the scrutiny of our historians." That something must have been a Convocation. He offered in evidence a portion of a document "discovered" by a Mr. Joyce "in the State Paper Office." The canon had read this extract but not the rest of the document. Maitland printed the whole; and it was at once apparent that it was valueless—at worst a lie, at best an idle guess. Even a canon may err. But he could have avoided this particular error by examining the relevant and accessible originals: the document itself, the journals of parliament, and the Act of Uniformity. Maitland warned him "and other honest controversialists" to beware of such evidence. "The argument from smoke to fire is a favourite with some minds, and, needless to say, it is sometimes legitimate . . . But Anglicans will run a needless danger if they argue that the paper at the Record Office, though not exactly truthful, must enshrine some core of truth. After all—or perhaps before all—men do endeavour to write history out of their own heads. Here, for example, is Mr. MacColl sending into a world in which Jesuits and Erastians live an argument which supposes that the Marian bishops sat and voted in the House of Lords after the Marian Acts had been repealed. We do not say that 'there must be some truth in this'. We say that the Canon's arm-chair was comfortable and that the statute book and the journals of parliament stood just beyond his reach . . . I would respectfully submit to him that evolving history from half a document when you know that the whole is close at hand and that you and others have a right to see it, is to expose yourself, your cause, your party to needless jeopardy. The party to which Canon MacColl belongs has been learned."

In the spring of 1901 Maitland accepted an invitation to give the Rede Lecture for that year. The lectureship had been founded at Cambridge by Sir Robert Rede, Chief Justice of the Common Pleas, who died in 1519, and it had been reorganized in 1858 "so that one lecture should be delivered annually by a man of eminence in science or literature." Like lesser men Maitland could regret an acceptance as soon as he had given it. "I have been idiot enough to take in hand the Rede lecture and know not what on earth to say."[38] If he had to linger in the Tudor Age, he would at least avoid religious asperities. Rede, after all, had been a judge; and if law has its own quarrels, they are prettier than the offspring of theology. In the closing pages of his *History of English Law* Maitland had suggested that the Common Law of the sixteenth century was in danger of foundering under the pressure of Roman Law, and he had repeated the suggestion in his article for the *Encyclopaedia Britannica.* The role of Justinian would have suited Henry VIII.[39] He decided to present his case under the title "English Law and the Renaissance."

Maitland invoked the shade of the Founder, gratified and puzzled, as he meditated on the passage of time. He had words to put in Rede's mouth. "Yes, it is marvellous and more than marvellous this triumph of the sciences that my modest rent-charge stimulates you annually to record; nor do I wonder less at what my lecturers have said of humane letters and the fine arts, of the history of all times and of my time, of Erasmus whom I remember and that age of the Renaissance (as you call it) in which (so you say) I lived. But there is one matter, one science (for such we accounted it) of which they seem to have said little or nothing; and it happens to be a matter, a science in which I used to take some interest and which I endeavoured to teach. You have not, I hope, forgotten that I was not only an English judge, but, what is more, a reader in English law."[40] Rede's death coincided with the reawakening throughout Europe of an interest in Roman Law. There was to be no "Reception" in England. But "a well-equipped lecturer might persuade a leisurely audience to perceive that in the second quarter of the sixteenth century the continuity of English legal history was seriously threatened." Such a lecturer would have more than one argument to offer. The common law was couched partly in bad Latin and partly in worse French, and it was easy for humanists to call it barbarous. Its courts were threatened by the new tribunals: the Council, the Star Chamber, the Court of Requests. "Might they not do the romanizing work that was done in Germany by the Imperial Chamber Court, the *Reichskammergericht*?" They were starving the common law of its suitors. In 1547, just after King Henry's death, "divers students of the common laws" complained to the Lord Protector of the encroachments of the civilians; and ten years later, according to Stow in his *Chronicles,* the judges in Westminster Hall had nothing to do but "to look about them."[41] In 1535 the Year Books came to an end. "The exact significance of this ominous event has never yet been duly explored; but ominous it surely is."

To these threats, direct or invidious, there was one force, one conservative principle, which could be opposed. In the rest of Europe there was little teaching of any law that was not Roman, "imperially or papally Roman." But medieval England had schools of national law. These she owed to the Inns of

Court which had evolved a scheme of legal education of the character dear to the middle ages—"oral and disputatious."

> For good and ill that was a big achievement: a big achievement in the history of some undiscovered continents. We may well doubt whether aught else could have saved English law in the age of the Renaissance. What is distinctive of medieval England is not parliament, for we may everywhere see assemblies of Estates, nor trial by jury, for this was but slowly suppressed in France. But the Inns of Court and the Year Books that were read therein, we shall hardly find their like elsewhere. At all events let us notice that where Littleton and Fortescue lectured, there Robert Rede lectures, Thomas More lectures, Edward Coke lectures, Francis Bacon lectures; and highly technical were the lectures that Francis Bacon gave. Now it would, so I think, be difficult to conceive any scheme better suited to harden and toughen a traditional body of law than one which, while books were still uncommon, compelled every lawyer to take part in legal education and every distinguished lawyer to read public lectures. That was what I meant when I made bold to say that Robert Rede was not only an English judge but, what is more, a reader in English law."[42]

"Law schools make tough law"; and the Inns of Court made the common law tough enough to survive the crucial years of the mid-sixteenth century. Once the crisis was passed, the formidable figure of Coke dominated the scene. "With an enthusiastic love of English tradition, for the sake of which many offences may be forgiven him, he ranged over nearly the whole field of law, commenting, reporting, arguing, deciding,—disorderly, pedantic, masterful, an incarnate national dogmatism tenacious of continuous life."[43] The most ardent Romanist would shrink from his embrace.

Maitland showed a sense of the occasion which his inaugural lecture, thirteen years before, had wanted. He insinuated his arguments with the deprecating air of counsel briefed to present an unfamiliar case. He charmed an academic audience with courtly references to two historians who had just died: Creighton, who had himself given a Rede Lecture on "The Early Renaissance in England," and Stubbs, whose great work ended just before the crisis developed. "I spoke warmly of W.S.," he told Poole, "and was rewarded by what French reporters call a movement of adhesion. I heard a purr from the Master of Trinity."[44] In the summer of 1901 the lecture was published, with a dedication to Thayer and adorned with notes to rebuke the naked text of the *Cambridge Modern History.* It has given general delight and provoked general dissent. "It is doubtful whether any legal historian familiar with the period would today accept its thesis."[45] Maitland exaggerated both the decline of the common law courts under the Tudors and the practical influence of the civil law in England. The disappearance of the Year Books was not in itself of great significance: the reports which immediately took their place resembled them closely. To Maitland's question whether the Prerogative Courts might not do the romanizing work done in Germany by the *Reichskammergericht* Bell pertinently replied that "they might have done but in practice they did not." Maitland would not have been distressed by this reaction and still less have resented it. He had raised an issue which demanded attention; and its importance was attested by the research incited, not least among the members of the Selden Society.

The lecture, indeed, is alive with personality, and the rejection of its thesis seems scarcely to lessen its appeal. But, as in the "Anglican Settlement" where, despite the learning so implacably pursued and so gallantly worn, there is an underlying sense of strain, so in the Rede Lecture, for all its abiding charm, the evidence is too brittle for the argument. Maitland was at home in the Middle Ages. There, when his imagination had been kindled by a theme in tune with his genius, he threw upon its development the full force of his mind. Success waited upon this necessity. In Tudor England, if not an intruder, he was no more than a guest. He did not move in it and live the life of its people, sharing their hopes and fears, their assumptions and preoccupations, as he did with Glanville and Bracton and the dramatis personae of the Year Books. In his own words, he liked most centuries better than the sixteenth.[46]

In these forays into an unsympathetic age Maitland was a historian who used the tools of a lawyer. But during these years he was also probing a concept or contrivance of the law. The exigencies of life demanded the recognition of groups not only as social and economic but as legal phenomena. Around them accumulated a mass of professional folklore. To assist or obscure analysis sixteen theories, of varying degrees of credibility, are said to have disfigured the pages of jurisprudence. Into this exhibition of morbid anatomy it will be necessary to peer only so far as it concerned Maitland.[47]

He had often felt the urge to explore the problem of legal personality. In 1890, when he warned Pollock of the depths he was plumbing in the *History of English Law,* he said that "for six weeks past I have had 'juristic persons' on my mind, have been grubbing for the English evidence and reading the Germans."[48] To the story of township and borough, which he chose for the Ford Lectures, an examination of these pervasive but contentious creatures was certainly relevant; but he declined the opportunity. "From a discourse on personality, the personality of the corporation aggregate, I shrink. Ought we to apply to it such adjectives as 'ideal', 'moral', 'mystical', 'juristic', 'fictitious', 'artificial'? Is it not, on the other hand, as real as the personality of a man? Foreign lawyers, Romanists and Germanists, are disputing strenuously. A great deal of what they are saying is interesting to students of English history, though it is sometimes couched in terms which are more abstract than we like. Just because our own legal history has been continuous, just because there has been no violent breach between 'folk-law and jurist-law', we have never been driven very far into what many of us would contemptuously call legal metaphysics, and I am not going to make the plunge."[49] In the winter of 1899 to 1900 the translation of Gierke and its accompanying introduction forced him to face the problem, and he pursued it further in four papers published between 1900 and 1904: "The Corporation Sole" in 1900, "The Crown as Corporation" in 1901, "Trust and Corporation" and "Moral Personality and Legal Personality" in 1904.[50]

"Group units" in one form or another had long been familiar phenomena in England and in other European countries. But it was in nineteenth-century Germany that they submitted to juristic analysis. Savigny began with an assumption. "All law exists for the sake of the moral freedom indwelling in every man. The original idea of a person, as the subject of a right, must therefore coincide with the idea of man, and the identity of both ideas may be expressed in this formula: every individual man, and only the individual man, is judicially capable." From this assumption it followed that when society required the introduction into the human compound of associations, these, though they might be called persons, were manifest fictions. The phrase *persona ficta* was itself of respectable antiquity. It was coined by Sinibald Fieschi, who in 1243 became Pope Innocent IV and who was not the man to fear the consequences of his words. Human beings could sin and commit delict; fictions could not. He drew a further conclusion. From the nature of the case "artificial personality" could be created only by sovereign power. Thus, said Maitland, "the Fiction Theory leads us into the Concession Theory. The corporation is, and must be, the creature of the State. Into its nostrils the State must breathe the breath of a fictitious life for otherwise it would be no animated body but individualistic dust." Such subordination was palatable not only to popes but to secular princes. They could keep the corporation "safe under lock and key."[51]

The Fiction theory, especially in the hands of Savigny, was attractive. But it did not pass unchallenged. An alternative, which might be called Realism, was devised by Beseler and developed by Gierke. "The new theory was to be philosophically true, scientifically sound, morally righteous, legally implicit in codes and decisions, practically convenient, historically destined, genuinely German and perhaps exclusively Germanistic." *Das deutsche Genossenschaft*—Fellowship, as Maitland rendered it into English—was "no fiction, no symbol, no piece of the State's machinery, no collective name for individuals, but a living organism and a real person, with body and members and a will of its own."

> The Realist's cause would be described by those who are forwarding it as an endeavour to give scientific precision and legal operation to thoughts which are in all modern minds and which are always displaying themselves, especially in the political field. We might be told to read the leading article in to-day's paper and observe the ideas with which the writer "operates": the will of the nation, the mind of the legislature, the settled policy of one State, the ambitious designs of another: the praise and blame that are awarded to group-units of all sorts and kinds . . . We might be referred to modern philosophers: to the social tissue of one and the general will, which is the real will, of another. Then perhaps we might fairly be charged with entertaining a deep suspicion that all this is metaphor: apt perhaps and useful, but essentially like the personification of the ocean and the ship, the storm and the stormy petrel. But we, the Realist would say, mean business with our Group Person, and severe legal logic. We take him into the law courts and markets and say that he stands the wear and tear of forensic and commercial life.[52]

To the German mind such analysis was congenial. Two devices spared English lawyers the pains of introspection. With fictions of many shapes and sizes they were indeed familiar. But Savigny's theory offered a consequence from which they shrank; they did not wish corporations to escape the penalties of tort. The principle of vicarious liability, as it was elaborated in the nineteenth century, enabled them to prevent any such immunity. An individual person was liable for the torts committed by his servant in the course of his employment not because he shared the servant's guilt but simply because he was the master. The question was not whether the master but whether the servant had been guilty of the negligence, the intent, or the malice which might be an ingredient of the tort. The master's responsibility required no abstruse rationalization. It was based on expediency. "There should be some person capable of paying damages and who may be sued by people who are injured."[53] If the master were not a human being but a corporation, no further analysis was wanted. Lord Lindley in 1904 deplored the attempt "to introduce metaphysical subtleties which are needless and fallacious. It is difficult to see why the ordinary doctrines of agency and of master and servant are not to be applied to corporations as well as to individuals."[54]

The development of the Trust supplied a second and comprehensive means of evading "metaphysical subtleties." Maitland, in the introduction to his translation of Gierke, explained why English readers might not readily appreciate the German preoccupation with theories of corporate personality.[55]

> For the last four centuries Englishmen have been able to say "Allow us our Trusts and the law and theory of corporations may indeed be important, but it will not prevent us from forming and maintaining permanent groups of the most various kinds: groups that, behind a screen of trustees, will live happily enough . . . If Pope Innocent and Roman forces guard the front stairs, we shall walk up the back." We will mention one example. If we speak the speech of daily life, we shall say that in this country for some time past a large amount of wealth has "belonged" to religious "bodies" other than the established church, and we should have thought our religious liberty shamefully imperfect had our law prevented this arrangement. But until very lately our "corporation concept" has not stood at the disposal of Nonconformity, and even now little use is made of it in this quarter: for our "trust concept" has been so serviceable. Behind the screen of trustees and concealed from the direct scrutiny of legal theories, all manner of groups can flourish: Lincoln's Inn or Lloyd's or the Stock Exchange or the Jockey Club, a whole presbyterian system or even the Church of Rome with the Pope at its head. But, if we are to visit a land where Roman law has been "received", we must leave this great loose "trust concept" at the Custom House . . . Then we shall understand how vitally important

> to a nation—socially, politically, religiously important—its Theory of Corporations might be.

This passage aroused great interest on the Continent; and in 1903 Maitland was invited by the Vienna Faculty of Law to elaborate it for Professor Grünhut's *Zeitschrift fur das Privat- und-Öffentliche Recht.* Dr. Josef Redlich, in acknowledging Maitland's acceptance of the invitation, wrote: "There is no juristic concept of English Law so much discussed now and yet so little known on the continent as the Trust. Since newspapers are almost daily talking about the immense economic power and shortcomings of the modern American trusts, German jurists also have become eager to learn the truth about their legal structure . . . Your essay will be regarded as a real *événement* and will be most gratefully accepted as the most important contribution to that old and, for us so vital, scientific feud raging around *persona ficta* and Genossenschaft." The paper on "Trust and Corporation" was written by Maitland in English, translated by Redlich, and published in 1904.[56]

Even in England lawyers could not hope altogether to escape the toils of jurisprudence. They had, moreover, darkened counsel by the invention of a "corporation sole." Before he could venture further to analyze legal personality, Maitland felt bound to examine, and if possible to eliminate, this insular eccentricity. In the sixteenth century a legal means had been sought of making a gift to the incumbent of a church and his successors. To transform the parson into a corporation seemed to offer the solution. Once the lawyers had committed themselves to this conceit, they might surely have used it to answer a second question. The patron of the living no longer owned the fee simple of the parochial glebe: might it not be vested in this corporate person? Coke toyed with the idea, but it came to pieces in his hands. He could not think of the abstraction and forget the man; and the man would insist upon dying and leaving the freehold in abeyance. "If our corporation sole really were an artificial person created by the policy of man, we ought to marvel at its incompetence. Unless custom or statute aids it, it cannot own a chattel, not even a chattel real . . . We are also told that in all probability a corporation sole cannot enter into a contract except with statutory authority or as incidental to an interest in land. What then can this miserable being do? It cannot even hold its glebe tenaciously enough to prevent the freehold falling into abeyance whenever a parson dies."[57]

In its original context the corporation sole was thus an ineffective solecism. But it was given another chance to be troublesome. Coke thought it would be comfortable if the king were to keep the parson company. Whether the state is itself a persona is still an enigma. "But what we see in England, at least if we look only at the surface, is not that the State is personified but (I must borrow from one of Mr. Gilbert's operas) that the king is 'parsonified'. Since that feat was performed, we have been, more or less explicitly, trying to persuade ourselves that our law does not recognise the personality or corporate character of the State or Nation or Commonwealth and has no need to do anything of the sort if only it will admit that the king, or, yet worse, the Crown, is not unlike a parson."[58] The simile would have been inconceivable in the Middle Ages. "The medieval king was every inch a king, but just for this reason he was every inch a man, and you did not talk nonsense about him." Simplicity dissolved in the welter of Henry VIII's ecclesiastical maneuvres. The "body spiritual" was to be part of the "body politic," and the "body politic" must coexist with the "body natural" of the king. "In Plowden's reports we may find much curious argument about the king's two 'bodies', and I do not know where to look for so marvellous a display of metaphysical—or we might say metaphysiological—nonsense." Maitland cited a passage from a case of 1561.[59] "The king has not a body natural distinct and divided by itself from the office and dignity royal, but a body natural and a body politic together indivisible; and these two bodies are incorporated in one person and made one body and not divers, that is, the body corporate in the body natural, *et e contra* the body natural in the body corporate." "Which faith," Maitland inclined to add, "except every man keep whole and undefiled, without doubt he shall perish everlastingly."

But with king as with parson the corporation sole stubbornly refused to do any real work. It did not separate the land that the sovereign held as king from the land that he held as man, nor the money in his pocket from the money in the Exchequer. It did not fill the gap made by the death of the human being who happened to be sovereign. "When on a demise of the Crown we see all the wheels of State stopping or running backwards, it seems an idle jest to say that the king never dies." The king played so poorly the part of a corporation that lawyers had been tempted to substitute his crown. But "the Crown," save as a synonym for the king, was not a person known to English law. It "never sues, never prosecutes, never issues writs or letters patent. On the face of formal records the King or Queen does it all."

To the parson and the king Coke added the Chamberlain of the City of London; and during the reign of Victoria other corporations sole, such as the Postmaster General and the Solicitor to the Treasury, were created by statute. Even with the aid of Parliament they did not earn their keep. "We have yet to be taught that the Solicitor to the Treasury never dies. When a Postmaster-General dies, what becomes of the freehold of countless post offices? . . . A critical question would be whether the man who is Postmaster-General for the time being could be indicted for stealing the goods of the Postmaster, or whether the Solicitor to the Treasury could sue the man who happened to be the Treasury's Solicitor." The corporation sole, indeed, is not a legal *persona* at all. "It is either natural man or juristic abortion."

In 1903 Maitland was asked to give the Sidgwick Lecture. He delivered it at Newnham College in the following year under the title "Moral Personality and Legal Personality."[60] Now that he had exposed the corporation sole as an unprincipled intruder, he felt free to attack the central problem. He must cross the boundaries of ethics and of jurisprudence. "That such a borderland exists all would allow, and, as usually happens in such cases, each of the neighbouring powers is wont to assert, in practice if not in theory, its right to define the scientific frontier. We, being English, are, so I fancy, best acquainted with the claims of ethical speculation and in some sort prejudiced in their favour. We are proud of a long line of moralists . . . and we conceive that the 'jurist', if indeed such an animal exists, plays, and of right ought to play, a subordinate if not subservient part in the delimitation of whatever moral sciences there may happen to be . . . But I shall attempt to indicate one problem of a speculative sort which (so it seems to me) does not get the attention it deserves from speculative Englishmen, and does not get that attention because it is shrouded from their view by certain peculiarities of the legal system in which they live." Maitland offered two texts. The first he took from the Sidgwick Lecture given by Dicey in the previous year. "When a body of 20 or 2,000 or 200,000 men bind themselves to act in a particular way for some common purpose, they create a body which, by no fiction of law but by the very nature of things, differs from the individuals of whom it is constituted." The second was a sentence by Balfour in the House of Commons. He had described a trade union as a corporation. Sir Robert Reid—afterwards Lord Loreburn—interrupted him. "Trade unions are not corporations." "I know," said Balfour, "I am talking English, not law."

Maitland expounded the rival theories, and reminded his audience that they were essentially of German origin. English law and English history were too rich and too untidy to submit to formulas. "We are not logical enough to be elementary." Nor are we prepared to carry a process of reasoning to inconvenient conclusions. "*Quasi* is one of the few Latin words that English lawyers really love." Maitland was a professor, not a politician, and must talk law as well as English. The corporation was a distinct legal unit in which rights and duties were reposed; in the trust the rights were exercised and the duties owed by human beings. But Mr. Balfour—not indeed a simple man—had expressed the instinct of his countrymen in his reply to Sir Robert Reid. "The less we know of law, the more confidently we Englishmen expect that the organised group, whether called a corporation or not, will be treated as a person." While it should be clothed with law, it is not in essence a legal phenomenon but represents a human need or desire which demands to be satisfied; and "trust" or "corporation" are but different instruments developed to meet it. To the men and women who use these devices the one is as real or as fictitious as the other. Maitland, if he had to make his choice, would be a realist. Law and philosophy alike must find their material, raw though it may be, in the thoughts and aspirations of ordinary people. The mind of the philosopher Maitland was too modest to explore. But "for the morality of common sense the group is a person. Let the moral philosopher explain this, let him explain it as illusion . . . He will not be able to say that it is an illusion which is losing power." Upon the lawyer he could pass judgment with less fear. "If the law allows men to form permanently organised groups, those groups will be for common opinion right-and-duty-bearing units; and if the law-giver will not openly treat them as such, he will make a mess and call it law."

With this lecture Maitland ceased to pursue the elusive concept of personality. He knew that in England at least he would persuade few lawyers and fewer philosophers to join in the hunt. But, if he had not killed his quarry, he had enjoyed the chase. He had chosen his epitaph, he told Figgis: *Hic jacet persona ficta.*[61]

Chapter XI

The Selden Society and the Year Books

As Literary Director of the Selden Society Maitland advised upon the choice of subjects and of editors. The former were easier to find than the latter; and when found, editors were inevitably of unequal quality. With such a scholar as Gross in America Maitland was concerned only to give the help that distance demanded and to coax from him as many volumes as possible. Some editors had to be encouraged, or be defended against unfair or untimely criticism. Others made heavy demands both upon Maitland and upon the indefatigable Lock, who, full of zeal if not tact, had replaced so efficiently the unhappy Dove. The relations of director, secretary, and editor may be illustrated from the story of Leach and the Beverley Town Documents.[1]

Arthur Francis Leach was a Fellow of All Souls from 1874 to

1881 and then became a Charity Commissioner. In 1896 he published *English Schools at the Reformation* and at intervals during the rest of his life produced monographs on individual schools. He offered to edit for the Selden Society "The Book of the Provost of Beverley," extracts from the manor rolls compiled in the year 1416. In April 1898 Maitland saw both Leach and the book. He was not impressed. "I yesterday saw Leach and the Provost's Book," he wrote to Lock. "I can not say that I think well of the latter for our purpose. It is a collection of extracts from manorial court rolls. The entries seemed to be of the ordinary dreary kind—and I do not think that the publication of them would to any appreciable degree advance our knowledge of legal history. On the other hand, Leach had in his house what seemed to me far more hopeful, namely a lot of records of the *town* of Beverley: town by-laws, ordinances of the gild merchant, ordinances of the craft gilds, etc.—15th and 16th century work. I am inclined to think that a good volume might be made of them. We have not done much for our boroughs, and Hudson's Norwich book does not touch all sides of the legal life of towns. Leach also told me that he could get at a good book of Lincoln ordinances. He further said that he was not unwilling to make a volume out of Beverley or out of Beverley and Lincoln. What think you? Will you have a word with Leach?"[2] In July the Council of the Society adopted the proposal for a volume on the municipal records of Beverley and Lincoln. In October Maitland had to leave in haste for the Canaries. Lock took over the control of this and of the other Selden projects; and he warned Leach that Maitland's illness might disrupt the Society's plans and that the book might be wanted for early publication.

In the following months Leach toiled manfully, and in September 1899 Maitland was confronted with a plethora of material. At his suggestion Lincoln was abandoned and the book confined to Beverley. During the second winter of Maitland's exile Leach showered upon Lock text and translation, proofs and revises. The Council could be told in February 1900 that the book was "well advanced and probably ready in early summer." With the text Leach was on comfortable terms; the introduction was less tractable. Lock bombarded him with queries and exhortations. "What is the position of your Introduction? When will it be ready? . . . The time is up when your volume should be published. If you wish Maitland to see it, you should be prompt. He is back, but has been ill since his return, and his stay in England is precarious." Leach sent the early pages of the introduction to Maitland, and Maitland wrote to Lock on July 4.[3] "Have you seen the beginning of Leach's Introduction? I don't like it at all. It is all higgledy-piggledy; even the grammar is hardly respectable. I should much like to tell him that this won't do for the Selden. But it seems necessary to press on with the volume. So what to do? Do you think this stuff too bad? I don't like suffragan or other bishops, but Leach's gird at them can hardly stand." Lock wrote severely to Leach. "You have again forgotten your instructions. Your description of the documents is scattered about the slips instead of collected under appropriate headings." Leach kissed the rod. "Please sir, I have been a very naughty boy, and I will try to be good next time." On July 17 Lock sent more of the introduction to Maitland. "Leach alleges a desire for *your* criticism. Please let him have it!" Maitland groaned over the new pages. "Eugh! I should like to get the book out, but really some of it is bad . . . After reading the new slips, I incline to tell Leach that he must leave all this out. He gives the rashest judgment about the most disputable matters." He sought, with small success, to dissuade Leach from voyaging without chart or compass into seas unknown. "I am failing to persuade him not to plunge into speculations about the craft gilds of cent.xii. He is perfectly civil, nay jovial, but sweet on his own stuff and has not read enough to know how thin it is. So I suppose that I must tinker it in detail."[4]

In October 1900 Lock reported with relief that the advance copy had been received from the printers, and in November the book was published. At the end of the introduction Leach paid his tribute to Maitland. "It is almost superfluous to acknowledge the care, courtesy and learning brought to bear by Mr. F. W. Maitland in the execution of his task as general editor. Are they not known unto all men?" With irrepressible spirits he at once suggested a companion volume on Lincoln. Maitland told Lock that he had received "a portfolio of prospectuses, advertisements, etc.—you know what it is like." He was not going to be caught a second time. "I think," he assured Lock, "that Leach will construe as a 'declension' of his offer the letter that I wrote to him, though in it I said that I would mention the matter to you. If he writes again I shall say that Lincoln is not wanted."[5]

Leach was an enthusiastic amateur. Turner—"Little T."[6]—was only too devoted to learning; and his relentless pursuit of the ideal was apt to exhaust all patience but his own. The Selden Society was the residuary legatee of a record in procrastination.

From 1889 to 1891 Maitland had been preparing *The Court Baron,* the fourth volume in the Society's series. In the course of his researches he had found a tract written in French in the middle of the thirteenth century which appeared in more than one manuscript under the title of *Brevia Placitata* and which contained forms of pleading for use in the King's court. "It deserved the attention of the Selden Society."[7] After Dove's death the Council surveyed its plans for the future, and among them was an edition of this tract. Maitland and Lock reported "that Mr. George J. Turner of Lincoln's Inn is at work upon the manuscript as a private undertaking with some prospect of its being printed by the Pitt Press of Cambridge; and we believe that Mr. Turner would be willing to edit it for the Selden Society. If so, we recommend it as an appropriate volume for the year 1900." In February 1896 Maitland told Lock that he "should like to find an early place for Turner's *Brevia.* I think that he will do them well."[8]

Turner, for reasons which remain obscure, preferred to resume his original design to publish the book for the Cambridge University Press. In November 1897 seventy-two page proofs existed and thirty-four galleys. By 1904 only forty-six more galleys had appeared. From 1904 to 1929 nothing seems to have been done. In 1930 the Press delivered thirty more galleys. These Turner kept for four years while he brooded over an introduction. He had his own methods and he took his own time. "As always, he sent his first draft to be set up and then began a serious revision of the proof—even for the text he had a transcript of one manuscript set up and then collated the proof with the other manuscripts, leaving it for the printers to take the type apart again and insert the variants."[9] In January 1938 the first part of the introduction was in paged slips, though it had not been finally revised or corrected. Part II remained in the galleys into which it had been put in 1935. Soon after 1938 Turner's eyesight failed; and he died in 1946. Miss Cam, who was his literary executrix, asked Plucknett to examine a trunk full of manuscripts and proofs. These were the *Brevia Placitata.* The second part of the introduction could not at once be found, but it was ultimately unearthed at Cambridge. In 1951—fifty-six years after the Council had recommended the work—*Brevia Placitata,* fostered by Plucknett, appeared as volume 66 of the Selden Society's publications.

These vicissitudes are a *reductio ad absurdum* of Coke's aphorism that "the most learned doubteth most." But they must not be allowed to overshadow Turner's solid work for the Society. He was partly responsible for three of its volumes and wholly responsible for three others.[10] *Select Pleas of the Forest* was his first individual contribution; and its history displays the differing reactions of Lock and of Maitland to his idiosyncrasies.

In February 1897 Turner accepted the invitation to prepare this volume for publication in 1899. During the next twelve months he was at work upon it. In April 1898 it was "well advanced," and in June the first batch of copy was in the hands of the printers. The book did not, indeed, progress as quickly as Lock had hoped; but in February 1899 he reported to the Council that most of the text was in print. Turner had still to write and then, *more suo,* to rewrite the introduction. Through the summer months Lock waited impatiently for it, and on September 25 he wrote to Turner. "I have been expecting to receive the remaining proofs from you and have received nothing. I should be obliged if you would supply them promptly—and give any explanation you may have of the delay." To complaints of unpunctuality Turner was impervious; but the last words of Lock's letter stung him to an immediate reply. He disdained explanation or apology. "I shall return all the proofs in my possession and leave the Society to find another editor." Lock answered him on the same day. "You must be well aware that I have no power either to terminate your agreement with the Council of the Society or to receive your proofs or to settle what may be the consequences of your throwing up the work, if you should persist in doing so . . . It will be my duty to explain the delay to the Council and I cannot do so without your assistance, which I still invite. But if you prefer not to give any explanation, by all means abstain: only complete the work at your earliest convenience and let me know when that will be. Excuse my adding that you should not answer this in a hurry or without full consideration. You are free to talk it over with me or (I have no doubt) with Maitland." Before Maitland could mediate there was a rapprochement. Lock called upon Turner, withdrew the offending expressions in his own letter, and telegraphed Maitland to say that all had been forgiven. Maitland, relieved but not doubting where the fault lay, wrote to Lock: "I am exceedingly sorry to hear of Turner's escapade. Certainly you have no cause for self-reproach—indeed I feel that you have carried patience and T. laziness as far as they should go. However, sometimes a little storm does good, and I hope that T. will get to work after it."[11]

In the first flush of reconciliation Turner thought that he might finish the book that same winter; but by the autumn of 1900 only the first sheets of the introduction were in print. Richard W. Hale, the Society's secretary and treasurer in the United States, complained bitterly of the failure to produce the promised volume. "The American subscriber is in full revolt and threatens a Declaration of Independence." Maitland, to whom Lock turned for help, could not hasten Turner or even break his silence. "A week ago," he told Lock on October 14, "I wrote to Turner a letter that, as I thought, would draw tears from a stone. No reply." A fortnight later he had to add: "He does not answer me though I wrote what I thought to be a sympathetic letter—i.e. I asked him to come here and to let me do all I could upon the book."[12] Lock devised a new plan. He arranged to pay for a secretary, Miss Martin, to help Turner with proofs and indexes, with a private understanding that each week she would report progress. The stratagem failed. Turner disliked women who invaded the province of men. He first diverted Miss Martin to subsidiary work where she could not entangle him and then dismissed her. In February 1901 Lock, driven against his nature to entreaty, asked if there was any chance of the book's appearance before the annual meeting in March. Turner made no answer. On April 18 Lock resumed reproach. "I see that you are still engaged on the foolish and hopeless task of revising the indexes before you have finished the text." But the end was in sight. On June 16 Maitland told Lock that he could pass everything for the press. *"Explicit foresta! Deo gracias!* I am suggesting to Turner that a qualified apology for delay would look better in the Preface than a discourse about *U.* and *V.*" The last fragments reached the printers in July, and the volume was published in October. "My heart rejoiced at the sight of Turner's book," Maitland wrote. "It looks very good. I am not sure that it is not the best book that we have issued."[13]

Maitland was unremitting in his quest for recruits. A rare and great success was the capture of Mary Bateson. Born in 1865, she was the daughter of the Master of St. John's College, Cambridge; her brother was a distinguished biologist. She was a student of Newnham College and, after obtaining a first class in the historical tripos, she taught and lectured there for the rest of her life. Mandell Creighton, when Professor of Ecclesiastical History at Cambridge, encouraged her to pursue research and enlisted her as a contributor to the *English Historical Review* of which he was editor. "I should like some ladies," he told Acton.[14] Her first work was a study in monastic history for the Norfolk Archaeological Society, and in 1898 she was engaged upon the archives of the Borough of Leicester. Maitland was impressed by her gifts. "I think," he wrote to Gross, "that you will like Miss Bateson's Leicester Records."[15] In 1901 he joined her in editing the charters of the Borough of Cambridge.

Already in 1898 he had thought of her for the Selden Society.

"Are you opposed to female labour?" he asked Lock. Three years later the Council agreed to commission a volume of Municipal Charters and Customs.[16] Of this project nothing more is recorded until December 1902. Lock was then again on the track of tardy editors and wished to have a book in hand in case of need. He approached Miss Bateson, and she undertook a volume of Borough Customs. She set to work with energy. On July 12, 1903, Maitland told Lock that she could produce the book in 1904, if required, and asked if she might be allowed a second volume. "Might Miss B. have two volumes for her borough customs? She is proposing a scheme that I like very much, namely to cut the stuff up and arrange it under legal titles: e.g. take 'Descent', then put under this title all the rules about descent that you get in the various custumals. She has made out what I think a very good scheme of titles and subtitles. But this plan cannot be adopted unless she may have a second volume within a reasonable time. I am inclined to back this proposal. I doubt we shall get more interesting matter or a better editor. But what think you?"[17] Lock approved the plan. In September Miss Bateson asked for "marching orders" and was told to send the copy for the first volume to the printers. In December the proofs were being sent to Maitland in Grand Canary, and in January 1904 Lock told him that "Borough Customs were prancing along gaily." But in March this happy collaboration was disturbed. Miss Bateson was hopefully contemplating a third volume; if Maitland had not abetted he had not discouraged her. Lock, when he wrote to Maitland, fortified an expostulation with an argument calculated to drive it home. A third volume would upset the Society's budget and delay the publication of Year Books. "I think you ought to know this if you are inclined to encourage her to add text to text and introduction to introduction . . . We must get her first volume out well before the end of the year. Please do not encourage her to shift the subject-matter of Volume I. The first printed material is excellent and even fascinating."[18]

Lock had his way, and the original distribution of material between two volumes was restored. In July Maitland read in Cambridge the proofs of Miss Bateson's introduction. "I tell her," he wrote to Lock, "that her last section will not do, as it states the disadvantages but not the advantages of our 'digest' plan. For the rest I think it good. (I tell her that, if she thanks me, it must be in a simpler style). If you have any criticism, now is your time."[19] *Borough Customs (Volume I)* was published on November 12, 1904. Lock, when he received the advance copy, wrote to Miss Bateson: "Your plan of the arrangement of the text looks in every way clear and admirable, and I congratulate you on its issue within the year."

Miss Bateson turned at once to the second volume, which she promised for 1906. In October 1905 she sent the introduction to Maitland for his criticism. Maitland found it "learned and instructive but formless" and returned it to her with "snarls and comments." Miss Bateson was grateful for stricture as for praise. "The snarls are gloriously helpful to me, and I believe I understand all of them." In November she had to give two lectures on Borough Customs in Manchester and these would take her away from her manuscript. But "as the audience will not know much, this will force me out of the cover of obscurity into the dangers of clearness, and something suitable for the introduction may come out of it."[20] By the end of 1905 the text of the second volume was in print. As Maitland was abroad, Lock offered to read the draft of the introduction. On January 31, 1906, he wrote to Maitland.

> I got Miss Bateson to send it to me, and I looked through a lot and agree with you that it wants recasting. I went so far as to recast in outline one section (on Compurgation) as a specimen. I did it in fear and trembling—but she likes it, I am glad to say, and is grateful . . . My object was to show that, by method and condensation, all the substance could be compressed into two-thirds of the space. She says that she will put in a story I told her of the value of the threefold oath, but you may think it too playful. Do you remember the old Eton interrogatory to test the veracity of a boy suspected of fibbing?
>
> Q. Take your oath? A. Yes.
> Q. Take your solemn oath? A. Yes.

Q. Take your solemn, dying oath? A. Yes.
Q. Bet a penny? A. N-n-no.[21]

Thereafter all went well. In March the introduction was in the press, and the volume appeared on August 7, 1906.

After the publication of *Bracton and Azo* Maitland's own contributions to the Selden Society were confined to the Year Books. In these he had long been interested; and he told Thayer in July 1895 that he would like to see a start made upon a new edition of them.[22] Thayer was enthusiastic and at once enlisted American support. There were, indeed, difficulties to be overcome. The first was to find a modus vivendi with the Record Office which, without undue haste, was seeking to supersede the so-called standard edition of the Year Books published between 1678 and 1680. With this edition Maitland had an unpleasing acquaintance. "It has," he had written in 1889, "as many faults as an edition can well have: it teems with gross and perplexing blunders."[23] As long ago as 1800 a Select Committee had inquired into the state of the Public Records and had recommended "that the Series of the Year Books from Edward I to Henry VIII be completed by printing those hitherto unpublished . . . and by reprinting the rest from more correct copies." The recommendation was ignored until 1863 when A. J. Horwood was commissioned by Lord Romilly, then Master of the Rolls, to edit the unpublished Year Books of Edward I and to close the gap which existed in the standard edition between the tenth and seventeenth years and between the eighteenth and twenty-first years of Edward III.

After editing five volumes Horwood died and was succeeded by Luke Owen Pike, who began the practice of supplementing the report in the Year Books from the record in the plea roll. Maitland had a high opinion of Pike and did not wish to upset him. "The Year Book project grows in my mind," he wrote to Lock in November 1896.[24] "But the matter . . . is complicated by this, that after a long interval Pike is being allowed to go ahead once more with the Year Books of Edward III. I have some reason to fear that if we announced a series of YBB the

Treasury would make this an excuse for stopping Pike's work and this I should regard as a grave disaster, for he is doing it very well. I should like to frame some treaty with the Deputy Keeper, but he could not bind the Treasury and (between ourselves) I fear that there is friction between him and Pike. I do not think that if we started with Edward II we ought to be prejudicing Pike's work, for it would be long before we could touch Edward III—but people become unreasonable when they don't like each other. So I feel that we have rather a difficult course to steer." Maxwell Lyte, the Deputy Keeper, was approached with success. He did not himself want any more Year Books in the Rolls Series and would gladly leave the field to the Selden Society. If he had his way, Pike would not be required by the Record Office, and the Society might gain an admirable editor. But, after vacillation, the Treasury sanctioned the continuance of the Year Books in the Rolls Series, and Pike was occupied with this work until 1911.

On December 15, 1896, Maitland proposed to the Council of the Society to reprint from manuscripts the Year Books of the reign of Edward II. The proposal was referred to a committee of which Lord Lindley was Chairman and both Lyte and Pollock were members, and by Lindley's casting vote action upon it was deferred "for not more than a year." Maitland was depressed by this decision or lack of decision. "One more effort a year hence, and, if that fails, I shall see whether an edition can be 'made in Germany'."[25] But at the annual general meeting on March 24, 1897, Maitland's proposal was accepted with only one dissentient, a Mr. Walter Rye of Golden Square who spoke of reprinting anything at all as an obsolete way of wasting money. On July 6 the Council resolved "that the reprint of the Year Books of Edward II be commenced and continued, as far as possible, in every alternate year in substitution for the ordinary publications, and that Professor Maitland should edit the first volume and superintend the whole project."

The resolution was satisfactory. Maitland at once examined the three relevant manuscripts in the Cambridge University Library, chose one as the basic text, and arranged for it to be copied. But in the first days of 1898 there was an Oxford diversion. On January 3 Maitland wrote to Lock:[26] "I have heard some important news about the Year Books which I must communicate to you. Thayer of Harvard has just paid me a visit after visiting Markby at Oxford, and Markby had given him to understand that the Clarendon Press would still be willing, as it was willing some years ago, to undertake the printing of the YBB and to bear the charge thereof wholly or at least in part. Now this of course may be very important news. I had thought that Markby's scheme had broken down a good many years ago owing to the backwardness of the Inns of Court and that no help was to be looked for in this direction. I should like to know what you think of this matter. I should dearly like to get this help towards the printer's bill, because if we could find relief in this quarter we might be able to make an offer to Pike: if we had money he would be the man for it."[27] Five days later he wrote again.[28] He had received a letter from Markby. "He has big ideas: much too big I fear to do much good in this day of small things. I am answering him in such a way as just to keep a correspondence alive, telling him of the humility of our finances and so forth. The practical question for us will be whether there is sufficient hope in this quarter to induce us to postpone our own little project. I feel that a failure or 'qualified success' on our part at the present moment might possibly damage the chances of a greater enterprise. So will you turn this over and in course of time give counsel?" Lock went to Oxford and saw Markby and other Delegates of the Clarendon Press. The Press was prepared to consider collaboration with the Society, and Markby was going to America in search of money. In July 1898 Lock reported voluminous correspondence with the Delegates, who would not move unless the Society shared in the cost of printing as well as of editing. In December Markby returned to England, and Lock asked him if his "crusade among the American millionaires" had been victorious. Markby had to admit failure; and on February 16, 1899, the Council of the Society decided to close the negotiations with the Clarendon Press and to implement at once the original design to reprint the Year Books of Edward II.

Apart from the writing of introductions, two major tasks

were involved: the discovery, transcription, and translation of the manuscripts; and the collation of the cases reported in the Year Books with the entries on the plea rolls. It was a special attraction for Maitland that the manuscripts, their copies, or their photographs, could be taken abroad each winter. In his preface to volume 17 he thanked Cambridge University for "the inestimable privilege of pursuing my task where the sun shines upon the Fortunate Islands." Even in this paradise illness might intervene or untoward accidents befall the copy. "We have been having rain," he wrote to Leslie Stephen,[29] "and when it rains here you find that the roof of your house has been surprised by the performance. I am now engaged in drying a boxful of copied Year Books which unfortunately was left beneath a weak point in the ceiling." But he could leave England each year with reasonable hope of fruitful hours. The second task must be done in London. To find someone at once ready and competent to search the records was not easy. Baildon, who had helped him in the past, was beginning to make his way at the Bar, and had more succulent fish to fry.[30] Others were approached in vain, and Maitland decided to ask Turner. "Little T.," if he consented, would be working for and with a friend, and would not have the chance to display his infinite capacity for taking and giving pains. The choice was progressively and abundantly justified. In April 1902, after Turner had been with him in the Canaries, Maitland had "some hopes of keeping him to the task by a system of payment by results." In May he could tell Lock "that little Turner is doing well. In a fortnight he has found a very respectable number of my cases, and if he keeps going for another fortnight the bulk of the work to be done at P.R.O. will be safe in note books." In August Turner was all that could be wished. "Do you remember that obscure third case on the specimen page? Little T. has found the record—I doubt if anyone else would have found it . . . I wish Turner would allow me to put his name on the title page —I must say something very handsome of him in the Preface."[31]

In the course of 1902 a second incursion, less orthodox than the negotiations with the Clarendon Press, distracted Maitland's attention. Charles Carroll Soule of Boston had published in 1901, under the title *Year-Book Bibliography,* an admirable monograph on the black-letter editions. Soule was not only a scholar; he was president of the Boston Book Corporation and an energetic and ingenious man of business. Professor Wambaugh of Harvard, when he visited Cambridge, regaled Maitland with "an amusing scene illustrating Soule's power of forcing people to buy even the old Year Books:—an imaginary Chief Justice of West Virginia finally capitulates before the argument that the Court of Vermont has a copy." On May 13, 1902, Soule wrote to Maitland that he proposed to reprint the printed Year Books with "a scholarly translation" and that "the professors of the Harvard Law School were very eager in the matter." He set sail for England, enjoyed "a satisfactory talk with Mr. Pike," and visited Edinburgh, where he saw Green who had recently begun to publish *The English Reports.* He was next traced to Oxford where he hoped to secure the support, if not the services, of Sir William Markby. On August 10 he wrote to Maitland. All to whom he had spoken thought well of his plan. "We have come to the conclusion that an editorial corps of ten or a dozen could get out a good preliminary translation in three or four years." If the printed text were obscure, Pike would compare it with the manuscripts. Ames and other American scholars "were eager to do what they could." He was only sorry that he had no time to visit Maitland, "the most scholarly of all," but hoped for his collaboration.[32]

Maitland sent this letter to Lock with a précis of his reply. Nothing of value could be done for the Year Books "without the formation of a good French text with sufficient notes from the records. I said that if this is meant I am friendly—but that if a 'reprint' is meant I am hostile." "And now what to do? Address ourselves to Green and inquire what is really being done—saying that our own arrangements may depend on the answer? . . . My own feeling is that perhaps Green might be induced to allow money and time enough for the production of something not discreditable—he seems to have secured Pike's adhesion and Pike would not allow what was very bad to appear over or under his name. Perhaps this may be the real solution of the Year Book problem, so far as this generation can solve it—and if the Society saw something tolerable appearing or likely to appear, the Society might well devote its money to other tasks."[33] Lock had no doubt of the course to be pursued. Maitland should warn Green "off Edward II as occupied ground." "Let him do the rest *if he can*. I don't believe that he can. Pike is a slow worker and, as you say, will not put his name to bad work. If we get our first volume out in good time next year we shall set up a standard which will put another strong drag on their pace; and before long they will have to come to you for help. Meanwhile let us concentrate on our own work and not worry about them. We need not be hostile—provided they leave Edward II alone . . . I do not think that the Society will now draw back from the work . . . unless you think candidly that the work will be better done if you were to throw in your lot with them and they were willing to give you a substantial salary: e.g. £1,000 a year. With us you are master of the situation (save for my occasional carping criticism) and that is something even if the money is still very poor."[34]

Maitland replied to Lock on August 13, 1902.[35] "I feel quite at ease now about Soule. You have I think a little misunderstood the trouble that his letter caused me. The thought of bargaining with him for a place in his scheme together with some shekels never crossed my mind—and a desertion of the Selden Society, so long as the Society can get any good out of me, I should regard as very base. What I did fear, perhaps unnecessarily, was that the Selden might within a few years consider that enough was being done for the Year Books by other hands. And I still think that hereafter this may be a reasonable, or at any rate a pardonable, opinion. I can't think that people like Ames or Pike will like to be mixed up with anything that is really discreditable, and it seems to me possible that they may screw up the scheme of translation to a decent pitch—so that people will be able to say, 'Well, we have in English the legal grit of these books and that is all we want.' (If they are wise they will begin with some late books—they are much easier, partly because they were soon printed, partly because the French has become a grammarless professional jargon with limited vocabulary). However all this lies in the future; and if even while

I live the Society says, 'We have had Year Books enough', I shall not be discontented." At the same time he summarized his position in a letter to Markby. "A scheme for translating the late books (in itself a pretty big task) would have my sympathy and at odd times I might be able to aid it, though Edward II will always have the first claim upon my time. But to putting out a French text that had not been laboriously made from a good supply of MSS compared with the record I will be neither party nor privy." In November 1902 the Council resolved to resist any encroachment upon their plans; and in March 1903 Maitland added a postscript in reply to a final letter from Soule. "I think it far better that we should go our several ways: that is to say the Selden Society on the one side and you and your associates on the other."[36] Soule's forays across the Atlantic were at an end.

Despite these alarms Maitland's Year Book was taking shape. In June 1902 he had sent to the press the first portion of the text; and in August he was writing a "discourse on language" for the introduction.[37] By the end of the following winter he had accumulated more text than he could use in one volume. In June 1903 he wrote to Lock: "I am getting a little frightened that I may not be able to cram in the whole of the Second Year. I am struggling to get rid of the fat, but this does not shorten the amount of copy . . . If I am pinched for room, shall I sacrifice the end of Year II or the French grammar?" Lock had no doubt. "By no means sacrifice the French grammar—leave out the end of Year II."[38] In July Maitland asked Lock for comments on the first part of the introduction. He feared that he might have been strident. "I shall be extremely grateful for criticism. Even if you only mark with red lead any passages that you dislike, I shall understand . . . Say if you think me too noisy—I can easily tone down. You know that some sober French grammar is to follow." He wrote also to Bigelow. "You will soon have before you a volume of Year Books—I am just finishing it. Often have I thought that it would never be done; but thanks to the Canarian sun I am through. I never work upon Year Books without thinking of Thayer. I should have liked to satisfy him. Shall I satisfy you?"[39] On October 23 the book was published as volume 17 of the Selden series and the first of their Year Books. By the time that Maitland left for the Canaries Lock had been able to judge the reaction of readers, and he wrote to Maitland. "Your book has taken the Society by storm—and not only the Society."[40]

Maitland was relieved and exhilarated. He had in hand the copy postponed from his first volume, and he pressed forward with the second. Within a year he had passed the whole book for the press, and it was published in December 1904. That winter in Madeira he completed the text and began the introduction of a third volume, which, "though buried alive in Year Books," he hoped to complete in the autumn of 1905. He had in fact to leave England in December on the eve of publication and asked Lock to send a copy after him. "It may help me when making Vol. IV."[41] A year later, before he left on his last voyage to Canary, he sent to the press the text and translation of this fourth volume. After his death Turner revised it and added an introduction on the judges and courts of Edward II, based upon material which he had been helping to prepare. Maitland also left behind him the rough transcript of an Eyre of Kent of 6 and 7 Edward II. Manuscripts of this Eyre had long been known to exist. They had been noted in Fitzherbert's Abridgment and a passage from them had been printed by Horwood in 1863. In 1900 Maitland had studied one such manuscript in the Cambridge University Library; in the winter of 1900–01 he transcribed it when he was in Grand Canary. The task was formidable. "Dios Todopoderosismo! What a record!"[42] It was not only prodigious but faulty; though it deserved the attention of the Selden Society, much must be done before it could be published. He never found the time to work on it, and after his death the transcript was found among his papers. The Council decided to include it in their Year Book series. Fifteen other manuscripts were discovered, and it appeared in three volumes in 1910, 1912, and 1913.

The Society and others were "taken by storm" not only by the editing of the first Year Book volume but by the introduction. Maitland shed light on many problems and asked many questions for his successors to answer. He discussed the origin of the Year Books and dismissed the belief, long held, that they were official reports. The belief was based upon a reminiscence of Edmund Plowden, who began to study the law in 1538 and who "had heard tell how in ancient days there were four reporters paid by the King." Coke proceeded to buttress this gossip. "The Kings of this realm did select and appoint four discreet and learned professors of law to report the judgments and opinions of the reverend judges." Blackstone improved upon Coke. "From the reign of Edward II to that of Henry VIII the reports were taken by the prothonotaries at the expense of the Crown and were published annually." Maitland showed the difficulties of such a story.[43] There was no record that any reporters had ever been appointed or had ever been paid or that their reports had been officially kept; the surviving manuscripts had always been found in private hands. There was not only negative but positive evidence against the tradition. "We should expect that manuscripts deriving from an official source would be very like each other, whereas, at least amongst those which belong to Edward II's time, there is wonderfully little similarity. From different manuscripts we sometimes obtain of one case two reports so unlike that we can hardly believe that they have been developed by transcription from a common original. At any rate the lawyers who copied Year Books, or employed professional scribes to copy them, exercised in full measure a right of omitting cases and parts of cases. Furthermore, we see a most remarkable contempt for the non-scientific detail of litigation: especially for proper names. These very often are so violently perverted that we seem to have before us much rather the work of a man who jotted down mere initials in court and afterwards tried to expand them than the work of an official who had the faithful plea rolls under his eye." Everywhere Maitland saw the outcome of private enterprise. The reporters interspersed the words of judge and counsel with comments and speculations of their own; and they did not scruple to criticize the judges who heard the case or to repeat the derogatory opinion expressed by one member of the court about another. Maitland quoted one passage out of many which would have looked strange in an official report.

Bereford is chief justice of the Common Pleas: Mutford and Stonor are justices. Stonor has been taking part in a debate with counsel. Then we read this:

Mutf. Some of you have said a great deal that runs counter to what was hitherto accounted law.

Bere. Yes! That is very true, and I won't say who they are. (And some people thought that he meant Stonor).

If the "official" theory must be rejected,[44] what was the origin and what the purpose of the Year Books? Maitland "strongly suspected that what was wanted was instruction and that these books were made by learners for learners, by apprentices for apprentices." Law for young barristers was not jurisprudence. It was a game of skill as intricate as chess and more lucrative. In court they could watch the technique of the serjeants, the masters of their craft. "What they desired was not a copy of the chilly record, cut and dried, with its concrete particulars concealing the point of law: the record overladen with the uninteresting names of litigants and oblivious of the interesting names of sages, of justices and serjeants. What they desired was the debate with the life-blood in it: the twists and turns of advocacy, the quip courteous and the countercheck quarrelsome. They wanted to remember what really fell from Bereford, C.J.: his proverbs, his sarcasms: how he emphasised a rule of law by *Noun Dieu!* or *Par Seint Piere!* They wanted to remember how a clever move of Serjeant Herle drove Serjeant Toudeby into an awkward corner, or how Serjeant Passeley invented a new variation on an old defence: and should such a man's name die if the name of Ruy Lopez is to live?"[45] The judges did not disdain to instruct them. Chief Justice Bereford more than once turned aside from the case before him to illustrate a point of pleading. One day he was interrupted by Serjeant Westcote. "Really," he said, "I am very much obliged to you for your challenge: not for the sake of us who sit on the bench, but for the sake of the young men who are here." On another occasion he gave a little lecture on avowry.[46] "Et jeo die une chose pur les jeones qe sont environ." "Les jeones," the young men standing around in court, might also be heard talking over technical questions "en le Cribbe." "What the Crib was we fain would know. Apparently this name might be given to a place where men fed, or again to a place that was wholly or partially enclosed by something that looked like basket-work. We have thought of a common dining-room, and we have thought of a part of the court set apart for students; but in the end we are asking for rather than giving information."[47]

In the introduction to volume 20, the third in the Selden series, Maitland said his last word upon the origin of the Year Books.[48]

> They, or rather the earliest of them (for we would not speak of an age that we have not observed), are students' note-books . . . Willingness to lend, to borrow, to co-operate, we may take for granted . . . We are among young Englishmen. Also we are among the founders of those societies, four of which become eminent as "the inns of court". These young men come up to London for term time; there is plenty of good fellowship among them; they club together; perhaps they jointly hire a house. Perhaps they are already devising "moots" or other exercises which are destined to become more and more academic, and, at all events, we may believe that they talk a good deal of "shop". This is the atmosphere in which note-books multiply. When, therefore, we have before us a dozen manuscripts purporting to contain the reports of a single year, we must not be surprised if the relationships between them are intricate in a very high degree. The assumption that every codex is the offspring of another codex is a natural starting-point if we would draw a pedigree; but in such a case as ours it may well be fallacious. Our case, indeed, is peculiar. The only people who want these reports live in constant intercourse with each other, and it is not at all impossible that all the copies that exist are to be found within one square mile of the earth's surface. A religious house may keep a Glanvill or a Bracton, a volume of statutes and a register of writs; but manuscript Year Books rarely come to us from monastic libraries. If, then, a man wanted to have a copy of his own,

> he might easily borrow two or three books from two or three friends, and then he could pick and choose what pleased him best, looking now at one book and now at another.'

After Maitland's death speculation continued and still exists upon the origin and purpose of the Year Books. Turner suggested that, though they were designed for instruction, they were compiled not by students but by experienced lawyers. They assume a knowledge of writs and of pleading beyond the reach of beginners. He thought that they were at first circulated in small pamphlets and were later copied into the larger volumes which now survive and which reflected whatever texts the compiler chanced to possess.[49] W. C. Bolland, who between 1910 and 1927 edited eight Year Books for the Society, thought them to have been a commercial speculation. "Some medieval capitalists, possibly a syndicate of Serjeants, saw their way to a profitable investment of capital."[50] They employed junior barristers to take notes in court of the crucial arguments—the pleas advanced and rejected and the reasons for their success or failure. These notes were taken to scriptoria, where they were dictated to a number of scribes. Several copies were thus produced for the use of anyone—serjeant or otherwise—who would pay for them. Such suggestions have their attractions and will doubtless have their successors. By whatever persons and for whatever purpose, the Year Books were produced for two and a half centuries. Maitland, as he warned his readers, was directly concerned with those of Edward II. It is rash to suppose that their character or their value remained constant throughout the years.[51]

Fifty pages of his introduction to volume 17 Maitland devoted to a study of "The Anglo-French Language in the Early Year Books"—the grammar which he had proposed to sacrifice if the volume were unduly swollen and which Lock had urged him to retain. He apologized for the experiment. He had been able to examine over many months three manuscripts which displayed the handiwork of a dozen clerks, and "observations of an empirical kind" had accumulated in his mind. "The publication of some of them, though they cannot pretend to phonological or grammatical science, may perhaps ease the labours of other students and transcribers." The French of the manuscripts might seem to modern eyes rough and uncultivated. But this in itself was a guarantee of fidelity to the spoken words. "No one has tried to polish and prune, or to make what is written better than what was heard. We fancy that learned men who explore the history of the French of Paris would sacrifice many a *chanson de geste* for a few reports of conversation that were as true to nature, as true to sound, as are our Year Books." The French spoken in the English courts in the last quarter of the thirteenth and the first quarter of the fourteenth century, if it was a dialect, was not an eccentricity and still less a jargon.[52] "In Edward II's day the educated Englishman was far more likely to introduce French words into his English than English words into his French . . . It is fairly certain that by this time his 'cradle speech' was English; but he had not been taught English and he had been taught French, the language of good society."

Maitland traced the creation of words to meet technical needs. "The lawyer was liberally exercising his right to make terms of art; and yet, if we mistake not, he did this in a manner sufficiently sanctioned by the genius of the language. Old French allowed a free conversion of infinitives into substantives. Some of the commonest nouns in the modern language have been infinitives: *diner, souper, pouvoir, devoir, plaisir.*" Words long imbedded if not hallowed in English legal dictionaries were made in this way at this time: voucher, disclaimer, interpleader, demurrer, tender, attainder, rejoinder, and, most significant of all, remainder. But it was one thing to admit these and many other words into regular use: it was another to stabilize orthography. "Whether this Anglo-French was being pronounced in different ways it is not for us to say. That it was being spelt in many different ways is certain." Maitland gave many instances of indiscriminate spelling. "No word was so short that it could not be spelt in at least two ways. The little word that means 'and' might be *et* or *e;* the little word that comes from the Latin *apud* and means 'with' might be *o, ov, ove* (written *ou, oue*), *of, od, oed;* the little word that in Modern French is *qui* might be *ki, ky, qi, qy, qui.* The following eight versions of the word that became our 'suit' were found in three reports of one short case: *siwte, siwete, sywte, suwite, suwte, sute, swte, seute.*"[53]

Maitland then explored the niceties and the permutations of grammar.[54] In the declension of nouns "the French of England hurried rapidly along a path which the French of France was to tread with slower steps. In our manuscripts the noun has no cases, and the accusative forms are already enjoying their complete victory." Gender was not, indeed, abandoned, but was in danger of confusion. "Englishmen were rapidly losing their sense of one of the chief means of distinguishing genders that the French language possessed. They were becoming careless of the final toneless *e*, the so-called *e* feminine." To the analysis of the Year Book verb Maitland devoted special attention. He filled six pages with variant forms, and examined in detail the use of the infinitive and the manipulation of the subjunctive mood in imperative, hypothetical, conditional, and negative clauses.[55]

In this venture into the field of the grammarian Maitland feared that he had displayed the audacity of ignorance. He was therefore pleased to have earned a word of praise from an expert. In January 1904 he wrote to Lock: "You will I think like to know (and will not think me vain for telling you) that I have a very pleasant note about Vol. I from the great Paul Meyer. I did not know him and he was the man whose judgment I most feared; so when he says that the task was difficult and could not have been better done I feel warm and comfortable."[56] Thirty years later Miss Dominica Legge, editing with Sir William Holdsworth the Year Books for 1316 and 1317, returned to the problem of language. She agreed that the manuscripts of Edward II faithfully recorded the speech of educated people, though his was the last reign of which this could be said. Anglo-Norman, as it might more properly be called, "was only one of many branches of the Langue d'oïl, and men like Bereford had no more call to be ashamed of speaking it than Froissard had of writing his native Hainault." The time had come to fill the outlines sketched by Maitland and to relate them more closely to the work of philologists. But "any fresh contribution to the subject must only be in the nature of a supplement to his masterly treatise."[57]

It was not until 1953—fifty years after Maitland's experiment—that Professor J. P. Collas called for a new, informed, and systematic study of Anglo-Norman vocabulary. Maitland's description "of the spelling, the morphology, and of much of the syntactical peculiarity of the language of the Year Books of the early fourteenth century has remained substantially as authoritative as it was when first it was penned. But by comparison the few paragraphs which were devoted to questions of vocabulary were fragmentary, discursive in the most general way, and ultimately destined to mislead." Vocabulary, indeed, "is notoriously the least tractable of all the aspects of language," and Maitland's observations upon it "were curiously mixed and incoherent." These are hard words. But Maitland had been as hard upon others; and if the words were just, they should be used against him. He would certainly have recognized and valued the scholarship with which Professor Collas weighted his judgment; and the correction of errors does not tarnish the courage of the venture.[58]

As philologist Maitland may have rushed in where experts had feared to tread. As historian he was master of the field. "If to the whole mass of materials for the history of the law England had nothing to contribute but the Year Books, England's contribution would still be of inestimable value. A stage in the history of jurisprudence is here pictured for us, photographed for us, in minute detail. The parallel stage in the history of Roman law is represented, and can only be represented, by ingenious guesswork: acute and cautious it may be, but it is guesswork still. Our 'formulary system', as it stood and worked in the fourteenth century, might be known so thoroughly that a modern lawyer who studied it might give sound advice, even upon points of practice, to a hypothetical client. We can bring the tissue of ancient law under the microscope; the intimate processes of nutrition, assimilation, elimination can be recorded year by year."[59] Maitland described with relish the shifts and devices of the serjeants, their search for premises, and the dialectical skill which matched the subtlety of the Schoolmen. But they did not work and argue in vacuo. The humanist might be tempted to complain that there was too much logic and too little life. "On the contrary we should claim on behalf of the Year Book that, when we consider that they were written by medieval lawyers for medieval lawyers, they show us a marvellous deal of the play of those moral and economic forces of which legal logic is the instrument, and often, if we may so say, the reluctant instrument. Our old lawyers were fond of declaring that 'the law will suffer a mischief rather than an inconvenience', by which they meant that it will suffer a practical hardship rather than an inconsistency or logical flaw. But it is an excellent feature of these Year Books that the unsuccessful argument is as well represented as the successful. We are forcibly told where the 'mischief' lies, where the shoe pinches, even when we are also told that the nonconformist foot that will not fit a shoe is a bad foot and should be pinched. And then, as we compare case with case, we see that more commodious shoes are made for growing feet: logic yields to life, protesting all the while that it is only becoming more logical."[60]

The Year Books mirror not only the legal and the economic, but the social life of their times. The reports of Edward II preserve the contemporary talk of the fourteenth almost as Boswell does that of the eighteenth and Trollope that of the nineteenth century. "Are they not the earliest reports, systematic reports, continuous reports, of oral debate? What has the whole world to put by their side? In 1500, in 1400, in 1300, English lawyers were systematically reporting what of interest was said in court. Who else in Europe was trying to do the like—to get down on paper or parchment the shifting argument, the retort, the quip, the expletive? Can we, for example, hear what was really said in the momentous councils of the Church, what was really said at Constance or Basel, as we can hear what was really said at Westminster long years before the beginning of the conciliar age?"[61] A trifling but revealing example of the faithful record of life is offered by the native proverbs with which the judges garnished their speech. A serjeant was protesting that, if his opponents had their way, they would both keep their land and get its price. "They would like," said Chief Justice Bereford, "to have the chicken and the ha'penny as well." In another case Bereford insisted that counsel, who had raised a number of inconsistent points, must choose the issue upon which he would be judged. If the court then ruled against him, "that would be for wine and candle": the case would be closed. "Wine and candle are the end of the day's work."[62]

But whether for language or manners, for legal or for social history, the Year Books would be waste land if there were not enough scholars to work upon them and harvest their fruits. To this task Maitland summoned laborers even at the eleventh hour. "What we want is a new and worthy edition of the Year Books undertaken as a national enterprise. We want a dozen men trained or in training to do the work: trained, if need be, at Paris under masters of the old French language: trained, if need be, at Harvard under masters of the old English law. It will cost money. It may fill a hundred, perhaps two hundred volumes. But we must have it, or England, Selden's England, will stand disgraced among the nations. The tide of conquest is advancing. The Anglo-Saxon laws are already German property. The Anglo-Norman law-books have been re-discovered—the word is not too strong—by Dr. Liebermann. A society that bears the name, not of Selden, but of Savigny, finds the money and finds the brains. A French librarian shows us how a Year Book should be read. As monuments of Germanic law they will look well, these English Year Books, among the 'Monumenta Germaniae'. As monuments of a French dialect they will look well, these English Year Books, among the 'Documents inédits sur l'histoire de France'. Lo! they turn unto the gentiles."[63]

Since Maitland's death devotion has added twenty-five volumes to the series of Year Books published by the Selden Society. But even now the reports of Edward II's reign have not been completed, and the claim of the Year Books upon the scanty time of scholars has been deprecated. Some, like A. L. Smith, have lamented that so much talent should be lavished upon such dismal material. Others have urged the greater value of the Plea Rolls. "The record," wrote Bell, "must always be superior to the report."[64] Maitland himself insisted that record and report must be read together; only thus can the dead be made to live again. In his fascinating book *The Oracles of the Law* Professor John P. Dawson has recently contrasted the crude ore of England with the golden age of Italy—"the wretched poverty of English Year Book learning" with "the wealth and range and intellectual power of Italian legal literature of the fourteenth century." Maitland paid his own tribute to the glories of Italian jurisprudence.[65] But the medieval common law, not meant nor fit for export, served well its own age and country; and Bench and Bar, shown at work in the Year Books, lacked neither intellectual power nor subtlety.

Chapter XII

The Life and Letters of Leslie Stephen. The Last Voyage

Maitland, if he had been free to choose, would have edited Year Books for the rest of his life. But he was caught by a cross-current and driven out of his course. In May 1895 Leslie Stephen's second wife Julia had died, and Maitland had written to him. "I have an irrepressible wish, however foolish and wrong it may be, to touch your hand and tell you in two words that I think of you. And yet you will know that, and will know also how my thoughts go back to what happened in your house nine years ago. Today you must feel that all men are strangers to you since none can help you to bear your grief; but some day believe that it is (let me say it) with something of filial love that

I think of you and write these useless words." Stephen wrote back to him:[1]

> Words are not useless, unless they are only words. Behind your words lay a kindness and sympathy which touched me deeply. No one can take me out of torment; but you, and one or two more, have soothed my sufferings.
>
> I cannot as yet write to any one except for some special reason. I have a reason for writing to you now. I have occupied myself for the last ten days or so with writing a little paper about my darling. It is intended entirely for her children: and while I live, must remain among us. It tries to fix some old memories and the thoughts that have come to me in reading many letters.
>
> I have, of necessity, spoken a good deal about myself—even of my earlier life—for reasons which would appear if you saw the document itself. This led me to think whether in the case of my death any use might be made of what I have written. I am quite clear, for reasons which I have more or less stated, that it would be not only silly but impossible to write a life of me. I am an expert in that matter and I know that the materials do not exist. But I think it possible that something might be said about me—e.g. if I die before the dictionary reaches my name.[2] Now here is my reason for writing to you. You are the only person who could speak of me to any purpose. I have more reasons for saying this than I choose to give. If, then, you should write something about me—not a set life, that ought not to be even thought of, but a notice—you ought to read the above document. I have said so much in it. Although the autobiography is only incidental, it would give you the key to all that is of any real importance. It could not be published, though possibly a passage or two might be quotable. But to you it would virtually tell the only things that would be necessary.

When Stephen himself died in February 1904, Maitland was in the Canaries. He had no immediate access to Stephen's papers, and his first thought was to do nothing. "He is too big for me for one sort of writing and too dear for another."[3] But when he returned to England and reread Stephen's letter, he felt that he must try to justify the trust reposed in him. Stephen's children gave him the fragment of autobiography to use as he thought fit. Only a short memoir was to be attempted. But even this would delay his work on the Year Books, and he warned Lock that he might be late with them. Lock could only deplore the interruption as unwise and superfluous. There was surely no lack of "literary gents" who could be hired to "polish off the job" at reasonable rates.[4]

As the months passed, Maitland came to realize the implications of his task. All who had known Stephen and who could and would offer their help must be approached, and it was as necessary as it was difficult to capture memories of him as a young man. On life at Cambridge Jackson was the obvious source of fact and legend; and his judgment must be sought on the value of available evidence. If an approach were made to one witness, "would it bring nothing or the wrong sort of thing?" If another "told a good story, would it be true?" Maitland had seen allusions to "one M. M. U. Wilkinson as a member of Stephen's 'set'." Was he still living and likely to be of service? "I think," said Jackson, "that M. M. U. Wilkinson (M^2U^3 or 'the squared cube' as he was called) may have been a member of the set; but, if so, he must have been the butt. He was a mathematical lecturer and bad at that. He played badly on the piano and had a face like a sun rising in a fog." Wilkinson was left undisturbed.[5] But it was the mass of letters found not only in England but in the United States which led Maitland, in the face of Stephen's warning, to "revolutionize his idea of the book." The short memoir became a full biography.[6]

When he went to Madeira in December 1904 Maitland took with him all the material that he had so far collected. He tried to reduce it to order, but longed for a second opinion. In February 1905 he wrote to Fisher.[7] "Oh! that we could talk of that biography or collection of letters or whatever it is to be! I can't make up my mind about plan or scale or anything else, but go on cop-cop-copying six or seven hours a day—and the ghost of the work visits me in the night-watches. The letters to Lowell, Norton and ('young') Holmes are so good—or seem to me so good while I am about them; and then comes the cold fit and I say that, though they interest you and me and a dozen others, the world will see no point in them; and then I hear the dear old philosopher himself damning my eyes for exposing all this 'trash' or 'twaddle' to the public gaze." By the end of the winter he had accumulated a mountain of manuscript. "I doubt I have ever written more in a given time." He feared that he must contemplate two volumes. But it was "so easy to be long," and he felt "that Leslie's vote, even if given quite impartially, would have been for one." He consulted both Fisher and Norton and, to his relief, each advised against a second volume.[8]

In Cambridge he could give the book only intermittent attention, submitting chapters to Jackson's criticism and seeking new light on dark places. But in December 1905 he left for Grand Canary, determined to complete the task. In February 1906 he could write that "in a kind of way he had finished his biographical job"; and in March that he should be ready to send the manuscript to the printers on his return to England. In the autumn he corrected proofs and compiled the index, and early in November the book was published simultaneously in England and in the United States.[9] It was well received and most cordially by those who had best known Stephen. Pollock wrote to Holmes at the end of 1906: "You will like Maitland's *Life of Leslie Stephen*. It is good that he lived to finish it and see it appreciated by the right people." Nearly fifty years later Noel Annan could still say that "Maitland did his work so well that a new biography would be superfluous."[10]

This verdict must be qualified. In spite or because of Maitland's anxious care, Leslie Stephen does not dominate the book. In a notice written within a week of Stephen's death Frederick Greenwood, the editor of the *Pall Mall Gazette*, had said that "if you got as far as friendship you went much further." Maitland had felt these words to be true, at least in Stephen's later life. "I don't know that it had always been so," he wrote to Jackson; "it was so when I began to tramp on Sundays in his company." But it was not easy to "get as far as friendship." Stephen, as he grew older, had built a barrier against acquaintances and especially against those whom he called "damned intellectuals," in whose presence "he shut up tight."[11] Apart from intimate friends a few percipient minds had sensed the truth. Thomas Hardy, calling upon Stephen in 1886, had found him "just the same or worse; dying to express sympathy, but as if suffering under some terrible curse which prevents him saying any but caustic things, and showing antipathy instead."[12] Maitland did not find it easy to lead his readers behind the barrier. He tried to set off against the bleak aspect of the later years the energy, physical and mental, of the younger man. Above all, he wished not to "destephenize Stephen."[13] But his inevitable reliance on Jackson's knowledge and judgment was not always helpful. In print at least Jackson's instinct was to soften words even if he blunted their edge. Stephen's ten years as a Fellow of Trinity Hall offered more than one awkward if revealing scene, and Jackson sought to make the rough ways smooth. "You shan't have to say," Maitland wrote, "that I ask for advice and yet don't take it. I have run my pen through the scene in chapel and the electoral proceedings—with some little regret because I wanted to suggest a certain 'levity' (that is about the right word—at any rate the word that would be used by unfriends) and also a certain enthusiastic and not precisely scrupulous partisanship in a friend's cause." Jackson would not even pass unexpurgated a tale of Stephen, while still in orders, reproving a man who had sworn in his presence with the indignant words "Damn your soul, Sir! Don't you know that I'm a parson?"[14]

If Maitland yielded too often to Jackson's scruples he was also too careful to keep himself out of the book. A biographer must not intrude upon his subject; but to sink his personality is to jettison a vital element. Maitland called many witnesses to character and reputation, and they stand between writer and reader. When he was content, as in the account of the Sunday Tramps, to rely upon his own knowledge and sympathy, the story at once becomes alive. In two pages almost at the end of the book Maitland trusted his judgment and, by disclosing his feelings, revealed Stephen's mind and heart. "I have scattered myself too much," Stephen had said. "I have been a jack-of-all-trades; and, instead of striking home, have only done enough to persuade friendly judges that I could have struck." If ever a history of English thought in the nineteenth century were written, Stephen added, his name would appear only in footnotes. Maitland took up these words.[15]

> I feel fairly sure that this is too strongly stated, and that Stephen will have a paragraph at the least, if the historian of English thought is, as he ought to be, a large-minded man, and by "thought" means as much as Stephen would have meant. But there is always truth in what Stephen says of himself; and when he adds that he lacked the requisite self-confidence, and in early days the requisite ambition, I can only agree with him. If in 1882, after the "Science of Ethics", he had settled down in a professorship or a secular deanery and had steadily philosophised, he would, I fancy, have earned a larger space than is likely to be his in forthcoming histories of philosophical doctrines, though historians might still be waiting for their biographical dictionary. But histories of systems are not the history of thought. I have said, and I believe it true, that Stephen thought of poetry while he read philosophy and of philosophy while he read poetry, and of stubborn fact, especially of the lives of concrete men and women, while he read everything.
>
> Now that, in these days of specialism, is not a prudent thing to do if you would see your name in the manuals. "Stephen", we were told after his death, "did not really care for poetry any more than Jeffrey, and consequently was not fully qualified to criticise it." Of course not: he was a philosopher. A distinguished philosopher[16] told me that he had not read the "Science of Ethics". Why should he? Its author was hardly a philosopher. Nor do we think of him as a historian to be likened to Stubbs or Gardiner. The country is well studded to-day with proclamations against trespassers. He who contemns them is no law-abiding man but a vagrant and a tramp. The preservation of open spaces is, let us admit it, a lost cause. The old common-fields must be en-

closed that two blades may grow where one grew before. And yet do we not like every now and again to see a broken hedge, a prostrate fence, a bit of barbed wire cut and cast aside? I hope so. By all means let the specialist specialise. And yet is it not well that every now and again a breath of cold fresh air should blow through his conservatories and try the hardihood of the plants that have been reared there? It is a probable opinion. In an untechnical as well as in a technical sense Stephen seems to me a free-thinker. Do many men think as freely? Not very many. He had a deep respect for professionals. The President of the Alpine Club, as we all know, was not the equal of a second-rate guide. And yet no guide could have written the "Sunset". Jack-of-all-trades is master of none. That is very true. By all means let Beckmesser score upon the slate every breach of the rules of mastery. Personally, I have a strong fellow feeling for Beckmesser. And yet, before the curtain falls, some one may say a good word for the "amateur".

Dem Vogel, der heut' sang,
Dem war der Schnabel hold gewachsen;
Macht' er den Meistern bang'—
Gar wohl gefiel er doch Hans Sachsen.

The book might well have ended with these lines from *Die Meistersinger*. But Maitland's misgivings returned, and he added yet more testimonials.

In time and in affection, as Maitland had said, he was too close to Stephen to see or to set him in perspective. In temperament he was too far removed. He was single-hearted and uninhibited. Stephen was compounded of unresolved tensions. His life invited a psychological study from which, had he been capable of it, Maitland would have shrunk.[17] From the moment when he decided upon a full biography, he had felt himself to be unprepared and unqualified for it. "I am perplexed as I never was before . . . I can no more draw a character than I can ascend the Schreckhorn." "I should have destroyed all that I have written were it not that Florence encourages me." "How to describe anybody! I can only shovel evidence into heaps and chuck it at the public." "The end is in sight. Never, never no more! Once and for one only!—or rather for two only."[18] He longed for publication as a release and shrank from it as an exposure. In April 1906 he wrote to Bigelow. "In a sort of a kind of a way the book is now written and the dreadful moment of publication may come before the end of the year. Dreadful it is. I have been writing books for a long while now, but only for a very small circle. If I blunder about the *writ of entry in the quibus* only you and two or three other learned fellows will find me out. Now I shall have the whole pack of reviewers in full cry after me."[19] But when the book appeared in November the reviews were kind. He was rid of his burden and the Year Books awaited him. From time to time in the last two winters he had turned to them for consolation. But medieval law was exigent: Chief Justice Bereford and Leslie Stephen could not be sandwiched. Now the Year Books might be resumed with a clear conscience and an undivided attention.

The strain of recurrent illness was aggravated by the burden of the book and by the need to crowd a year's lectures into the summer and autumn months. Professor Hollond recalled a day in the Long Vacation of 1905 when he sat in the Law School newly built in Downing Park and suffered with Maitland as he "halted in his lecture gasping for breath, with a shadow of pain passing over his lined face."[20] This impression must not be allowed to distort the picture of Maitland in his last years. There were indeed moments when dejection bordered on despair. In April 1906 he was ill in the Canaries when he should have been in Cambridge; and he wrote to Lock that he was "tired of stopping the leaks of this crazy boat . . . Now at last I am *definitely* in default as a professor. How I am to go on I don't well see."[21] But such moods passed; and in the summer and autumn of 1906 he lived as full a life as in previous years. He is not to be thought of as a man sentenced to an early death. In May 1906 he accepted the invitation to be the Sandars Reader in Bibliography for the academic year 1906–07 and proposed, when he returned to Cambridge in the following spring, to speak of the legal manuscripts in the University Library.[22] He not only fulfilled his present and looked forward to future duties but, save when cold or damp kept him indoors, enjoyed social engagements, dining in his own and other colleges and attending the meetings of societies to which he belonged. He relished especially the Eranus Society. It had been founded in 1872 and met five or six times a year in the house or rooms of one of its twelve members, when the host read a paper and provoked a general discussion. In December 1905 Maitland wrote to Jackson that he was determined "to dine with the Society on Monday, as the devil himself cannot now prevent me from keeping this term."[23] He read his last paper to the Eranus on the eighth of May, 1906. Its theme is uncertain. The minutes of the Society give the title as "Do Poets Sing?" According to Fisher its name was "Do Birds Sing"—a "speculation as to the conditions under which articulate sound passes into music."[24]

On the morning of November 16, Florence and Ermengard left Cambridge for the Canaries. A house had been taken in Tafira and they wished to make all things ready for Maitland when he followed them after the end of term.[25] They were to stay the night in the Midland Hotel at St. Pancras and sail the next day by a Blue Anchor boat from the East India Docks. Maitland's sister Kate came to stay with him in Downing. On the evening of the sixteenth Maitland wrote to Florence.

Downing College, Cambridge.
16 Nov. 1906.

Beloved,

I hope that you have not had quite so much rain as we have had. The court is a lake. It has been very cold and cheerless. So I stopped at home all this afternoon working at proof-sheets . . . Well, you are on your way to the sun, and very soon you will be cheered by a sight of it. I am dreadfully sorry about our poor Goose. You must certainly take a first class if the second looks very bad—don't scruple to do so—we can live cheaply when we are out in Canary. Now good-bye and a happy voyage to you. I shall soon be with you.

Give my love to the Isleta as soon as you see it. I do hope and trust that you are going to be happy.

So with many kisses good-bye.

Your own

F.[26]

A second letter, written on November 27, survives.[27]

Downing
27 Nov. 1906

My best beloved,

I don't know in what order you will get your letters or in what order you will open them. First let me tell you that I get very good reports of our dear child at Bex both directly and indirectly. Nothing could be better. I have given her careful instructions as to sending me letters for you. Next I can tell you that I am well; no aches or pains.

When I wrote to you last I was very sad indeed. Thoby's death was heart-rending and I could think of nothing else. Now I am not so sad but I am perplexed. Perhaps you will know from your mother what is coming. However I will tell you. Yesterday I had a short note from 'Ginia saying that Nessa is engaged to marry Mr. Clive Bell, Thoby's great friend.[28] Apparently they exchanged promises before the funeral. Well, it isn't conventional but it seems to me all natural and right and beautiful. My only fear is that Nessa may have caught rather hastily at the first support that offered itself. Your mother from whom I had a note to-day says that she rejoices, but adds that she doesn't know Mr. Bell. I have great faith in Nessa and guess that all will go well. But there will be some exclamations, won't there? My next sentence was going to be "What will Milly say?" At the moment that I was beginning it the enclosed note came. I send it to you, and it may amuse you; it has amused me. Milly has a soft heart for lovers[29] . . . I can't help thinking of poor 'Ginia. If her head stands all this anxiety and sorrow and joy, it is a good steady head.

Have I expatiated too much on this affair? I have precious

little else to tell you. I was really glad to get your telegram —it seems to have been delayed; as it is I fear that your voyage was long and rough. I like to think of you and the dear duchess sallying forth into Triana. My fate will be the Durham. I am sorry to spend so much money, for I am quite well enough to face a second class, but I don't want to wait another week. The Durham calls, as I hoped, at both islands: so I may hope to be with you late on the Friday and happy shall I be when I see you once more.

I have had some kind letters about the book—Hardy is very laudatory, so is Bryce. Last night I ate a Society dinner and am no worse for it. We have had some really warm days —almost muggy.

I look forward to a letter, then to a meeting.

Your own

F.

Three days later Maitland had to face a heavy loss. Mary Bateson had seemed as vigorous as ever. She had been appointed one of the three editors of the projected *Cambridge Medieval History* and was full of plans. On November 30 she died. Maitland was deeply moved; and his last task was to write a notice of her and of her work.[30]

> To many residents at Cambridge it still seems hardly credible that Miss Mary Bateson is no longer at work among them. We thought it so certain that twenty years hence her generous enthusiasm for learning, her dogged tenacity of purpose, her cool and sober common sense would still be serving mankind, that we might well be dazed by the disaster that has befallen us. Yet some things are clear. If we have to think of promise, we can also think with some comfort of performance. For much more we confidently hoped; but we have much that cannot be taken away. I shall not endeavour to tell the whole tale but will speak only of the last book. The admirably edited *Records of the Borough of Leicester* and the brilliant papers on the "Laws of Breteuil"[31] had shown that Miss Bateson's knowledge of the

history of our medieval towns was almost, if not quite, unrivalled. Thereupon she was asked to undertake for the Selden Society a sort of digest of the borough custumals, published and unpublished. The first volume appeared in 1904; the second and last appeared this summer with a long and learned introduction, which is in truth a full and elaborate commentary . . . Such a book cannot make its mark in a couple of months, nor yet in a couple of years. It cannot attract "the general reader"; it can be only a book for a few students of history. Moreover, Miss Bateson, a true daughter of Cambridge, felt such scorn for what she would call "gas" that it was difficult to persuade her that a few sentences thrown in for the benefit of the uninitiated are not to be condemned by the severest taste. Of such a work I should not like to speak confidently at short notice. But it was my good fortune to see this book in every stage of its growth: in manuscript, in slip and in page. Good fortune it was. The hunger and thirst for knowledge, the keen delight in the chase, the good-humoured willingness to admit that the scent was false, the eager desire to get on with the work, the cheerful resolution to go back and begin again, the broad good sense, the unaffected modesty, the imperturbable temper, the gratitude for any little help that was given—all these will remain in my memory, though I cannot paint them for others. As to the book—friendship apart—I do think it good. Given the limits of space and time, which were somewhat narrow, I do not see how it could have been much better. Given those limits, the name of the Englishman who both could and would have done the work does not occur to me. Unless I am much mistaken, that book will "sup late", but in very good company. I see it many years hence on the same shelf with the *History of the Exchequer* and the *History of Tithes*. Neither Thomas Madox nor yet John Selden will resent the presence of Mary Bateson.

Maitland was now impatient to join Florence and Ermengard. On December 6 he left Cambridge for London in good health and two days later went on board the *Durham Castle* at Southampton. Either in London or at sea he caught influenza, was neglected by the ship's doctor, and by the time he reached Las Palmas on Friday December 14, was desperately ill with pneumonia. He was carried ashore to Quiney's Hotel and, when Florence was told and hurried to him, he did not know her. For twenty-four hours he was delirious with short intervals of consciousness: he would answer a question put directly to him, only to wander off into disconnected words.

The English doctor in Las Palmas attended him; but Florence could get no other help and for five nights and six days nursed him herself.[32] On the morning of Wednesday the nineteenth of December he seemed a little better and asked for his *Leslie Stephen*. "All the day until he died it was by his side and he sometimes held it up and turned over the pages and said how bad the light was and that he could not read in bed . . . Oh, I never realised what a strain of anxiety that book had been to him." The doctor, when he paid his morning visit, was pleased. But Florence felt sure that he was too optimistic. "I thought there were many signs which showed me he was really most desperately ill." She asked for a second opinion; and later in the day a Spanish doctor came with a nurse. "He told me that the treatment and nursing had been right but that the pneumonia was double—both lungs entirely covered. It was very dangerous but he had held out wonderfully and if I could only keep his heart going another three or four days he would pull through. He said that there was the greatest danger, but I must count every hour he lived as to the good."

Florence felt immediate confidence both in the doctor and in the nurse. At half-past eleven that night she put on her dressing gown and "went into Fred's room. He was then lying quiet and comatose—his eyes open but in a sort of sleep . . . I lay down again in the next room and fell asleep. At half-past twelve I felt the nurse seize my arm. She said, 'Come quick—the end.' I said, 'No, it is only one of the usual attacks of faintness, we will pull him through.' I rushed in with her. We gave him brandy and an injection of strychnine and then injections of brandy. But it was all useless. At a quarter to one he died. He was unconscious, and the end came quietly and painlessly. I knelt by the side of his bed and had my face on his arm and held his hand."

In the afternoon of the next day, the twenty-first of December, Florence and Ermengard laid him in the little English cemetery close to the sea on the Telde road which he had loved so much.

Notes and Index

Abbreviations

BNB	Maitland, *Bracton's Note Book* (London: Cambridge University Press, 1887).
Buckland	W. W. Buckland, "F. W. Maitland," *Cambridge Law Journal,* 1:279.
C.P.	*The Collected Papers of Frederic William Maitland,* 3 vols. (Cambridge University Press, 1911).
CLJ	*Cambridge Law Journal.*
Child's-Eye View	Ermengard Maitland, *A Child's-Eye View* (Bernard Quaritch, London: Selden Society memoir, 1957).
Domesday Book	Maitland, *Domesday Book and Beyond* (Cambridge University Press, 1897).
EHR	*English Historical Review.*
Fisher	H. A. L. Fisher, *Frederick [sic] William Maitland: A Biographical Sketch* (Cambridge University Press, 1910).
Henry Sidgwick	*Henry Sidgwick: A Memoir by A.S. and E.M.S.* (London, Macmillan, 1906).
Hollond	Henry Arthur Hollond, *Frederic William Maitland* (Bernard Quaritch, London: Selden Society Lecture, 1953).
Letters	*The Letters of Frederic William Maitland* (Selden Society, Cambridge University Press and Harvard University Press, 1965).
LQR	*Law Quarterly Review.*
Life of L.S.	Maitland, *The Life and Letters of Leslie Stephen* (London: Duckworth and Company, 1906).
M. de P.	Maitland, *Memoranda de Parliamento: Records of the Parliament Holden at Westminster . . . in the Thirty-third Year of the Reign of King Edward the First* (London: Rolls Series, 1893).
Pollock and Maitland	Pollock and Maitland, *The History of English Law before the Time of Edward I* (Cambridge University Press, 1st edition 1895; 2nd edition 1898, reissued with an introduction and bibliography by S. F. C. Milsom, 1968). References, unless otherwise stated, are to the 2nd edition.
Roman Canon Law	Maitland, *Roman Canon Law in the Church of England* (Cambridge University Press, 1898).
S.S.	Selden Society
Township and Borough	Maitland, *Township and Borough* (Cambridge University Press, 1898).

Notes

Chapter I. Parentage

1. Much of the information used in this chapter is derived from documents and recollections recorded by Samuel Roffey Maitland and John Gorham Maitland, and put at my disposal by Miss Ermengard Maitland.

2. She was a descendant of Richard Busby, Headmaster of Westminster School from 1638 to 1695, of whom Dr. Johnson wrote that he "suffered none of his scholars to let their powers lie useless." *Lives of the Poets* (Life of Nicholas Rowe).

3. Betty Miller, *Robert Browning* (London: John Murray, 1952), p. 4.

4. Geoffrey Faber, *Jowett* (London: Faber and Faber, 1957), p. 21.

5. Letter from Maria Webb, daughter of Samuel Roffey's friend William Hodge Mill, to Mrs. Reynell (Selina Maitland), dated April 3, 1891.

6. Manuscript fragment of autobiography in family papers, on which the following account of Samuel Roffey's life is based.

7. Maitland House, The Spa.

8. V. H. H. Green, *Oxford Common Room* (London: Edward Arnold, 1957), pp. 23–24.

9. June 17, 1891; W. H. Hutton, *Letters of William Stubbs* (London: Constable, 1904), pp. 364–365.

10. "An index of such English Books, printed before the year MDC, as are now in the Archiepiscopal Library at Lambeth." It is annotated with biographical references and is still in use; letter of Geoffrey Bill, Librarian of Lambeth Palace Library, to Miss Maitland, February 5, 1966.

11. Maitland had been elected a Fellow of the Royal Society in 1839.

12. *Letters,* no. 98.

13. W. D. Christie, "The Cambridge 'Apostles'," *Macmillan's Magazine,* Nov. 1864, p. 18. See also below, Chapter III.

14. I am indebted for this and other information to the courtesy of the present Secretary of the Civil Service Commission and to H. Boggs-Rolfe, C.B.E., of the Lord Chancellor's Office.

15. Letter from Spedding, dated November 20, 1855, Maitland family papers.

Chapter II. Early Years

1. For this and other information I am indebted to the kindness of the Librarian, Eton College.

2. These are two of the boats in the Fourth of June procession. *Letters,* no. 1.

3. Gwen Raverat, *Period Piece* (London: Faber and Faber, 1952), p. 22, quoting her mother on her first visit to England from America. See also *Letters,* no. 489.

4. *Life of L.S.,* pp. 95, 101–102.

5. Fisher, pp. 5–6. The "closest school friend" was presumably Gerald Balfour.

6. B. B. Rogers (see Fisher, p. 16) and Ermengard Maitland (*Child's-Eye View*) gainsay both epithets.

7. *Letters,* no. 384 (April 27, 1904); see also below, Chapter X.

8. Rev. E. D. Stone to Mrs. Reynell, Sept. 25, 1907 (Maitland family papers).

9. See Leslie Stephen's *Life of Sir James FitzJames Stephen* (London: Macmillan, 1895), pp. 77–86.

10. *Life of L.S.,* pp. 29–36.

11. Pollock, *For My Grandson* (London: John Murray, 1933), pp. 20–25.

12. *The Adventurer,* June 4, 1869.

13. *Life of L.S.,* p. 35. See also Stephen's *Jowett's Life, Studies of a Biographer* (London: Duckworth, 1931), II, 146.

14. *Child's-Eye View,* p. 9.

15. H. E. Wortham, *Victorian Eton and Cambridge* (London: Arthur Barker, 1956), p. 179.

16. *Letters,* no. 1.

17. Wortham, *Victorian Eton and Cambridge,* pp. 62–63.

18. *Letters,* no. 2.

19. Wortham, *Victorian Eton and Cambridge,* pp. 134–135.

20. *A Writer's Recollections* (London: Collins, 1918), pp. 96–99.

21. "Miss Buss and Miss Beale
Cupid's darts do not feel.
How different from us!
Poor Miss Beale and Miss Buss."

22. "Ladies" became "Girls" in 1871. The school is vividly depicted by Mrs. M. V. Hughes, *A London Girl of the Eighties* (London: Oxford University Press, 1936), chaps. I to V.

23. Raverat, *Period Piece,* p. 61.

24. They are given here in the order in which they appear in the diary.

25. See below, Chap. X.

26. *London Music in 1888–89* (London: Constable, 1937), pp. 40, 51, 311.

27. *Letters,* no. 16.

28. William Rogers, *Reminiscences* (1881), p. 42. For what follows see pp. 51–90, 127–167.

29. *William Wetmore Story and His Friends* (1903; edition cited, London: Thames and Hudson, n.d.), II, 278.

Chapter III. Undergraduate

1. *Life of L.S.,* pp. 46, 49.

2. *CLJ,* 1: 282.

3. Evans came from Somerset. She had charge of Kate from babyhood and then remained as a combined lady's maid and confidante. The family were devoted to her and she to them. She nursed Aunt Louisa in her last illness; and after Sela and Fred had both married, she and Kate depended on each other. The diaries kept by Kate and Sela form part of the Maitland family papers.

4. *Some Early Impressions* (London: Hogarth Press, 1924), pp. 63–66.

5. D. A. Winstanley, *Later Victorian Cambridge* (London: Cambridge University Press, 1947), p. 212.

6. Page 63.

7. *Period Piece,* chap. I. After his retirement Taylor became blind and devoted himself to the provision of Braille books on mathematics and natural science.

8. *An Autobiography and Other Essays* (London: Longmans, 1949), p. 16.

9. *Letters,* no. 373 and note.

10. Trevelyan, *Autobiography,* p. 15; *CLJ,* 1: 297.

11. Hollond, p. 7.

12. *Cambridge University Reporter,* Dec. 7, 1900. Henry Sidgwick (1838–1900) was a Fellow of Trinity College from 1859 to 1900 and Knightbridge Professor of Moral Philosophy from 1883 to 1900.

13. Sir John Pollock, *Time's Chariot* (London: John Murray, 1950), p. 146.

14. *Letters*, no. 323; and see *Letters*, no. 11. Leslie Stephen suggested that Gurney might have been the prototype of George Eliot's *Daniel Deronda;* see *Letters*, nos. 322 and 323.

15. *Walter Leaf, Some Chapters of Autobiography* (London: John Murray, 1932), pp. 85–87, 95.

16. Fisher, p. 7.

17. *Letters*, nos. 229, 288.

18. Hollond, p. 8.

19. Letter of March 14, 1907.

20. *Autobiography*, p. 22.

21. *The Athenaeum*, Jan. 12, 1907; *Saturday Review*, Dec. 27, 1906.

22. *Walter Leaf*, pp. 86–87.

23. Fisher, p. 13.

24. *Letters*, no. 468. Moulton became a Lord of Appeal in 1912.

25. Fisher, pp. 13–14.

26. Harold Nicholson, *Tennyson* (London: Constable, 1923), pp. 72–77.

27. *Life of Sir FitzJames Stephen*, pp. 99–106.

28. *Henry Sidgwick*, pp. 29–30.

29. On the Chitchat Club see M. R. James, *Eton and King's* (London: Williams and Norgate, 1926), p. 242.

30. *Walter Leaf*, pp. 85–90.

31. Pollock, *For My Grandson*, pp. 30–38.

32. *Letters*, nos. 10, 318, 402.

33. They were soon divorced for incompatibility: Winstanley, *Later Victorian Cambridge*, pp. 189–190, 206–207.

34. Buckland, *CLJ*, 1: 279; letters of Jan. 18, 19, 1907, from the Deputy Registrary, University of Cambridge, to Mrs. Reynell.

Chapter IV. London Years

1. *Henry Sidgwick*, pp. 322, 499; *Letters*, no. 53.

2. Letter to Mrs. Reynell, March 14, 1907 (Maitland family papers).

3. Rogers, *Reminiscences*, pp. 80–85; E. L. Woodward, *The Age of Reform* (London: Oxford University Press, 2nd ed., 1962), pp. 493–496.

4. *Henry Sidgwick*, pp. 272–273.

5. Fisher, p. 23, quoting H. Solly, *These Eighty Years* (London, 1893), II, 440. B. F. Lock, in his prefatory memoir to S.S. vol. 22, wrote that Maitland lectured at Rochdale on Political Economy; but no trace of this is to be found in the local archives.

6. *Letters*, no. 477.

7. See *Letters*, nos. 239, 253.

8. G. C. Coulton, *Fourscore Years* (London: Cambridge University Press, 1943), p. 324.

9. *Letters,* no. 255. It later became the first essay in the *Collected Papers.* "The infant Grotius" had written, but not published, *De jure praedae* in 1604; in 1868 it was found and edited.

10. Hollond, p. 8; see above, Chap. III.

11. "Two Lectures," *CLJ,* April 1966, p. 68. In January and February 1876 Joshua Williams delivered in Gray's Inn Hall twelve lectures on "The Seisin of the Freehold."

12. Verrall offered an additional paper on Common Law. They could have sat, had they wished, for the Honours examination.

13. Fisher, pp. 15–16.

14. *Letters,* no. 373.

15. Buckland, p. 280.

16. (1880) 15 Ch. D. 143.

17. (1880) 16 Ch. D. 49.

18. Fisher, pp. 16–17.

19. Augustine Birrell, who was called to the Bar a year before Maitland recorded his impression of Jessel at this time. "His judicial strength seemed irresistible and his pace was tremendous. He got through a great deal of work in a very short time and made the fortune of his principal leader, that excellent lawyer who afterwards became Lord Justice Chitty": *Things Past Redress* (London: Heinemann, 1933), pp. 95–96.

20. See Maitland's obituary of Stubbs, *EHR,* July 1901; *C.P.* III, 495–511.

21. *Letters,* no. 4. In 1882 the Settled Land Act made an important contribution to the reform of Real Property, but drastic changes had to wait until 1925.

22. *C.P.,* I, 162, 190.

23. George Saintsbury, *A Last Scrap-Book* (London: Macmillan, 1924), pp. 203–205.

24. He had been secretary of the Leander Club, had written upon legal topics, and had been Chief Justice of the Ionian Islands.

25. Florence Hardy, *The Early Life of Thomas Hardy* (London: Macmillan, 1928), pp. 172–173.

26. *Letters,* no. 10.

27. Letter to the *Athenaeum,* Jan. 18, 1907; see also *Letters,* no. 11.

28. *BNB,* i.103.

29. Chapter XVII. In Appendix II is given a list of the Tramps as recorded by Stephen.

30. Cited by Edward Thomas, *A Literary Pilgrim in England* (London: Jonathan Cape, 1928), p. 48. Meredith wrote for the Tramps the *Stave of Roving Tim.*

31. Maitland named them: Edmund Gurney, Shadworth Hodgson, F. W. Maitland, F. Pollock, Corveth Read, G. C. Robertson, Leslie Stephen, James Sully.

32. Jan. 1881, *Letters*, no. 7.

33. Sir John Pollock, *Time's Chariot*, p. 57.

34. Sir Maurice Powicke, *Modern Historians and the Study of History* (London: Odham's Press, 1955), pp. 9–18; *The Collected Papers of Paul Vinogradoff, with a Memoir by H. A. L. Fisher*, 2 vols. (Oxford University Press, 1928), I, 14–15.

35. Pollock to Maitland, 9 Nov. 1887; C. U. Add. M.S. 7006.

36. *Letters*, no. 9.

37. *Letters*, no. 7; quoted above.

38. Reprinted *C.P.*, I, 202, 230, 304.

39. *Letters*, no. 10. The lectures were followed in the session 1884–85 by a further twelve on "The Courts of Law and Equity and Their Jurisdiction." He also took a class with Snell's *Equity* as textbook.

40. See F. H. Lawson, *The Oxford Law School, 1850–1965* (London: Oxford University Press, 1968), pp. 79–80.

41. Vinogradoff's obituary of Maitland, reprinted in Vinogradoff, *Collected Papers*, II, 252–253; *Letters*, no. 97; Fisher, p. 24.

42. *Letters*, no. 12.

43. Fisher, pp. 24–25.

44. T. F. T. Plucknett, *Early English Legal Literature* (London: Cambridge University Press, 1958), pp. 8–10; Powicke, *Modern Historians*, p. 10; H. E. Bell, *Maitland: A Critical Examination and Assessment* (London: Adam and Charles Black, 1965), pp. 3–4; Sir Cecil Carr, *The Mission of the Selden Society* (London: Bernard Quaritch, 1960), pp. 10-11.

45. *LQR*, 1 (1885): 189, 324.

46. *Letters*, no. 12A.

47. *Letters*, no. 97; Vinogradoff, *Collected Papers*, I, 254.

48. *Letters*, no. 14. The "rubbish" was the edition of Bracton by Sir Travers Twiss, 1878–83. At long last Maitland's fears have been allayed by the devoted scholarship of Professor Samuel E. Thorne, whose great edition of Bracton is in course of publication.

49. *Letters*, no. 214. See S.S. vol. 59.

50. Winstanley, *Later Victorian Cambridge*, pp. 303–304, 323–324.

51. Fisher, p. 29; Carr, *Mission of Selden Society*, p. 12; Vinogradoff, *Collected Papers*, I, 254.

52. Fisher, p. 23.

53. See especially vol. I, pp. 33–35.

Chapter V. Return to Cambridge

1. Bell, *Maitland*, p. 140.

2. Boswell, *Life of Samuel Johnson*, April 15, 1781.

3. "Two Lectures," *CLJ*, 1966, pp. 56, 57–58.

4. *Letters,* no. 17.
5. See *Letters,* no. 41.
6. Oct. 31, 1885, *Letters,* no. 14.
7. *Letters,* no. 32. See also *Letters,* nos. 21, 27, 29.
8. *Letters,* nos. 34, 44, 56.
9. *Letters,* no. 27.
10. Mark DeWolfe Howe, ed., *Holmes-Pollock Letters* (Cambridge, Mass: Harvard University Press, 2nd ed., 1961), I, 15.
11. *Letters,* nos. 27, 33, 44.
12. *Letters,* no. 33.
13. "Two Lectures," p. 65.
14. Page v.
15. *Letters,* no. 27.
16. *Letters,* no. 38.
17. "Two Lectures," p. 54n.
18. The letter was reprinted in *BNB,* I, xvii–xxiii; Vinogradoff, *Collected Papers,* I, 297.
19. *Letters,* no. 12A.
20. *Letters,* no. 15.
21. *Letters,* nos. 14, 17, 20, 21, 22, 28.
22. *BNB,* I, 103.
23. *BNB,* I, 107.
24. S.S. vol. 53, pp. xi–xiii; *BNB,* I, 76–77. See also S.S. vol. 53, p. xxiii, note 1, and S.S. vol. 56, p. xii.
25. *Letters,* no. 39, Maitland to Ames; see also *Letters,* no. 35. The letters from Thayer, Ames, and Bigelow are in Cambridge University Mss.
26. Fisher, p. 52; Pollock, *For My Grandson,* p. 190; *Table Talk of John Selden* (S.S. 1927), p. viii.
27. Letter from Pollock to Dove, Dec. 14, 1887 (S.S. Correspondence).
28. Lord Justice Fry was interested in legal history and particularly in Selden, whose life he wrote for the *Dictionary of National Biography.*
29. Maitland to Dove, April 27, 1887, *Letters,* no. 26. The letter on the Year Books is mentioned earlier in the present chapter.
30. "In the Record Edition of Domesday Book, vols. I and II (1783), it was attempted by a special record type to reproduce the original abbreviations of the manuscript." V. H. Galbraith, *The Making of Domesday Book* (London: Oxford University Press, 1961), p. xi.
31. Maitland underestimated the amount of material. When S.S. vol. 1 was published, the years covered were 1200–1225.
32. *Letters,* no. 44; see "The Materials for English Legal History" (1889), *C.P.,* II, 8–11.
33. *Letters,* nos. 31, 33, 35.
34. *Letters,* nos. 37 and 41.
35. *Letters,* no. 39.
36. *Letters,* nos. 49, 51, 58; and see preface to S.S. vol. 2.

37. S.S. minutes for Nov. 29, 1888.

38. *Letters,* no. 54. See also *Letters,* nos. 58, 60, 65.

39. S.S. vol. 1, pp. ix–xx.

40. S.S. vol. 1, pp. xxiv–xxv.

41. S.S. vol. 2, pp. lix–lx. Maitland in this volume speaks of "villan" and "villan" status, though in Pollock and Maitland he speaks of "villein" and "villeinage."

42. *Letters,* no. 57.

43. S.S. vol. 2, pp. 130–131.

44. S.S. vol. 23, pp. 91–92.

45. See *Life of L.S.,* chap. XV, and Noel Annan, *Leslie Stephen* (London: MacGibbon and Kee, 1951), pp. 73–74, 296.

46. An amusing account of the episode is given by Rothenstein in *Men and Memories* (London: Faber and Faber, 1931), I, 97–99.

47. *Letters,* no. 16.

48. *Letters,* no. 18.

49. Sela and Vincent Reynell lived from 1883 to 1887 in Cambridge, where Reynell was Headmaster of King's College Choir School.

50. *Letters,* nos. 28 and 62.

Chapter VI. Downing Professor: 1888 to 1898 (I)

1. See generally Stevens, *Downing College* (London: F. E. Robinson, 1899), in the series Cambridge University, College Histories.

2. His brother, Fletcher Christian, took the lead in the mutiny of the *Bounty.*

3. Stevens, *Downing College,* pp. 109–111.

4. Fry to Maitland, June 7, 1888, and Stubbs to Maitland, June 7, 1888, Cambridge University Mss; Maitland to Thayer, *Letters,* no. 42.

5. *Letters,* no. 46.

6. *C.P.,* I, 480.

7. Above, Chapter IV.

8. Plucknett, *Early English Legal Literature,* pp. 12–14.

9. *Letters,* no. 377.

10. Plucknett, *Early English Legal Literature,* pp. 13–14.

11. *C.P.,* III, 495–511.

12. They were issued in a single volume in 1909 and, after seven reprints, were published separately in 1936.

13. Fisher, p. 69.

14. Plucknett, *Legislation of Edward I* (London: Oxford University Press, 1947), pp. 26–28, and *Columbia Law Review,* 31: 778; A. K. Kiralfy, *Action on the Case* (London: Sweet and Maxwell, 1951), pp. 19–31; S. F. C. Milsom, *LQR,* 74: 95, 407, 561; H. G. Richardson and G. O. Sayles, S.S. vol. 60, esp. pp. cviii–clv.

15. *Letters,* nos. 359 and 455.
16. Carr, *Mission of the Selden Society,* pp. 7–8.
17. *The Athenaeum,* Jan. 5, 1907.
18. *Letters,* no. 222.
19. *Child's-Eye View,* p. 8.
20. *Quarterly Review,* 1907, p. 411.
21. *Letters,* no. 373, and see above Chapter III.
22. Bell, *Maitland,* pp. 142–143.
23. *Letters,* no. 106.
24. *Saturday Review,* Sept. 10, 1910; Carr, *Mission of the Selden Society,* p. 14; *Letters,* no. 274.
25. Charlton pasted in the front of the first volume of the *Note Book* the following plea which Maitland had sent to Bate to accompany an umbrella left by Bate in Maitland's house. "Et predictus J.P.B. venit et dicit quod predictus F.W.M. cepit et asportavit umbrellam suam precii xxj sol. nequitur et in felonia et contra pacem, etc. Et predictus F.W.M. dicit quod non cepit nec asportavit dictam umbrellam sed invenit eam latitantem et discurrentem in aula sua; et dicit quod umbrellae sunt quasi res nullius et ferae naturae." This copy of the *Note Book* is now in the Library of The Queen's University of Belfast. Professor F. H. Newark has kindly given this information.
26. I am deeply indebted to Professor E. L. G. Stones of the University of Glasgow for telling me of this letter and for sending me a copy. The letter is in the custody of the Librarian of the University of Glasgow.
27. *Letters,* nos. 133, 161.
28. *Letters,* nos. 175, 176.
29. An address delivered on July 9, 1890, and published by the Cambridge University Press.
30. Armitage Robinson, *Cambridge University Reporter,* June 22, 1907.
31. *Henry Sidgwick,* p. 180.
32. *Letters,* nos. 188, 191.
33. *CLJ,* 1: 290.
34. *Letters,* no. 194; and MS letter to C. H. S. Fifoot.
35. *CLJ,* 1: 292.
36. Sir John Pollock, *Time's Chariot,* p. 52.
37. R. C. K. Ensor, *England, 1870–1914* (London: Oxford University Press, 1936), pp. 116–117, 284–285.
38. *Letters,* no. 345.
39. *Quarterly Review,* 1907, p. 411.
40. *Letters,* nos. 64, 66, 69. Pell had also lent Maitland the rolls of his manor. See "The History of a Cambridgeshire Manor," *EHR,* July 1894; *C.P.,* II, 366–406.
41. Preface to S.S. vol. 4; *Letters,* no. 86.
42. Jan. 1891, pp. 63–69; *C.P.,* II, 190–201.

43. "Lesch" is sedge. See S.S. vol. 4, pp. 12, 107–118.

44. *Letters,* no. 118. Maitland reviewed the essay on the coroner in *EHR,* 1893, pp. 758–760; he had already reviewed *The Gild Merchant* in the *Economic Journal* for June 1891, reprinted *C.P.,* II, 223–231.

45. *Letters,* no. 224.

46. *C.P.,* II, 32; *Letters,* no. 94; S.S. vol. 8, introduction, p. ix.

47. *Letters,* nos. 140, 141.

48. *Letters,* no. 143.

49. See S.S. vol. 85, introduction, pp. xii, xv, xvii, xix.

50. Maitland printed A. W. Verrall's English version of them at p. xxi of his introduction to the *Mirror of Justices,* S.S. vol. 7.

51. *Letters,* no. 279; Howe, *Holmes-Pollock Letters,* I, 31; *Bracton and Azo,* S.S. vol. 8, introduction, p. xxvi.

52. "The Roman Elements in Bracton's Treatise," *Yale Law Review* 32 (1923): 751–756; Vinogradoff, *Collected Papers,* I, 239.

53. Samuel E. Thorne, *Bracton on the Laws and Customs of England* (Cambridge, Mass.: Harvard University Press, 1968), vol. I, Translator's Introduction, pp. vii–xlviii. See also H. Kantorowicz, *Bractonian Problems* (Glasgow: Jackson, 1941), pp. 36–58, 78–127; and Plucknett, *Early English Legal Literature* (Cambridge University Press, 1958), pp. 55–57, 65–72.

54. Maitland's plea, whatever its weight as mitigation, is not unwarranted. See Thorne, *Bracton,* I, Translator's Introduction, xxxiii–xxxvi.

55. *Letters,* nos. 369, 492, 495; see also no. 164.

Chapter VII. Downing Professor: 1888 to 1898 (II)

1. "The Body Politic," *C.P.,* III, 285–303.

2. *Letters,* no. 28.

3. *Letters,* nos. 59 and 61; Vinogradoff, *Collected Papers,* I, 20, 30–31. Seebohm's book was *The English Village Community* (1883).

4. *Letters,* no. 149. The Regius Professorship of Modern History at Cambridge was vacant through the death of Sir John Seeley. Vinogradoff's letter to Maitland, dated Jan. 12/24, 1895, is in Cambridge Add. Mss.

5. E. J. Tardif, visiting England in 1892, had just missed Maitland. "By an unhappy misfortune we have crossed ourselves on the way from Cheltenham to London" (Letter to Maitland, Sept. 30, 1892, Camb. Add. Mss.).

6. *Letters,* no. 177. See also Liebermann's letter of July 6, 1892 (Camb. Add. Mss.), and Buckland, *CLJ,* 1: 281.

7. Powicke, *Modern Historians,* p. 154.

8. Hutton, *Letters of William Stubbs,* p. 134.

9. Letter of Dec. 11, 1892 (Camb. Add. Mss.).

10. Letter of March 28, 1895 (Camb. Add. Mss.).

11. *Sussex Archaeological Collections,* XLII, 63, where Round gives a bibliography of the conflict. See also *Letters,* nos. 134, 147, 252.

12. *Letters,* nos. 179, 224. On the incident see Helen M. Cam, *Selected Historical Essays of F. W. Maitland* (Cambridge University Press, 1957), pp. xxiv–xxvii.

13. Reprinted in Cam, pp. 259–265.

14. *Letters,* nos. 252, 264. It is fair to add that Round paid tribute to Maitland four years after his death (Cam, pp. xxvi–xxvii).

15. F. M. Stenton, *Anglo-Saxon England* (London: Oxford University Press, 2nd ed., 1943), p. 703.

16. Letter of Jan. 8, 1896 (Camb. Add. Mss.).

17. *Letters,* no. 238.

18. *Men and Memories,* I, 48.

19. *Letters,* no. 79.

20. *Letters,* nos. 234, 238.

21. David Ogg, *Herbert Fisher* (London: Edward Arnold, 1947), pp. 43–44, 142–143.

22. *Letters,* no. 62.

23. A characteristic review under the title "Tenures in Roussillon and Namur," appeared in *EHR,* Oct. 1892; reprinted *C.P.,* II, 251–265. Maitland here examined two books on local history by French historians, their aims and achievements and the wider issues involved. Botched or pretentious work he sought to kill with ridicule; see his review of *The History of Marriage, Jewish and Christian, in Relation to Divorce,* by H. M. Luckock, Dean of Lichfield (*EHR,* 1895, pp. 755–759). In Maitland's words he had here "played the savage with the Dean"; *Letters,* no. 150.

24. *Letters,* nos. 218–220, 244; *C.P.,* III, 114.

25. The full title is *Records of the Parliament Holden at Westminster in the Thirty-third Year of the Reign of King Edward the First.*

26. P. M. Winfield, *The Chief Sources of English Legal History* (Harvard University Press, 1925), p. 258; Vinogradoff, *Collected Papers,* I, 79; *Letters,* nos. 186, 187.

27. V. H. Galbraith, *The Public Records* (London: Oxford University Press, 1934), p. 70.

28. *Letters,* no. 73. See also *Letters,* nos. 55, 57, 70, 72, 78.

29. *Letters,* no. 100. See also *Letters,* nos. 102, 108, 115, 119, 120.

30. *Letters,* no. 134. There had in fact been a short notice in *Notes and Queries.* The Scottish "word" may have been spoken by George Neilson or Joseph Bain (Cam, *Selected Historical Essays,* p. xvi). Bain was the editor of the *Calendar of Documents Relating to Scotland Preserved in the Public Record Office.*

31. The importance of the *Memoranda de Parliamento* has been emphasized by many historians. See Galbraith, *Studies in the Public Records* (London: Nelson and Sons, 1948), pp. 4, 6–7; Cam, *Selected Historical Essays,* pp. xv–xx; Powicke, *The Thirteenth Century* (London: Oxford

University Press, 2nd ed., 1962), pp. 348–351, 747. Bell, *Maitland,* chap. VI, is less enthusiastic.

32. *Letters,* no. 36; "The History of a Cambridgeshire Manor," *C.P.*, II, 336.

33. Sir John Pollock, *Time's Chariot,* pp. 81–93.

34. *Letters,* nos. 78, 83; Howe, *Holmes-Pollock Letters,* I, 32.

35. *Letters,* no. 87.

36. In December 1897 Pollock told Holmes that he thought to write a short elementary book on English legal history; and in November 1898 he published two installments in the *Harvard Law Review.* See Howe, *Holmes-Pollock Letters,* I, 81, 89.

37. In the result the *History* ended at the death of Henry III.

38. *Letters,* nos. 96 (Nov. 1, 1891) and 109 (May 29, 1892).

39. Pollock to Maitland, Feb. 15, 1893 (Cam. Add. Mss.). Pollock was no party to the contract with the Cambridge University Press, which paid all the author's share of profits to Maitland. Maitland always in fact sent Pollock one fifth of such profits; and, in a memorandum accompanying his will, wrote that his representatives should continue the practice. See *Letters,* no. 138.

40. Howe, *Holmes-Pollock Letters,* I, 52; Stephen to Maitland, July 26, 1894 (Camb. Univ. Add. Mss.).

41. *Letters,* no. 138.

42. *Letters,* nos. 140 and 150.

43. Howe, *Holmes-Pollock Letters,* I, 60–61.

44. Powicke, *Modern Historians,* p. 165.

45. *Letters,* nos. 165, 178. The second edition was reprinted in 1911, 1923, 1952, and 1968, on the last occasion with a valuable introduction and bibliography by S. F. C. Milsom.

46. Maitland to Lord Acton, Nov. 11, 1896 (Camb. Univ. Lib. Add. 6443).

47. "The Materials for English Legal History" (1889), *C.P.*, II, 6. Reeves's *History of English Law from the Times of the Saxons* was published in 4 volumes from 1783 to 1787.

48. From a review of *The Gild Merchant,* June 1891, *C.P.*, II, 223–224. Madox published *Firma Burgi* in 1722. On him and his contemporaries see D. C. Douglas, *English Scholars* (London: Jonathan Cape, 1939), esp. Chapter XI.

49. *Letters,* no. 98; see above, Chapter I.

50. "The Survival of Archaic Communities," *C.P.*, II, 337–338.

51. Faber, *Jowett,* p. 418.

52. I am most grateful to the Librarian of Glasgow University in whose custody this letter is, for telling me of its existence and allowing me to have a copy of it. The letter is undated, but from its contents must have been written at some date in July, August, or September 1896; see *Letters,* nos. 177 to 180.

53. *Pollock and Maitland,* I, xxxv (p. cv in the 1968 reissue).

54. *Letters,* nos. 93, 106, 109, 147.

55. See *Domesday Book,* pp. 3 and 5, and Vinogradoff, *English Society in the Eleventh Century* (London: Oxford University Press, 1908). The chief critic of Maitland's conclusion upon the purpose of the Domesday survey is V. H. Galbraith; see *Studies in the Public Records* (1948), chap. IV; *The Making of Domesday Book* (1961); and the citations from these two books in Bell, *Maitland,* pp. 21–25.

56. See *Domesday Book,* Essay I, sect. 9, opening paragraph.

57. Tait's review is in *EHR,* 12 (1897): 768–777. Maitland had been especially attracted by F. Keutgen's *Untersuchungen über den Ursprung der deutschen Stadtverfassung,* which he had discussed in *EHR,* 11 (1896): 13–19.

58. *Letters,* no. 200. No new edition of *Domesday Book* was called for, and in 1900 Maitland wrote to Poole: "I now regret that I did not take occasion of Tait's review to explain my guesses about the manerium" (*Letters,* no. 264). See Powicke, *Modern Historians,* pp. 54–56, and Bell, *Maitland,* chap. II.

59. *Domesday Book,* Essay II, sect. 6, last paragraph.

60. Powicke, *Modern Historians,* p. 75; *Letters,* nos. 109, 211, 271.

61. *Letters,* nos. 188 and 194, and a letter from Maitland to Poole of Feb. 28, 1897, in Camb. Univ. Lib.

62. See Maitland's review of Gross, *The Gild Merchant* (1891), *C.P.,* II, 223–231.

63. "The Survival of Archaic Communities: I. The Malmesbury Case," *LQR,* 1893, pp. 36–50; *C.P.,* II, 313–337.

64. *The Antiquary,* chap. 4.

65. Preface, *Township and Borough.*

66. *Township and Borough,* pp. 4–7. Maitland, had he thought and wished to do so, might have put in evidence Thomas Hardy's portrait of Dorchester in *The Mayor of Casterbridge,* published in 1886.

67. *Township and Borough,* pp. 36–37, 40–41, 42–43, and Appendix, notes 149–151.

68. *Township and Borough,* pp. 18, 80–81.

69. *Township and Borough,* p. 24.

70. *Township and Borough,* pp. 21–22. See Maine, *Ancient Law,* 6th ed., p. 184.

71. *The Bookman,* Feb. 1907.

72. *Letters,* no. 201.

73. *Letters,* no. 99; see also *Letters,* nos. 95, 97, 98. The paper was "Henry II and the Criminous Clerks," *EHR,* 1892, p. 224; *C.P.,* II, 232.

74. 10 C. and F. 534 (1843); followed in *Beamish v. Beamish,* 9 H.L.C., 274 (1861), where, however, Willes, J., was critical of *The Queen v. Millis.*

75. *Pollock and Maitland,* II, 373–374.

76. Hutton, *Letters of William Stubbs,* pp. 204–234.

77. In a different context Professor Galbraith has also doubted the "evolutionary" character of the sixteenth century. Comparing the skill of medieval with the sloth of Tudor archivists, he suggested that the Tudor period was "a greater breach with the preceding age than Whig historians have cared to admit"; *Studies in the Public Records,* pp. 87–88.

78. William Lyndwood (1375?–1446) finished his book about 1430 and it was first printed 1470–1480; the standard edition is that of 1679. It contains the provincial constitutions of fourteen Archbishops of Canterbury.

79. *Letters,* nos. 168, 170, 173. *EHR,* 1896, pp. 446, 641; 1897, p. 625.

80. *Letters,* no. 225.

81. *LQR,* 1896, p. 174; *LQR,* 1886, p. 153.

82. Robert Grosseteste, Bishop of Lincoln from 1235 to 1253, was an indefatigable reformer and a wide scholar. He wrote books on theology, on philosophy, and on husbandry; commented on Aristotle and on Boethius; and composed French poems.

83. See Hutton, *Letters of Bishop Stubbs,* p. 206.

84. *Letters,* no. 239. G. F. B. was Dr. G. F. Browne, Bishop of Bristol; "my lord of London" was Mandell Creighton.

85. See C. R. Cheney, "Legislation of the Medieval English Church," *EHR,* 1935, p. 202; Bell, *Maitland,* chap. VIII, and authorities there cited, pp. 115–120.

86. *Letters,* no. 418.

Chapter VIII. Family Life

1. For the material of this and the succeeding chapter I am greatly indebted to the late Ermengard Maitland: her Selden Society memoir, *F. W. Maitland, A Child's-Eye View* (1957), her manuscript essays, and her conversations with myself. I have drawn also upon *Fredegond and Gerald Shove* (privately printed, 1952), written by Fredegond with a preface by Ermengard Maitland, and upon Florence Maitland's diaries and letters.

2. *The Maitland-Bigelow Letters,* ed. Warren O. Ault, *Boston University Law Review,* 37.3 (Summer 1957): 308.

3. *A Child's Eye-View,* pp. 6, 11.

4. *Fredegond and Gerald Shove,* pp. 13, 21.

5. *Period Piece,* p. 195.

6. F. W. H. Myers was a pupil and friend of Henry Sidgwick. He was interested in psychical research and author, with Edmund Gurney, of *Phantasms of the Living* (1886). His wife was an accomplished amateur photographer; two portraits by her of Florence Maitland are reproduced in *Fredegond and Gerald Shove.*

7. Ursula Vaughan Williams, *Ralph Vaughan Williams* (London: Oxford University Press, 1964), pp. 35–36. In 1897 Adeline married Vaughan Williams and the Maitland children were her bridesmaids. When Mait-

land died in Las Palmas, Vaughan Williams went out to bring Florence and Ermengard home. His setting of Whitman's *Toward the Unknown Region* in 1907 was in memory of Maitland and dedicated to Florence. In 1925 he set to music four poems by Fredegond.

8. Florence Maitland's diaries; *Letters,* no. 166; *The Maitland-Bigelow Letters,* pp. 304, 305, 310.

9. *A Child's-Eye View,* pp. 10–11.

10. *Period Piece,* pp. 63–64, 269–272.

11. See above, Chapter II.

12. *Fredegond and Gerald Shove,* p. 2.

13. *A Child's-Eye View,* p. 6.

14. *Henry Sidgwick,* p. 454; letter of August 1, 1905, from Jackson to Maitland, Camb. Add. Mss.; *Letters,* no. 444; *Life of L.S.,* p. 278.

15. *Letters,* nos. 121, 122. Thayer visited Horsepools once: see *Letters,* nos. 204, 307.

16. *A Child's-Eye View,* p. 15.

17. *A Child's-Eye View,* pp. 14–15; Ermengard Maitland's recollections.

18. *A Child's-Eye View,* p. 8.

19. Ermengard Maitland's recollections.

20. "An Agnostic's Apology," *Fortnightly Review,* June 1876; reprinted with other papers under the same title in 1893. Thomas Hardy, like Maitland, had been nurtured on the services and traditions of the Church of England and was steeped in the thought and language of the Book of Common Prayer; and he, too, felt the agnostic influence of Leslie Stephen. See *The Early Life of Thomas Hardy,* pp. 132, 139, 269.

21. *Henry Sidgwick,* pp. 227–228, 347–348.

22. Faber, *Jowett,* p. 140.

23. *A Child's-Eye View,* p. 10; Ogg, *Herbert Fisher,* p. 12.

24. *Letters,* no. 239.

25. *A Child's-Eye View,* pp. 9–10; *Fredegond and Gerald Shove,* p. 26.

26. *Letters,* nos. 215–219, 222.

27. The University appointed Courtney Stanhope Kenny, who had succeeded Maitland as Reader in English Law in 1888 and who was to succeed him again as Downing Professor in 1907.

28. *The Maitland-Bigelow Letters,* p. 312.

Chapter IX. Winter Exile

1. *Letters,* nos. 230, 231. *The Life of Henry Fawcett* (1888) was by Leslie Stephen.

2. *Letters,* nos. 235, 237, 239, 240.

3. *Letters,* nos. 245–250; Buckland, p. 285.

4. Maitland gave Quiney's Hotel, Las Palmas, as his postal address.

5. *Letters,* no. 261.

6. "Maitland-Bigelow Letters," p. 313.

7. *Letters,* no. 278.

8. *Letters,* nos. 300, 350, 412.

9. *Letters,* no. 253. The article is reprinted in Cam, *Selected Historical Essays,* pp. 97–121.

10. *Letters,* nos. 253, 254, 259; *Henry Sidgwick,* pp. 578–579.

11. See above, Chapter III.

12. *Letters,* nos. 259, 261.

13. *Life of L.S.,* pp. 465–466, 469, 485–486.

14. *Letters,* nos. 380, 385. The book was reissued as an Ann Arbor Paperback by the University of Michigan Press in 1961.

15. *Fredegond and Gerald Shove,* pp. 23–24.

16. *Letters,* nos. 348, 350, 377.

17. *Letters,* nos. 252, 259, 281, 350, 353.

18. MS shown by Ermengard Maitland to C. H. S. Fifoot.

19. *Letters,* no. 260.

20. *Fredegond and Gerald Shove,* p. 22.

21. *Letters,* no. 345.

22. Buckland, p. 285.

23. Buckland, pp. 282–284.

24. See his obituary by Sir Cecil Carr in *Proceedings of the British Academy,* 40 (1954): 207–218; *Letters,* no. 181.

25. *Letters,* no. 500.

26. S.S. vol. 66, p. viii.

27. *Letters,* no. 308.

28. Verrall to Maitland, Jan. 31, 1903, Camb. Add. Mss. For Peter Featherstone and his relations see George Eliot, *Middlemarch,* chaps. 35 and 53.

29. *Letters,* nos. 466, 468, 470; R. St. J. Parry, *Henry Jackson, O.M.* (London: Cambridge University Press, 1926), pp. 72, 78.

30. Leonard Woolf, *Sowing* (London: The Hogarth Press, 1960), p. 198.

31. See the controversy over the Squire Law Library, below, Chap. X.

32. *A Child's-Eye View,* p. 10.

Chapter X. Downing Professor: 1899 to 1906

1. *Letters,* nos. 266, 289, 313, 332, 334, 363, 365, 385, 386.

2. *Letters,* no. 426. See also *Letters,* nos. 420, 422, 423, and Jackson to Maitland, March 10, 1905, Camb. Univ. Mss.

3. *Henry Jackson,* p. 152.

4. *Cambridge University Reporter,* Dec. 17, 1904; *Letters,* nos. 408, 414.

5. *Letters,* no. 426.

6. *Letters,* nos. 344, 352.

7. Stevenson to Maitland, Nov. 17, 1902, Camb. Add. Mss.; *Letters,* no. 383. Stevenson's edition of *Asser's Life of King Alfred* was published in 1904; *The Crawford Collection of Early Charters and Documents,* by Stevenson and A. S. Napier, had been published in 1895.

8. *Letters,* no. 373; Vinogradoff, *Collected Papers,* I, 23–30; Powicke, *Modern Historians,* pp. 9–18.

9. *Letters,* nos. 370, 372, 373, 374; Vinogradoff to Maitland, Feb. 24, 1904, Camb. Add. Mss. Maine was the first occupant of the Corpus chair.

10. *Letters,* nos. 413, 427; Buckland, p. 296.

11. Powicke, *Modern Historians,* p. 130. H. D. Hazeltine, who succeeded Kenny as Downing Professor in 1919, visited Maitland for a day in 1902 but only became his colleague in the Cambridge Law Faculty in the Michaelmas Term, 1906.

12. *Essays on the Teaching of History* (Cambridge University Press, 1901), Introduction by Maitland, pp. xiv–xv; *C.P.*, III, 404. Gray was Professor from 1768 to 1771, but did not lecture.

13. *Henry Sidgwick,* p. 313.

14. G. P. Gooch, *History and Historians in the Nineteenth Century* (London: Longmans, 2nd ed., 1952), pp. 344–349; Trevelyan, *Autobiography,* pp. 16–17; *Life and Letters of Mandell Creighton* (London: Longmans, 1906), I, 277–278.

15. Sir Charles Oman, *On the Writing of History* (London: Methuen, 1939), pp. 209–210; see also David Matthew, *Lord Acton and His Times* (London: Eyre and Spottiswoode, 1968), pp. 100–105.

16. *Life and Letters of Mandell Creighton,* I, 368–376. *Henry Sidgwick,* pp. 569–570.

17. *Letters,* no. 176; Trevelyan, *Autobiography,* p. 18.

18. *The Cambridge Modern History, an Account of Its Origin, Authorship and Production* (1907); G. N. Clark, Introduction to *The New Cambridge Modern History,* p. xviii.

19. Letters by Maitland to Acton, Camb. Add. Mss. 6443; Oct. 26, 1896 (196), Nov. 20, 1896 (197), Nov. 25, 1896 (198), Nov. 27, 1896 (199), Nov. 28, 1896 (200). Mr. A. E. B. Owen of the Cambridge University Library most kindly brought these letters to my notice and gave me copies.

20. Camb. Add. Mss. 6443 (197).

21. Maitland to Acton, Camb. Add. Mss. 6443; Dec. 3, 1897 (203), Nov. 4, 1898 (204); *Letters,* no. 261.

22. *Letters,* no. 332.

23. *The Cambridge Review,* Oct. 16, 1902; *CP,* III, 512.

24. *Letters,* no. 343. John Bagnell Bury became Regius Professor of Modern History, and Maitland "thought the appointment very good"; *Letters,* no. 348.

25. *Cambridge Modern History,* II, 565.

26. *Cambridge Modern History,* II, 569. "Elizabethan Gleaning V," *EHR,* July 1903; *C.P.*, III, 185.

27. *Cambridge Modern History,* II, 570–571.

28. *Cambridge Modern History,* II, 587–588.

29. *Cambridge Modern History,* II, 550.

30. *Cambridge Modern History,* II, 577.

31. *Cambridge Modern History,* II, 580.

32. *Cambridge Modern History,* II, 562–563.

33. A. L. Smith, *Frederic William Maitland: Two Lectures and a Bibliography* (London: Oxford University Press, 1908), p. 25: Sir J. E. Neale, "The Elizabethan Acts of Supremacy and Uniformity," *EHR,* 1950, p. 165, and *Elizabeth and Her Parliaments, 1559–1581* (London: Jonathan Cape, 1953), pt. I, chaps. II and III. See Bell, *Maitland,* chap. IX.

34. A. L. Smith, *Maitland,* pp. 23, 28.

35. Cam, *Selected Historical Essays,* p. 210; *Cambridge Modern History,* II, 592.

36. See Bell, *Maitland,* pp. 129–130; Cam, *Selected Historical Essays,* p. 216, n. 1.

37. *Letters,* no. 239. *Dictionary of National Biography,* "MacColl, Malcolm." "Canon MacColl's New Convocation," *Fortnightly Review,* Dec. 1899; *C.P.,* III, 119.

38. Maitland to Poole, April 29, 1901, *Letters,* no. 283.

39. See also Maitland's review of *The Records of the Honourable Society of Lincoln's Inn* in *EHR,* 1898, p. 576.

40. *English Law and the Renaissance* (Cambridge University Press, 1901), pp. 1–2. Rede was Reader at Lincoln's Inn in 1486.

41. *English Law and the Renaissance,* p. 22, and notes 51, 52.

42. *English Law and the Renaissance,* pp. 27–28.

43. *English Law and the Renaissance,* p. 25. "History of English Law," *Encyclopaedia Britannica,* 10th ed., supplement 1902, reprinted in Cam, *Selected Historical Essays,* pp. 112–113.

44. *Letters,* no. 287.

45. Bell, *Maitland,* pp. 131–137. See also Holdsworth, *History of English Law,* IV, 255–282; Cam, *Selected Historical Essays,* p. xiv; Plucknett, *Concise History,* pp. 298–299; John P. Dawson, *A History of Lay Judges* (Cambridge, Mass.: Harvard University Press, 1960).

46. *Letters,* no. 233.

47. Martin Wolff, "On the Nature of Legal Persons," *LQR,* 54 (1938): 494.

48. *Letters,* no. 87.

49. *Township and Borough,* p. 14.

50. *LQR,* 16: 335, and *C.P.,* III, 210; *LQR,* 17: 131, and *C.P.,* III, 244; *C.P.,* III, 321; *C.P.,* III, 304. Two other papers read to the Eranus Society may be noted but add little: "The Unincorporate Body," *C.P.,* III, 271; and "The Body Politic," *C.P.,* III, 285.

51. Gierke, *Political Theories of the Middle Age,* pp. xix, xxv, xxx. Maitland more than once suggested that, at the close of the Middle Ages, the common law had borrowed the fiction theory from the canonists: see *Pollock and Maitland,* I, 489–491; Gierke, *Political Theories of the Middle Age,* p. xiv; "The Corporation Sole," *C.P.,* III, 211. The evidence adduced is not convincing, and the suggestion has not been accepted; see Pollock, *Essays in the Law* (London: Oxford University Press, 1922), p. 151.

52. Gierke, *Political Theories of the Middle Age,* pp. xl–xli.

53. Willes, J., in *Limpus v. London General Omnibus Co.,* I. H. and C. (1862), at p. 529.

54. *Citizens Life Assurance Co. v. Brown* [1904] A. C. 423.

55. Gierke, *Political Theories of the Middle Age,* pp. xxix–xxx.

56. See Redlich to Maitland, Aug. 5, 1903, Camb. Add. Mss; *Letters,* nos. 364, 366, 420. For Maitland's original version see *C.P.,* III, 321.

57. "The Corporation Sole," *LQR,* 16 (1900): 335; *C.P.,* III, 210.

58. "The Crown as Corporation," *LQR,* 17 (1901): 131; *C.P.,* III, 244.

59. Plowden, *Case of the Duchy of Lancaster,* p. 213.

60. *C.P.,* III, 304.

61. Cited by A. L. Smith, *Maitland,* pp. 54–58.

Chapter XI. The Selden Society and the Year Books

1. S.S. vol. 14. For an example of Maitland's loyal support of an editor see *Letters,* no. 161.

2. *Letters,* no. 212. For Hudson's Norwich book see S.S. vol. 5.

3. *Letters,* no. 268. Selden Society correspondence, June 1, 1900, June 18, 1900, July 16, 1900 (Lock to Leach); July 17, 1900, July 19, 1900 (Lock to Maitland).

4. *Letters,* nos. 269, 270.

5. *Letters,* nos. 273, 275.

6. See above, Chapter IX.

7. S.S. vol. 4, p. 11.

8. S.S. minutes, May 22, 1895; *Letters,* no. 174.

9. Preface to S.S. vol. 66, where Plucknett told the story.

10. Volumes 13, 22, 26, 42, 45, 63.

11. S.S. correspondence, esp. Lock to Turner, Sept. 25 and 26, 1899; *Letters,* no. 246.

12. *Letters,* nos. 273, 275, 284.

13. *Letters,* nos. 288, 292. A "qualified apology" and a note on the medieval use of the letters U and V both appeared in the preface.

14. *Life and Letters of Mandell Creighton,* I, 341.

15. *Letters,* no. 226. The first volume of the Leicester Records was published in 1899, the second in 1901, and the third in 1905.

16. *Letters,* no. 212; S.S. minutes, June 25, 1901.

17. *Letters,* no. 355.

18. March 4, 1904, S.S. correspondence.

19. *Letters,* no. 397.

20. *Letters,* no. 449, and Miss Bateson to Maitland, Oct. 26, 1905, Camb. Add. Mss.

21. S.S. correspondence. See also S.S. vol. 21, p. xxix.

22. *Letters,* no. 165. See also *Letters,* no. 39.

23. "The Materials for English Legal History," pub. in *Political Science Quarterly* and reprinted in *C.P.*, II, 1–60; see esp. p. 54.

24. *Letters,* no. 182; see also *Letters,* nos. 183, 204, 207, 326.

25. *Letters,* no. 185.

26. *Letters,* no. 204. Sir William Markby (1829–1914), after having been a Judge of the High Court of Calcutta, was Reader in Indian Law at Oxford and a Fellow of All Souls College. See F. H. Lawson, *The Oxford Law School, 1850–1965* (London: Oxford University Press, 1968), pp. 73–75.

27. Pike was receiving for his work on the Rolls Series "a wage the like of which we could not pay"; *Letters,* no. 183.

28. *Letters,* no. 205.

29. *Letters,* no. 347.

30. *Letters,* nos. 296, 297, 311.

31. *Letters,* nos. 308, 315, 329. In the preface to S.S. vol. 17, Maitland wrote of Turner: "Of the learning, skill and industry that he showed in searching the Plea Rolls for cases reported in the Year Books I cannot speak too highly or too gratefully."

32. *Letters,* nos. 316, 327, 339, and Soule to Maitland, Camb. Add. Mss. Eugene Wambaugh (1856–1940) was professor at Harvard from 1892 to 1925; he published his *Study of Cases* in 1892 and edited Littleton's *Tenures* in 1903.

33. *Letters,* no. 327.

34. Lock to Maitland, Aug. 12, 1902, S.S. correspondence.

35. *Letters,* no. 329.

36. *Letters,* nos. 331, 351.

37. *Letters,* no. 326. Maitland had long been at work upon his discourse; see *Letters,* no. 279.

38. *Letters,* nos. 355, 356. S.S. vol. 17, is entitled *Year Books 1 & 2 Edward II;* vol. 19, *Year Books 2 & 3 Edward II.*

39. *Letters,* nos. 360, 361, 362. Thayer had died in March 1902.

40. Dec. 11, 1903, S.S. correspondence.

41. *Letters,* nos. 442, 460.

42. *Letters,* no. 280. See Rolls Series, Year Book 30–31 Edw. I, pp. lv–lxi, and Pollock and Maitland, II, 646, n. 3.

43. S.S. vol. 17, pp. xi–xiv. The references to Plowden, Coke, and Blackstone are given in a footnote to p. xii.

44. Pike (Rolls Series, Year Book 20 Edw. III, pt. 2, vol. I, p. lxxii) suggested that the Year Books may have been the semiofficial work of four clerks of the Common Bench. The suggestion has not been accepted; see Turner, S.S. vol. 26, pp. xxv–xxviii, and W. C. Bolland, *The Year Books* (London: Cambridge University Press, 1921), pp. 33–35.

45. S.S. vol. 17, p. xv; and see p. xiii.

46. S.S. vol. 17, p. xv. When a lord distrained his tenant for services or rent, the tenant—if he challenged the distress—brought an action of replevin; and the lord might admit or "avow" the distress and justify it by alleging that the rent or services were in arrear.

47. S.S. vol. 19, p. xvi. If the Crib could not be identified, a case of 1310 at least locates Hell. An assault had been committed "here in the hall in the place under the bench that is called Hell"; S.S. vol. 19, p. xvi.

48. Pages x–xv, esp. pp. xii–xiii.

49. S.S. vol. 26, pp. xxxvi–xl.

50. Bolland, *The Year Books,* pp. 35–42; A. W. B. Simpson, in *LQR,* 73: 492.

51. On their changing nature and outlook see Plucknett, *A Concise History of the Common Law,* 5th ed. (London: Butterworth, 1956), pp. 268–273.

52. Contrast the French of the later Year Books: *Letters,* no. 329, and S.S. vol. 17, pp. xvii, xxxiii–xxxvii.

53. S.S. vol. 17, pp. xxxvii–xliii.

54. Pages xlv–liii.

55. Pages liv–lxxvii.

56. *Letters,* no. 375. Paul Meyer (1840–1917) was Director of the Ecole des Chartes and a distinguished philologist.

57. S.S. vol. 52, p. xxx.

58. S.S. vol. 70, esp. pp. xvii and xxi–lxiv. See also the extensive introduction by Professor Collas to S.S. vol. 81.

59. S.S. vol. 17, pp. xvii–xviii.

60. Pages xviii–xix.

61. Pages xvi–xvii.

62. S.S. vol. 17, pp. xv–xvi; S.S. vol. 20, pp. lxix and 190. As a modern variant or reminiscence of "wine and candle," a friend told Maitland that Devonshire people still said "That's supper—beer and bed," meaning "That's all over."

63. S.S. vol. 17, pp. xxxii–xxxiii. The French librarian was Maurice Prou (*Manuel de Paleographie,* planche 4).

64. A. L. Smith, *Maitland,* p. 39; Bell, *Maitland,* pp. 106–107. *Contra,* see V. H. Galbraith, *Introduction to the Use of the Public Records* (London: Oxford University Press, 1934), 51.

65. *The Oracles of the Law* (Ann Arbor: University of Michigan Press, 1968), 143; Pollock and Maitland, I, 21–24, 111–124, 207–208.

Chapter XII. The Life and Letters of Leslie Stephen

1. *Letters,* no. 157 and Camb. Add. Mss. It was in Stephen's house that Maitland had proposed to Florence Fisher.

2. *Dictionary of National Biography,* of which Stephen was the first editor.

3. *Letters,* no. 381.

4. *Letters,* no. 397.

5. *Letters,* nos. 400, 414, 417; Jackson to Maitland, Jan. 16, 1905, Camb. Univ. Mss.

6. *Letters,* no. 404. Stephen's chief correspondents in the United States had been Oliver Wendell Holmes, James Russell Lowell, and Charles Eliot Norton.

7. *Letters,* no. 418; and see *Letters,* no. 416.

8. *Letters,* nos. 418 and 419.

9. *Letters,* nos. 468, 469, 480, 485, 486. It was published by Duckworth and Company. Gerald Duckworth was Stephen's stepson.

10. Howe, *Holmes-Pollock Letters,* I, 136; Annan, preface to *Leslie Stephen.* Both Thomas Hardy and Lord Bryce congratulated Maitland; *Letters,* nos. 493, 494.

11. *Letters,* nos. 379, 417. Stephen had contributed many papers to the *Pall Mall Gazette.*

12. *The Early Life of Thomas Hardy,* p. 238.

13. *Letters,* no. 410.

14. *Letters,* nos. 402, 441. The electoral proceedings concerned Henry Fawcett and Trinity Hall, when Stephen persuaded the Fellows to break the College statutes. See also *Life of L.S.,* pp. 106–107.

15. *Life of L.S.,* pp. 491–492. Stephen recalled the *History of Thought in the Eighteenth Century,* which he had published in 1876.

16. J. M. E. McTaggart, Fellow of Trinity College, Cambridge; see *Letters,* no. 428.

17. It is one of life's ironies that Stephen's daughter, Virginia, should have been, in another generation, the writer most richly endowed for such a study.

18. *Letters,* nos. 418, 428, 444, 464. "For two only": Stephen and Florence. For Stephen's ascent of the Shreckhorn, see *Life of L.S.,* pp. 83–85.

19. *Letters,* no. 472.

20. Hollond, p. 4.

21. *Letters,* no. 471; and see *Letters,* no. 472.

22. Maitland to F. J. H. Jenkinson, May 18, 1906, Camb. Add. 4403. I am indebted to Mr. A. E. B. Owen of the Cambridge University Library for the notice of this letter.

23. *Letters,* no. 459. On the Eranus Society see *Henry Sidgwick,* pp. 223–224.

24. Fisher, p. 22. I am indebted to Professor C. D. Broad for the reference to the minutes and for other kind help.

25. A previous winter had been spent in Tafira. Fredegond, on medical advice, was spending the winter of 1906–07 at Bex in Switzerland.

26. *Letters,* no. 491. "Goose" or "Duchess" were Maitland's pet names for Ermengard.

27. *Letters,* no. 494. It appears from its contents that an intermediate letter has been lost.

28. Thoby was Leslie Stephen's elder son by his second wife. Aged twenty-six, he had died in the previous week of typhoid caught in Athens. Ginia and Nessa are Virginia and Vanessa Stephen. Thoby and Clive Bell had met at Trinity College, Cambridge, where, with others (including Leonard Woolf, later married to Virginia), they had founded in 1899 "the Midnight Society which met on Saturdays at that hour to read plays and poetry"; Annan, *Leslie Stephen,* p. 123n.

29. Milly was Caroline Emelia Stephen, Leslie's sister; see Annan, *Leslie Stephen,* p. 296. She was a Quaker and "as good as gold"; *Letters,* no. 478. In the enclosed note she had written: "Oh indeed I *do* agree with you, dear F. W. M. (but I am longing badly to know more!). Yes, we may be quite sure of Nessa—even of her choosing wisely—and that is the one thing that matters."

30. *The Athenaeum,* Dec. 8, 1906; *C.P.,* III, 540.

31. Published in *EHR,* vols. 15 and 16 (1900–01); see *Letters,* no. 234.

32. The material and quotations which describe the last voyage and the last days in Las Palmas are taken from a letter written by Florence to her mother on December 21, 1906, and shown to me for use in this book by Ermengard Maitland.

Index

Index

Index

Index

Index

Bei Fragen zur Produktsicherheit wenden Sie sich bitte an:
If you have any questions regarding product safety,
please contact:

Walter de Gruyter GmbH
Genthiner Straße 13
10785 Berlin
productsafety@degruyterbrill.com